Our Precious Corn

makwa enewed

Makwa Enewed is an imprint of the American Indian Studies Series, at Michigan State University Press.

Gordon Henry, *Series Editor*

Makwa Enewed stands dedicated to books that encompass the varied views and perspectives of people working in American Indian communities. In that light, books published under the Makwa Enewed imprint rely less on formal academic critique, argument, methodology, and research conventions and more on experientially grounded views and perspectives on issues, activities, and developments in Indian Country.

While work published in Makwa Enewed may resound with certain personal, speculative, conversational, political, and/or social concerns of individuals and groups of individual American Indian people, in a larger sense such concerns and their delivery reflect the import, strength, uniqueness, and potential viability of the imprint.

The imprint will gather its strength from the voices of tribal leaders, community activists, and socially engaged Native people. Thus, each publication under the Makwa Enewed imprint will call forth from tribally based people and places, reminding readers of the varied beliefs and pressing interests of American Indian tribal people and communities.

Our Precious Corn

Yukwanénste

Rebecca M. Webster

Makwa Enewed | East Lansing, Michigan

Makwa Enewed
Michigan State University Press
East Lansing, Michigan 48823-5245

Library of Congress Cataloging-in-Publication Data
Names: Webster, Rebecca M., author.
Title: Our precious corn = Yukwanénste / Rebecca M. Webster.
Other titles: Yukwanénste
Description: East Lansing, Michigan : Makwa Enewed, [2023] | Series: American Indian Studies Series | Includes bibliographical references and index.
Identifiers: LCCN 2022024196 | ISBN 9781938065309 (paperback) | ISBN 9781938065316
Subjects: LCSH: Oneida Indians—Food—Wisconsin—Oneida. | Corn—Folklore. | Corn—Social aspects. | Corn—Religious aspects. | Oneida Indians—Wisconsin—Oneida—Social life and customs.
Classification: LCC E99.O45 W43 2023 | DDC 305.897/5543—dc23/eng/20220615
LC record available at https://lccn.loc.gov/2022024196

Cover design by Anastasia Wraight
Cover art is *Grandma's Corn*, by Rebecca M. Webster.

Visit Michigan State University Press at www.msupress.org

Contents

Preface

SHEKOLI SWAKWE·KÚ. KANYΛʔTAKE·LU NÍ· YÚKYATS UKWEHUWEHNÉHAʔ. Rebecca Webster ní· yúkyats oʔslunikéhaʔ. Wakkwáho niwakiʔtaló·tʌ. Onʌ́yoteʔa·ká ní· wakuhwʌtsyó·tʌ. Talukowa·nué nitwake·nú·. (Hello everyone. My Oneida name is Kanyʌʔtake·lu, which means "snow scattered here and there." My English name is Rebecca Webster. I'm wolf clan. People of the standing stone is the clay I'm made from. I grew up near Duck Creek in Oneida.)

Ne· yakʌ latuhákwe (and so it is, they say), history is told from the viewpoint of the victor. In Haudenosaunee history, we were rarely the victor. Our voices have been drowned out and mainstream society has repeatedly tried to make us disappear. Today, we have a chorus of Haudenosaunee scholars rising up and letting the world hear their voices. I hope this book adds to that chorus by including the words of our Haudenosaunee people, especially of those in Oneida, Wisconsin, the Duck Creek Oneidas. A significant portion of this book consists of the voices of Oneida people from the past and the present. In addition to archival data, I conducted interviews with over fifty Oneida community members to gain a better understanding of our relationship with corn. Their thoughts, opinions, and stories are woven throughout this book to help explore our historical relationship with corn since the beginning of time. Corn has walked alongside us since creation. She continues to teach about our original instructions and our place within creation. When we forget, she reminds us. When we get sick, she heals us. When we have to lay something down, she makes sure our grandchildren can pick it up.

As corn is constantly teaching us and reminding us of our original instructions, we also need to be mindful that none of us hold the rights, so to speak, of that which is contained in our original instructions or in any other part of our history or our culture. So much of it is subjective. So much of it comes from being passed down without finding its way to a written page. Each chapter starts off with a phrase from Bob Brown, Oneida Bear Clan Chief, "ne· yakʌ latuhákwe." This is a tribute to all those who have said these things in the past. It is also a recognition that I am writing and interpreting other people's stories and sharing my own story based on my understanding at this particular moment in time. At its core, it is an admission that I have a lot to learn still and rely heavily on those around me to continue to guide me and help me on this path.

It's quite appropriate, then, that the first quote in the book come from Bob Brown. I met with Bob and my mentor, Toni House, quite often while I was writing this book. A few times our discussion turned to brainstorming the titles of the book chapters and of the book itself. I was worried about the marketability and recognizability of using an Oneida word in the book's title. Bob and Toni encouraged me to go ahead and use an Oneida word. In particular, Bob kept coming back to the word "yukwanʌ́ste."[1] He explained it had two meanings: "our corn," and "our precious." During one of our many conversations, it clicked, and I understood. I went back to my interview transcripts from over a year prior, and there it was:

> I remember an older gentleman back in the day talking about the words about things and saying "corn." He said, "Do you know how to say 'corn'?" And you know, we're talking in the language, of course. So, he says, "Sanuhtekʌ nahte ne tat ahsilu nahte kʌte onʌst? Wakilu hen ohnʌste ki wa." So,

> I'm saying, "Oh yeah, I understand it's corn. You say it like that." Then he goes on and says, "No that's not really what I mean. What I mean is, what the corn is." So, it's kind of like he's got me duped, you know? So, I have to say I don't really understand what he's asking. Then he says, "Well, the thing about it is tat ʌsatnikulayʌtane tat tsi nahte kwah I kʌ sanʌste kwah akweku tsi nahteshu sanʌste̲. Ne kwi kaikʌ tho nu twetha tsi nahte aoliwa wahanatuhkwe Shukwayaʔtísu o·nʌsteʔ ne tsi kwah akweku ukwanʌste kihwa." In a sense, he was telling me that if you think about it, it's something that is very precious to you. You do your very best to take care of it. You watch over it. You make sure that nothing happens to it. So, he was saying when the Creator created the corn, o·nʌsteʔ, he says he thought it would be something that is very precious to people. If you think about it, the word "o·nʌsteʔ," it's almost like saying "yukwanʌ́ste," our corn is something that is very precious to us. So, he said, "When you see an apple, it's out there and you can take it and you don't have to do anything other than wipe it off or whatever and eat it. In order for you to eat the corn, there's a lot you need to do. And it's got all of these things that are growing around it, you know. All these husks are together around the cob to protect it." So, he was explaining that to me back when I was younger, and I never really realized what he was saying until much later.[2]

I posted an update on my progress in writing this book on social media. It was the first time I posted about the title. My mom and aunt were quick to remind me of a childhood story. I was an only child and the first grandchild. It's fair to say I was spoiled. My family had me convinced my name was Becky Precious. When I was fifteen months old, my mom and I were at a department store. A woman asked my name. I told her it was Becky Precious. She was surprised I could talk because I was so little. She turned to my mom and said, "What a nice daughter you have, Mrs. Precious."

> Looking back, this story reminds me of the analogy between our corn and our children. As Bob explained, corn is protected by layers of husks. Likewise, we

> try to shelter our children from the outside world and slowly peel the layers back to get them ready for their transition to adulthood. When they are adolescents, we say they are "under the husk." As a child, my family placed me under many layers of protection because I was precious to them. I am now doing the same for my own young children.

Corn remains very precious to our community. She is the eldest of the three sisters, the one we rely on the most for sustenance. She, along with sisters beans and squash, is feminine in nature as she presented herself as a sister and as a woman time and again in our stories. Even in our language, she is female. In our language, there is the presumption that everything around us is feminine unless specifically noted otherwise. We are a matrilineal people, with our clans and family ties being traced through the women. Women are the bringers of life. As you will see throughout this book, corn brings forth life and helps sustain us physically, mentally, emotionally, spiritually, and culturally.

As corn is just one of the three sisters, the focus of this book shouldn't be read to dismiss the other sisters, nor any of our other traditional Indigenous foods. Rather, I use corn as a symbol we can relate to through time. Corn helps sustain our bodies, but she does so much more than that. Corn takes us on a journey through our history to help us understand where we are today. Corn helps us confront those traumatic aspects of our past in order to help heal as we move into the future.

Writing this book was a beautiful learning experience. My hope in sharing what I learned is that it might serve as an open hand to guide some people back to our community and our culture. Just as corn has walked with us throughout all of history, by our side, holding our hand, I feel the corn has helped bring my family and friends closer to understanding and embracing our original instructions. She helped forge connections with people I may not have had a connection with in the past. She served as a gateway, and granted a permission of sorts, to feel safe in asking questions and listening to stories about our history and our community. I didn't realize how profoundly our history and culture were connected to corn until I began to gather stories and piece them together. As I wrote this book, I could feel her holding my hand through the entire learning process. I hope she reaches out and pulls you in as well. She is loving, forgiving, wise, and patient. She is waiting for you to help her fulfill her responsibilities.

As you begin the book, I leave you with these thoughts: Né· katsaʔ Ok nu·tukwató·ktʌ né· waʔtkatʌ́·nukeʔ né· ʌskwatílhekeʔ né tho niyo·lé· waʔkkwe·ní· né· elhúwa. Wakewyʌtehtaʔuhátyehseʔ. ta· tho niyohtúhak né· yukwaʔnikúhlaʔ. Táneʔ tho. (Now whatever I've left out or made a mistake, you will forgive me because that is as far as I am able to do this just now. I'm continuously going along learning. This is how it shall be our minds. That is all.)

CHAPTER 1

Tsiʔtsyotáshawau

(Of Where It Began)

NE· YAKʌ LATUHÁKWE, YUKWANUHSYU·NÍ[1] (WE ALL BUILD A HOUSE) ORIGINAL instructions derive from our stories of creation. During our ceremonies, we practice our original instructions by giving thanks for all of creation. This is an acknowledgment of the relationships among everything in creation, and an opportunity to reaffirm our responsibilities to all of creation. This chapter focuses on how storytelling educates us about our relationship with corn in various contexts. In order to do this, it is imperative to begin with an introduction of our Yukwanuhsyu·ní creation story. This chapter begins by illustrating and setting the context of how our path was intended.

Variations on Oral Tradition

Our creation story was first told during a time of oral tradition. The Yukwanuhsyu·ní people share an overarching story with slight variations throughout the otherwise consistent timeline of main events. Linguistically, the

Yukwanuhsyu·ní people (Mohawk, Oneida, Onondaga, Cayuga, Seneca, and Tuscarora) speak Iroquoian languages, although each tribe had and continues to have a distinct language. The conversion of any Yukwanuhsyu·ní community's creation story to English results in the loss of meaning. Committing an oral creation story to writing, even in its original language, has the potential to distort and dilute it. In addition, we must all keep in mind that Western culture often looks to quantify the truthfulness or correctness of history. In contrast, we are storytellers relating the story from generation to generation with the awareness that both the storyteller and the listeners are at various developmental stages in their own lives, so they will understand and interpret our stories differently.

More than forty written versions of the creation story were recorded over the span of three hundred fifty years.[2] One of the written versions explains the competing dangers and significance of writing down our oral traditions: "This written version is just that—a single version. This telling of the Story is no more or less perfect or pure than any of the other repetitions that have ever been spoken by any elder."[3]

Weaving the Story of Corn

This chapter relies on a number of different oral and written versions of Yukwanuhsyu·ní stories. I heard our creation story from different people on different occasions. My greatest exposure to our story has been from Bob Brown, Oneida Bear Clan Chief. Each time I heard him tell the story, I made new connections with the things he talked about. Even before I started writing this book, he was open to answering questions and having discussions about different segments of the story. That two-way communication is vital to our understanding of the world around us, and something that can get lost if we rely solely on the written word. In addition to the creation story, this chapter also looks at two versions of the cornhusk doll story told by different Oneida community members and a story about the three sisters told by Bob Brown.

FIGURE 1. Bob Brown taking a break from making a corn pounder to pet our dog, Stella. Photo credit Ruth Plenty Sweetgrass-She Kills.

For the written versions of our creation story, I relied most on three in particular. First, the late Amos Christjohn wrote a brief version of the story. Christjohn was an Oneida first-language speaker who helped the Oneida community in language revitalization efforts starting in the 1970s. Together with his sister, Maria Hinton, and a team of other first-language speakers, he worked tirelessly to ensure that our language could survive by developing curriculum and other language materials, including an Oneida dictionary. Second, the late Demus Elm, an Oneida elder, told the Oneida creation story to Floyd G. Lounsbury, an Oneida linguist, in 1971.[4] Harvey Antone, a relative of Demus Elm, worked with Bryan Gick, a linguistics professor, to transcribe and translate Elm's story for a book titled *The Oneida Creation Story. This book contains the creation story in the Oneida language with a translation in English.*[5] Third, the late John Arthur Gibson (1850–1912), Seneca chief from the

Six Nations Reserve in Canada, wrote down a lengthy version of the creation story.[6] His goal to preserve Yukwanuhsyu·ní culture also led him to publish a written version of the Great Law of Peace (more about this later) as well as host a number of scholars interested in writing about Yukwanuhsyu·ní culture.

I weave together portions of oral and written versions of our creation story to explore our relationship with corn. I start with a brief portion of the story as told by the late Amos Christjohn to provide an overview.[7]

"Long ago, before there was any land here, there was water all over. The only things were the creatures that lived in the water and the birds that flew above the waters. Now, further above there was land which was called the Sky World, and there were people living there, but these people had supernatural powers. In the middle of the land was a great tree which gave them their light. There were many different fruits on the tree; this is where their light came from, the fruits.

"Now the rule was that no one could cut into the tree, or a great punishment would be given to that person, whoever was caught harming the tree. Now there was this young couple, and the young woman was to have a baby. This woman started to crave things, and one of the things she craved was the roots and bark from the tree, so she asked her husband to go and gather these for her. He was afraid to get these because he would surely be punished. He waited for the people to go from the tree. As they all left, he went over and started digging.

"As he was digging, suddenly the ground caved in, and it left a big hole in the ground by the tree. The man got very scared of what had happened, so he went back and told his wife what had happened, and she asked if he got what she had wanted. He told her he did not because he got so scared. She got very mad and said she would get it herself.

"As she got to the tree, she saw the hole. She went over to get a closer look. As she was looking through, she saw all the water down below. She did not know that her husband followed her. As she was looking through, she fell through the hole. As she was falling, she tried to grasp hold of something so she would not fall. All she could get was some of the ground and roots of the tree. But she could not hold on and she fell through. As she fell through, the birds and water animals saw a light through the hole that was made, and they could see something falling. So, the birds went up to see what it was, and they noticed that it was a woman from the Sky World.

"So, they sent one of the birds back down to tell the water animals to see which one of them was able to support her upon their back. Then they talked among one another to see who was able to support her. So, they turned to the great turtle and she agreed. All the birds went up to bring the woman down safely on the turtle's back.

"As the woman fell, she got very frightened and fainted. She never woke until she was on the turtle's back. All she saw was water, all the birds, and the water animals. She asked where she was, and they told her that they saw her fall through the hole up there. She looked to where they had pointed and saw the light shining through the hole.

"So, she asked if they knew where there would be any mud or dirt so she could mix it with what she had grabbed as she fell. Some of the animals said they were not sure but there might be some at the bottom of the water.

"First the otter said he would go down and see if there was any. Then he went underwater and was gone. Everyone waited patiently for the otter. Soon he came floating to the top but didn't get any mud. So, the loon said it would try and went underwater. Everyone waited patiently for the loon to come up, and soon she came up and she too did not have any. So, the beaver said he would try and away he went. Soon he came up with none and felt very sad. The woman told him not to feel bad and that he had tried his best. So, the muskrat said he would try, and he went down. For a long time, the muskrat was gone. They became worried, and then the muskrat came floating to the top with a little bit of dirt in between his claws. The woman took it and put it with the dirt she had and placed it upon the back of the turtle. It began to grow and grow, and different things began to grow too.

"Then the woman began to gather things, for she was getting ready to give birth to the child she was to have. As the time came, she gave birth to a girl, and she was very happy. The woman and her daughter walked about the earth, and she taught her daughter the different things that grew and what they were used for. As the days and years went by, the young girl grew to womanhood, and she looked very beautiful. As she was walking about far from her mother, there was a man that appeared before her. She became very terrified at seeing this man and she fainted.

"As she came to, she noticed that there were two arrows on her stomach. One had a sharp point on it and the other a dull point. She took them home with her. As time went on, she felt funny inside her and she told her mother of this man that she had seen and of the two arrows he had left behind. So, the mother told her of what had happened to her and how they got to where they are now.

"As the days went by, the young woman did not feel too good because there was a great commotion within her body. When she finally gave birth to her twins, the one called the right-handed twin was born the way all children are born, and the left-handed twin came from his mother's armpit. This is what killed their mother. Right away the left-handed twin spoke up and said it was the right-handed twin that killed their mother. Then the right-handed twin spoke up and explained to their grandmother what had happened. He told her that he and his brother were arguing about who was going to be born first. He told his grandmother that he told his brother that he was going to be born the way all children are born, and his brother said he was going any way he wanted to, and so therefore he came out of their mother's armpit and that is what killed her. It was the left-handed twin that killed their mother. But the grandmother did not believe him and took the side of the left-handed twin and got very angry with the right-handed twin. She told him to bury their mother. And so, angrily, he started to bury his mother. As he finished, there immediately grew corn, beans, squash, and Indian tobacco. Then the twins went about their own ways.

"The thing different about the two was that they had powers to create things and they would grow rapidly. As the right-handed twin was walking about, he was creating the grasses and different medicine plants and giving them names. The left-handed twin would go around and give poison to some of the plants and also distort some others. Now as the right-handed twin was going around, he was creating different plants that could be used as food and also different kinds of trees. Some were tall and straight, some big and wide, and he gave them different uses. And his brother would go around changing the edible plants by making them smell awful. He would give the tall trees rough bark and the big ones small and stout with sharp thorns. Then the right-handed twin started to create different animals, small ones and big ones. These animals would eat the plants to help them grow. Then the left-handed twin came around and made animals that would eat the other animals that his brother had created.

"Then the right-handed twin made different areas where the waters would flow. He made streams, rivers, springs, lakes, and the big oceans. Some of the rivers he made, the water currents flow in both directions and the springs with sweet tasting water. Then the left-handed twin came by and made the rivers have rough and jagged rocks that caused the rivers to have very rough rapids. Some of the springs breathed poison and heat, which made them smell very bad. As the right-handed twin finished with the waters, he went to the different birds and gave them beautiful colored feathers and songs that they could sing. Soon the left-handed twin came and saw the birds. He changed some of the birds and the songs they sang. Later, the right-handed twin went back to look at all the things that he had created. He noticed the other different things in his creations and knew he didn't create those things. He looked at everything he made and saw the changes. This made him very angry. As soon as he finished checking the things out, he set out to look for his brother. Soon he found him amusing himself by the ocean. The right-handed twin spoke very sternly to his brother and told him that he had no right changing the things that he had created. Then the left-handed twin replied to his brother and said that he wanted to create things too. He shouldn't be the only one to be creating things. So, the right-handed twin said it was time that they decided who would be the creator of all the things on Turtle Island.

"So, they decided that they would challenge each other with a game of lacrosse. So, the right-handed twin made a big golden ball of sand and threw it in the east and said that this golden ball would be the one to start the game when it came up in the east and end the game when it went down in the west. So, they agreed and went their own way to get ready for the game.

"When the golden ball rose from the east, they began the game and became rough with one another. When the ball set in the west, the game stopped, but neither one won the game. So, they said they would play the peach stone game when the golden ball came up from the east and end the game when the ball set in the west. When it rose from the east, they began to play. It was going back and forth, but when the ball set in the west, still no one had won. Then they said that they would think of something when the ball rose from the east. When it did rise, the left-handed twin said the only way that anyone was going to be creator of all things was that one of them would have to be killed. So, they would have to fight with one another. They began to fight, but it was still even; no one was winning. They went to reach for something to kill the other with. The right-handed twin reached for the deer antlers and the left-handed twin reached for an old stick. As this happened, the right-handed twin knocked his brother to the ground. He thought he had killed his brother. He made him a raft and set him on it and put him out to sea. Then the right-handed twin was considered the creator of all things. He was called the Holder of the Sky. The left-handed twin was called Flint because of his rigidness. The left-handed twin was not killed; he survived and established new land across the ocean and created his own things, the things he liked."[8]

What follows are different segments of the creation story that discuss corn, laid out in a linear fashion as time progresses in the story. These early segments occur before Yotsiʔtsísaʔas becomes pregnant. They begin when she is a young woman.

Cornbread Marriage Cakes and Corn Mush

At one point in the story, Yotsiʔtsísaʔas's uncle tells her that he is going to pass away, and he asked the people to put him in a log box [coffin] and place him in a tree. Yotsiʔtsísaʔas went up the tree to talk to her uncle. Her uncle told her what was going to come in her future, including that she would marry the guardian of the tree, Hotahéy. Her uncle told her that she and her mother needed to make cornbread marriage cakes and bring them to Hotahéy. So, she and her mother made the marriage cakes and put them in a pack basket. In Gibson's version, the cornbread wedding cakes are made with huckleberries.[9]

Yotsiʔtsísaʔas took the pack basket of cornbread wedding cakes to Hotahéy as a gift and told him they were supposed to get married. In the past, Hotahéy had other women tell him that they were to become his wife, but each one turned out to not be the one he was supposed to marry because each one was only interested in herself and what she could get from him as the guardian of the tree. So, when Yotsiʔtsísaʔas told him that she was supposed to marry him, he didn't believe her right away and put her through some tests. One such test was to cook corn mush.

Hotahéy instructed her to fill up a pot of water, start a fire, and heat up the water over the fire. She did this. When the water started to boil, Hotahéy told her to go in the other room and take the braids of corn and take the cobs off the braids and shell the corn.[10] She did this. Then, Hotahéy told her to cook the corn. She did this. Then he told her to take the corn out and grind it into flour. She did this. Then he told her to refill the pot with fresh water and boil it and put corn flour in the boiling water and make mush. She did this.

As the water was boiling and the corn flour began to cook, he told her to undress. She thought that was an unusual request but undressed knowing that she was being tested. Hotahéy explained that the test he was giving her was to see whether she had an endurance for pain and to make sure that she was strong. She was to not flinch or yell out in pain and to stay as calm as she could as she cooked the corn. As the mush was cooking, it started to bubble up and splatter all over. Pieces of the mush began to splatter all over her body, and she didn't flinch or cry out in pain. After the mush was done cooking, Hotahéy summoned his two large pet dogs and instructed her to stay still while the dogs cleaned her. The dogs had rough tongues with sharp, razorlike edges. As they licked her body clean of the mush, she began to bleed from their scraping tongues. Hotahéy then gave her a small pot of sunflower oil and told her to wipe herself with the oil to soothe herself. The oil helped heal her right away. Hotahéy watched her endure the pain and told her she passed the test. He then told her to get dressed and feed the dogs the mush.

This test wasn't necessarily meant to prove her worth to Hotahéy. It was to prove that she had the strength that would become crucial later in the creation story. As Brown explained it, this story may sound horrific, but it is a way to foretell about what women will endure after they are created below on earth. Women endure menstrual cycles, give birth to children, and need to be strong to endure these things. Women also need to know what medicines to use and take to heal and soothe themselves and those around them.

Loretta Webster, an elder and retired land attorney for Oneida, explained how she thinks of this story every time she makes corn mush. "This morning, I made corn mush. Every time I make corn mush, I think about Sky Woman as a young girl making corn mush for the man she was supposed to marry. I also think about how painful it was for her to get through that whole thing, and she did! It reminds us what a rough life we have come from, how lucky we are, and that our ancestors are sky people. Our ancestors are from the spirit world. Sometimes it's hard for us to remember that, but I do. I do think of her every time I make corn mush. I also think of how careful I have to be."[11] Loretta's story demonstrates that these stories live on in our daily lives.

After Yotsiʔtsísaʔas passed the mush test, Hotahéy told her to go back home. He instructed her that when she got back home, she was to wait three days and have the people in the village take their roofs off because he had a gift for them. When she returned home, she told her mother what they were supposed to do. After three days, they took their roofs off their houses. They stood outside, watching what would happen. Then, dark clouds started to roll toward them. The people began to panic and wonder what kind of gift would come with the dark clouds after they took their roofs off their houses. The clouds came to be right over them, and it started to rain but instead of rain, corn came down from the clouds and filled up all their houses in the village. The gift was the corn, our sustenance. As Bob explained the lesson here, for the corn to become a gift, we must have rain. We also must trust that when it does rain, our plants are being nourished.

Celestial Tree

The celestial tree is the tree that was uprooted to make way for a hole for Sky Woman to fall through.[12] This tree had all sorts of fruits, flowers, and lights growing from it. Some accounts of this story acknowledge that this was all part of the plan and that her descent to the world below was not an accident or the act of a jealous husband. Some versions explained that the people noticed the lights on the celestial tree blinking and fading out. They knew that this meant that a change was coming.

Right after I finished the interviews for this book, I had a dream about a life-sized cornhusk doll with long braided hair. Her hair had all the colors in it: brown, black, yellow, red, and gray. She wore a yoke with the celestial tree on the front. I was dreaming about how the Oneida people prospered and floundered together over time. Throughout that history, corn was with us, experiencing our joy and our heartache right along with us. Having just finished up the interviews with our community members, I felt so hopeful for our future and the future of our corn sister that I could feel a change coming. I made a cornhusk doll bust with a beaded yoke just like in my dream. Some of the lights are dim, but they are coming back on. On her back are three sisters gardens. I named her "She Will Relight the Tree." She is telling our current story about how corn is experiencing a resurgence in our community.

Mother Earth Garden

Most versions of the written creation story begin when a pregnant Yotsiʔtsísaʔas fell through a hole in the sky. As she fell, she grabbed at the roots of the tree. Different versions describe the event a little differently. One version

FIGURE 2. Three cornhusk dolls I made in 2019. The first is a doll with writings pulled from Arthur C. Parker's historical works. The second is a large bust with a beaded yoke. The third is a doll wearing traditional clothing, a backpack, and sunglasses. She is also holding math and science textbooks and a corn braid.

explained that Hotahéy threw seeds down the hole with her.[13] Another version explained that a beast gave her a pot, a mortar and pestle (corn pounder), a marrowbone, and an ear of corn as she was falling through the hole.[14] Gibson's version explained that the Fire Dragon (Comet) gave Yotsiʔtsísaʔas dried corn and dried meat before she fell through the hole.[15]

As Yotsiʔtsísaʔas was falling, the birds got together to catch her and ease her descent until the turtle became ready to hold her. Then, the animals tried to swim to the bottom of the water to bring up dirt. Only the muskrat was successful. She took the dirt from his paw and mixed it with the roots of the tree and began to dance around as the dirt grew and spread out beneath her feet over the back of the turtle.

Later in the story, she gave birth to a baby girl, Yenʌhliʔnése (she leads the groups). Yenʌhliʔnése grew into a woman and later became pregnant with two twin boys. Unfortunately, she died during childbirth. After the birth of the twins, we refer to Yotsiʔtsísaʔas as lohsótha (his grandmother) or lotihsótha (their grandmother). Lotihsótha was distraught and instructed her grandsons to help her bury their mother's body. The roots that lotihsótha initially brought with her and incorporated into the expanding earth were dormant until they buried Yenʌhliʔnése. Mohawk elder Tom Porter explained the burial as follows.

> and her daughter was lying on the ground. So the mother took a container . . . and she went and got dirt. She carried it back and she began to put the dirt on her daughter. She began to cover her body. And then she got some more. She kept doing that until the dirt piled up over top of the daughter. She didn't bury her under the ground. She put dirt on top, like a mound. That's different.
>
> This is when we begin calling it "our Mother, the Earth" because this is the first time these people became part of the earth. And it's the first time that anyone had babies from this earth.[16]

As Porter explained, the body of Yenʌhliʔnése became the nourishment for things to begin to grow. Potatoes grew from her feet, beans grew from her fingers, squash grew from her stomach, strawberries grew from her heart, corn grew from her breasts, and tobacco grew from her mind. Other versions discuss these main plants but in slightly different orders.[17]

Since 2018, children in Oneida participating in a rites of passage initiative, Tetwatunhatenyehse (we are changing our lives), plant a Mother Earth garden in the spring. This initiative was modeled after Ohero:kon (under the husk),[18] an Akwesasne Mohawk rite of passage initiative lea by Louise Wakerakats:se Herne, Bear Clan Clanmother. In preparing the Mother Earth Garden, the boys prepare the garden by shaping her body. The girls sing seed songs and plant the seeds in their respective parts of the body. Then they recreate a part of the creation story where Yotsiʔtsísaʔas has to prove herself to Hotahéy and he sends his dogs in disguise to try to distract her, seeing if she will follow his instructions. This was another one of his tests. In the recreation, the girls fetch water in wood and clay bowls to water the garden and the boys try to distract the girls by playing lacrosse and talking to them. Planting the Mother Earth garden is a way to help the children remember parts of the creation story and to understand their responsibilities.

Breast Milk and Corn

When Yenʌhliʔnése passed away after giving birth and was buried, corn grew from her breasts. Corn was even used as a substitute for breastmilk. In the early 1940s, Mrs. Thomas Elm commented on this practice, "Many years ago the babies were never fed by a bottle. If a baby did not get enough from the breast of the mother or if the mother died, the baby was fed by a spoon such as gruel of the ground white corn."[19] While that practice may not be as common as it once was, women today still see the relationship between breastmilk and corn, as the following three stories show. Carol Elm and Vickie Cornelius both worked for the Oneida Cannery and helped bring more corn into the community. Stephanie Stevens is a member of **Ohe·**láku (among the cornstalks), a co-operative of ten Oneida families growing corn together. These stories illustrate how women today are learning about and understanding our relationships with our foods and with our stories.

> Before I started learning about the culture and the traditions of the longhouse, I didn't really recall our relationship with corn. We really just ate it for food and for sustenance. After I learned, I saw how the corn is related to us. The mother corn nourishes us as people. Think back to how our mothers fed us. Back in the day, we were breast-fed, we weren't bottle-fed. Then after a certain time, we didn't breast-feed anymore, and we went and bought formula. That

> time is coming back again where we relate to the directions from our corn. It's like the mother, the mother corn. I get that same feeling that the corn is precious to us, and we need to take care of it.[20]

Vickie told me,

> When I think of the white corn, the first thing that comes to mind is our creation story when the mother passes and the corn, beans, and squash grow from her. When I had my sons, I had a midwife. She really encouraged us to nurse. It wasn't until years later that I learned about the green corn, the milky part of the corn. That relates back to the nourishment for us just as our breasts are sustaining our babies. I began looking at it as a more holistic view of how that corn really takes care of us. If you put more time and care into your garden, then it's going to come back and take care of you.[21]

Stephanie described the different stages of corn and how they correlate with our changing needs, "And just like my breastmilk nourished each of my children, that corn nourishes them in a similar way. It provides sustenance to the people. At different stages of its life, the corn provides different nutrients, for example, during the green corn phase, the corn is milkier. Similar is true of breastmilk, at different stages of a baby's growth and development, breastmilk provides different nutrients that a baby needs to survive and thrive."[22]

Lotihsótha and Shawíhskla Want the Corn

The twins, Okwiláse (sapling) (sometimes referred to as the right-handed twin or Skyholder) and Shawíhskla (flint) (sometimes referred to as the left-handed twin), grew fast just like their mother did. After the twins grow up, they began to explore their gifts of being able to create. In one portion of the story, Shawíhskla found his brother roasting some corn.

"Skyholder busied himself creating all kinds of plants that provide what we know as foods. Then he decided he should eat and rest before finishing his work. He built a fire and began roasting his latest creation, corn.

"It was at this time that the wind began to carry from his fire a very appetizing aroma. Just at that time, Flint was walking around outside, and it happened that he could smell the aroma of roasting corn. In a moment he told his grandmother about the aroma, and she directed him to follow it to his brother's lodge.

"Soon he arrived at its source. There he found Skyholder roasting an ear of corn and as he watched it seemed that streams of oil were dripping from the cooking ears. 'What are you cooking?' he asked.

"'I am preparing food that will sustain human beings who will live on this earth in the future,' was the reply.

"'Can you spare me some?' Flint continued.

"'It is not yet time. Soon food will be plentiful on the earth and then all who have need may eat.'

"'As Flint turned to go, he looked all around his brother's lodge. To his astonishment he saw many things growing, and many of these had produced flowers. He saw a beautifully colored shrub and asked, 'What kind of thing is this?'

"'I have planted that. Soon it will bear fruit.' Flint returned to the lodge of Iohsótha and told her all that he had seen. 'You must keep watch,' she said, 'and when he is gone from his lodge, alert me and I will come to see these things.'"[23]

Gibson's version continued with Okwiláse receiving a warning from his father about his brother and Iohsótha plotting against him. His father tells him to trade some corn for some flint that comes from his brother's mouth. The trade would prevent his brother from spoiling his work. His father explained, "Only that will make it possible that you will be successful in what you are doing, and he will not be able to spoil your work. He will attempt to take control, but he will not be able to do it when you control the substance of his life."[24]

As predicted, when Okwiláse began to cook corn again, his brother came to visit. His brother agreed to the trade. After Shawíhskla let Okwiláse break off the flint from his mouth, Okwiláse gave his brother two kernels of corn and told him to eat one and give the other to their lotihsótha. When Shawíhskla brought the corn to his lohsótha, she commented, "This tastes good. This tastes very good! You will tell me the next time you sense your brother is making food, and I will go there."[25]

As the brothers were going about creating the beings in the world around them, Okwiláse would make something and Shawíhskla would alter his creations. After Shawíhskla gave Okwiláse some flint, Shawíhskla was no longer able to interfere as much with the creations Okwiláse came up with.

Grandma Throws Ashes

In both Brown and Gibson's versions, Okwiláse roasted some corn again some time later. Shawíhskla approached his brother and asked for some. His brother denied his request and told him it was not ready. Shawíhskla went back to lohsótha and told her about his experience. Grandma got mad that her one grandson denied the other grandson his request for corn. So, she went to ask him if she could have some corn. Again, his response was the same. He told her it was not ready for them to eat and refused the request, explaining that if she waited, the corn would be ready later. She got mad and grabbed some ashes and threw the ashes onto his corn. As Brown explained, this part of the story instructs us that we have to utilize the ashes to clean the corn and make sure it is edible and soft. Even today, when we cook our corn, we boil it in water with hardwood ashes to remove the hulls of the kernels. The ashes act like a lye and dissolve the hulls. Using the ashes also makes the niacin in the corn available for our bodies to absorb, making the corn even more nutritious.

Gibson's version provided an additional lesson about patience and sharing food. In this version, when lohsótha asked for corn before it was ready, Okwiláse responded:

"'It is not our custom,' Skyholder said. 'We must wait until it is cooked. We will eat it together. It is well known we all have an equal right to it.'

"The old woman said, 'It is such a small matter that you should let me have the small undeveloped end of the ear.'

"'It is not a custom which should come to pass,' he replied.

"Skyholder replied, 'We will be together when we eat, and each will have an equal right to the food.'

"'I can't believe how stingy you are,' the old woman said. Then she went to stand near the fire. She picked up a handful of ashes and threw them on his roasting com.

"As soon as she did this, the appealing aroma ceased and she said, 'Is it only human beings who should be pleased? Is it not possible that I should ever be pleased?'

"'What you have done is not good,' Skyholder rebuked.

"'You have spoiled something that will bring happiness to people.'

"When the corn was cooked, they ate together. When they finished, Skyholder said, 'Now I will show you all the things that are growing here.'"[26]

Even though Okwiláse knew he was not the favorite grandson, he did not deny Iohsótha the food that was appropriate to eat. He also showed her patience when she got angry with him. He also rewarded her (involuntary) patience by showing her all the things he created since she last visited him. After the twins were done creating, we refer to Okwiláse as Shukwayaʔtísu (he made our bodies) and as Creator and Skyholder.

Conclusion

Our creation story paints a vivid picture of our relationship with corn and of corn's relationship with us. It links us to our past and reminds us of our ancestral knowledge. Corn is so prevalent in all versions of our creation story, it is clear that she has always been there for our people, guiding us through this journey over time. If we truly perceive her as the spiritual being she is, we can also see how she has been our nurturer and educator. We are strong, resilient, and intelligent because of her presence, lessons, and guidance.

Our creation story serves as the beginning of the roadmap that tells us where we came from, who we are, and where we are going. It demonstrates how intelligent and thoughtful our ancestors were. Mainstream society wants us to think our ancestors were simple, backward savages. We are so much more than that. The rest of our story confirms that we were and continue to be a strong, resilient, and intelligent people.

Kanehelatúksla

(To Extend Greetings and Thankfulness)

NE· YAKΛ LATUHÁKWE THE ORIGINAL INSTRUCTIONS OF THE YUKWANUHSYU·NÍ teach us to be mindful and thankful for the world around us. Our instructions have deep connections to our ceremonies and stories that are structured around celebrating our thankfulness. The focus of this chapter will include our responsibility to give thanks for creation through the Kanehelatúksla, how this relates to our ceremonies, and stories supporting our responsibilities, especially those about corn. This chapter then moves into a description of husking bees and how they embody those lessons prescribed in our original instructions and corn stories. Husking bees are the annual celebrations where communities come together to share in the work of the corn harvest, again giving thanks for what creation has provided. They serve as community gatherings where we see a contemporary progression of our storytelling.

Giving Thanks

The responsibility to give thanks is prevalent throughout all our original instructions, stories, and ceremonies. It is the foundation of who we are as Yukwanuhsyu·ní people. Our way of life is centered around this acknowledgment that we need to understand our relationship to the world around us and that we have a responsibility to everything in creation. The Kanehelatúksla, also referred to as the Ukwehu·wé tehethwanuhwehela·túhe? Shukwaya?tísu (Oneida Thanksgiving Address to the Creator) and the Kanehelatúksla (to extend greetings and thankfulness), is a way to acknowledge and give thanks for all of creation. Even within the same community, people will share the Kanehelatúksla in their own way, using their own words. The late Maria Hinton provided a written version of the Kanehelatúksla. She was a first-language speaker who worked tirelessly with other first-language speakers to preserve the Oneida language and create curricula and resources for future generations. One section of her account gives thanks for corn, beans, and squash: "Áhsʌ nya?tekutʌhnu·téle? né· tyohʌ·tú ne? akwe·kú kákhwa? kʌ́·tho ohwʌtsyá·ke. Úskah tsi? ʌtwahwe?nu·ní· yukwa?nikúhla?. Ta· tho niyohtúhak yukwa?nikúhla?. The Three Sisters are the leaders of all the foods here on earth. Let's put our minds together as one. This is how it shall be our minds."

Curt Summers, an Oneida-language teacher, explained how we plant the three sisters, including giving thanks for them.

> There's a protocol to growing our gardens. Our main food sources are áhsʌ nya?tekutʌhnu·téle? [three sisters]. As a people, we have a responsibility for them. Every spring, whether it's the men or the women preparing the garden for planting, before we turn the ground, the men gather their families and they go to their garden site. They recite a speech they prepared, thanking those foods that will grow there. We thank them that for still being here and continuing on with the responsibilities. . . . This is done early in the morning when the sun is coming up. Then the women sing seeds songs as we plant. Those songs acknowledge those foods that sustain us. We plant

> the corn, beans, and squash together, those three sisters, because they have responsibilities to each other as they grow.[1]

With the songs, we give thanks to the seeds when we plant to encourage them to sprout and grow. Lexi Levinson, a young Oneida woman, emphasized how important it is to interact with the corn when she is just a seed and as she grows. "Corn has a spirit and that's why you are supposed to sing to it when you're planting," Lexi explained. "There are certain songs for when it goes into the ground. When you touch it, you are giving it life. As it grows, you're supposed to go past it and feel the leaves. Play with the silk when it comes out. Touch it and feel it so it knows that you were there supporting it."[2] Similarly, Toni House shared a story about how she and her granddaughter, Xyleigh, learned seed songs.

> I went to this conference in Toronto and Raven Swamp sang some seed songs and I asked her if I could record her. She gave me two songs and she translated them. All summer I would go outside, and I would put my phone on and play this and Xyleigh would come with me. I didn't ever try to teach her the songs. I was trying to learn them. She started to sing that song, and her dad, he's this great singer. He can sing all different kinds of songs, and then one day he came in and he goes, "Oh, Xyleigh, sing something else. We can't get her off that one song," and I was listening to her. Here she was singing that seed song and I'm laughing. I never tried to teach her, it just happened because she was with me and she wanted to play outside all summer. So, finally her dad said to her, "Here, Xyleigh, we're going to give you a new song." So, he sang a song for her and she's looking at him and she goes, "No, that's your song. This is my song." . . . This corn is teaching us and it's going really, really, slow. Really, really, slow. Then all of a sudden, bang! Two years old and she's singing the seed songs.[3]

Randy Cornelius, Oneida Bear clan Faithkeeper, also talked about the importance of giving thanks, especially as it relates to our foods.

> What the Creator gave to our people, those ceremonial songs, they are honor songs. What our people were doing back then, and a lot of people are still doing today, is that they turn their back to them. That's how they feel. It's the same feeling that we get when we get the cold shoulder, when we get mad at somebody and we won't acknowledge them for whatever reason. That hurt that comes with it is the same thing that creation experiences when we don't show that respect, when we don't have that relationship. We don't get back that reciprocity. That's what our ceremonies are all about. It's giving back and honoring them and holding them up. That's encouragement right there, to be honored like that. We are always to be thankful of that and it's every time we put anything in our mouth, any kind of food, water, whatever, "yawʌ."[4] We talk about being thankful. That's what we would say even if it's just in our mind when we finish a meal. When our ancestors did this, they would be saying that thank you to the spirit of the food "yawʌ." We are honoring it because it knows that it's here to sustain us. It knows its responsibility. Everything in creation knows its responsibility of what the Creator has put here.[5]

Ceremonies

All our ceremonies celebrate and honor all of creation. At all these ceremonies, we give thanks to our corn by serving some type of corn soup. Of all our ceremonies, there are three in particular that are dedicated to giving thanks to our three sisters: corn, beans, and squash. One is our seed ceremony. This ceremony honors all of plant life and takes place before we plant our gardens. We play the peach stone game to entertain Shukwayaʔtísu, and, in a certain way, seeds are what we wager. The men play against the women. We play the game in a flat-bottom bowl and use six peach stones. One half of each stone has been painted black. We use beans to keep score. We earn beans from the other side by shaking the bowl and having the stones land all on the same color or all but one on the same color. The side that loses all their beans loses the game.

Gibson's version of the creation story described the origins of the peach stone game for the seed ceremony.

"Then the elders said, 'We will seek aid through the Great Gamble. Our Mothers, the Three Sisters, the corn, beans, and squash, shall be the chief personalities represented at this time. We will wager for them, and after the game, we will plant. Then we shall do as Skyholder has ordered done.'

"Another came forward with an idea. 'This will be a good thing. We will commemorate that which happened in the past, when Skyholder and his Grandmother, Mature Blossoms, bet together. The two wagered all that which grows on the earth. So the way we will do this, we menfolk will wager against our mothers, the women.'

"The elders agreed to the matter. Now they did play the game, and the male human beings won and now they said, 'It shall come to pass, when these anniversaries recur, the first thing to be done is that the Great Gamble will be performed. At that time, our Mothers shall become the central persons.'

"Now the people planted and when they finished, they assembled and held a Great Feather Dance. They offered up thanksgiving for having finished planting their fields.

"When the seeds sprouted, the people hoed their gardens and then gathered together. They gave thanks that the seeds had sprouted, and they held the Great Feather Dance. It was decided that there would be performed when the harvest was in, and for a long time the people were at peace."[6]

If the women win the peach stone game at the seed ceremony, they win the seeds, and the men are responsible for planting. If the men win, they win the seeds, and the women are responsible for planting. This ceremony solidifies the balance and shared responsibility for our gardens. If agriculture was exclusively a woman's role, as many anthropologists claim, this portion of the ceremony would be very different.

Another ceremony is the green corn ceremony. At this ceremony, we give thanks for Shukwayaʔtísu for providing us with food to sustain us. This ceremony occurs when our corn is not fully ripe but still perfect for eating. The corn is not actually green at this stage; rather the term is used to describe the corn as not being fully ripe. The final ceremony is the harvest ceremony. This ceremony is to give thanks for our bountiful harvests from our gardens.

In Gibson's version of the creation story, there came a time when people did not practice the ceremonies, and families did not respect each other. Shukwayaʔtísu came to deliver a series of instructions to serve as reminders to the people. He told them, "When the earth grows warm, you must apply hard labor to this task. You will learn the custom of planting," Gibson wrote.

> You will have the corn, beans, and squash. When you plant, you will make use of the ceremony of which you have become accustomed, repeatedly giving thanks. The Great Feather Dance will take place. When the plants have sprouted you will continue by taking care of them and when they are ready you will again employ a ceremony to give a thanksgiving. Thus, when the green beans are ready, you will put aside a kettle of these cooked, enough for the entire assembly, and then one will be appointed to speak with a unanimous voice in the ceremony of thanksgiving. And the same shall happen when the green com is ready and the squash puts forth fruit.[7]

Gibson's version also described the importance of sharing the work and harvest with each other. He explained that Okwiláse instructed that a young woman be chosen to take a corn and bean plant and a young man be chosen to take a bean plant in a place where Okwiláse would later be buried. Time passed, people chose a young woman and a young man, and they completed the task. Upon their return, they shared their story, and there was great discussion about what to do next. Gibson's story continues:

> At that time the Elders said, "You have gone to a great deal of trouble to get these things. We assembled here have made preparations to greet you with thanksgiving now that you have completed the task of bringing Our Mothers here. We now with one voice give thanksgiving. We shall now go along the path of ritual he has

> set out for us. Also, we will greet with thanksgiving all the things which support our lives. What shall we do with these things which have come among us?"
>
> Then someone said, "I think we all have an equal right to them. It would be a good thing if we all assist one another when we plant, and again when we must cultivate and then at harvest. When we have plenty, we will divide it up among us." After that the people helped one another in this work.[8]

The ceremonies and this segment of Gibson's version of the creation story reminds us that we must be thankful and that the whole community, not just the women, helped with growing our foods. Like all things in life, growing our foods takes balance and requires the effort of everyone in the community.

Corn Stories about Responsibility

In addition to our creation story and our ceremonies, Yukwanuhsyu·ní people have a number of stories that teach us valuable lessons and remind us of our original instructions. Three such stories are about the seven dancers who formed the constellation Pleiades, why the cornhusk doll has no face, and how the three sisters came to have a reciprocal relationship with the people.

The story about how the Pleiades formed is as follows.

"Once upon a time there was a Native village by the river. There were eight boys that played together all the time. Every day they met at the same place. They even had their own chief. Whenever they met, the chief would play his drum. Then the others would start to dance. When they got tired of dancing, then they would eat.

"One day the chief said, 'Tomorrow we will have a feast and I want to ask for different kinds of food.' One boy asked for corn soup. His mother said, 'Why do you want to take it over there when you can eat it here? No, you can't have any.' One boy asked for deer meat. His mother got angry with him and said, 'Why do you want to take the deer meat over there? No, you can't have any.' One boy asked for corn and his mother said no we don't have any.

"All the boys met at their place where they played all the time. Then they told their chief that they couldn't have a feast because their mothers wouldn't let them bring any food. The chief said to them, 'Don't feel bad, I'll play, and you can still dance.' The boys said, we are too hungry to dance. The chief said, don't think about anything, just dance. When I play faster, you dance faster.

"They began to dance, and they danced so fast they began to rise up and soon they were over the trees. Finally, the parents looked up and saw their children dancing so far off the ground. They hollered at them to come back. Their chief said don't look down just dance faster. One boy looked down and he fell back down. This day if you look up to the sky you will see the seven dancers dancing."[9]

Pleiades marks time for the Yukwanuhsyu·ní. When the new moon appears and the seven dancers are directly overhead us in the sky at sunset, then it is time for Midwinter Ceremony. This story also conveys a lesson about the need to feed our children and to not withhold food from them.

As with the creation story, there are many variations on the story about why cornhusk doll has no face. A young elder and well-known storyteller, Brian Doxtator, and a thirteen-year-old boy, Ernest Stevens IV, shared their versions with me. There are a lot of implied messages that address our culture within these stories. The Yukwanuhsyu·ní people rely on various medicinal societies to help people with their physical, spiritual, and mental well-being. Corn, including corn husks, is used in all of them. "This woman was so beautiful," Brian said as he began his story.

"She had a gift to take care of all the children and they loved her. The old people called her to their longhouse, and they told her it was obvious that she had this gift with children. So, they told her it was her responsibility to watch over the children during the day. So, while the women were in the fields and the men were away in the woods . . . One day, she took the children to the pond to go swimming, and for the first time in her life, she actually looked into the water and saw her reflection. She never knew how beautiful she was because she never saw herself. She couldn't believe that she was so beautiful, so she ended up staring at herself all day long. When the parents came back at the end of the day, the kids were hungry and tired, so they went to the old people and they complained about her. The old people . . . called her to the longhouse and reminded her of her gift and reminded her that it was her responsibility to care for the children. She agreed to fulfill her responsibility.

"The next morning, the yearning to see her own beauty was so powerful that that's all she could think about. She took all the children to the pond, and again she stared at herself all day long because she couldn't believe how beautiful she was. At the end of the day, a little girl was so tired that she was almost going to go to sleep in the water, and then the parents and other adults came back just in time to save this little girl. They were all so angry because this woman was clearly not fulfilling her responsibilities. So they went to the old people a second time to complain again. The old people . . . called her to the longhouse, and they said this is the third time they told her what her responsibility to the children was and the second time they had to warn her to fulfill that responsibility. She again agreed to fulfill her responsibility.

"The next morning, the yearning to see her own beauty was so powerful that that's all she could think about again. She took all the children to the pond again. Like the day before, she didn't take good care of them and forgot to feed them. This time, a little boy was swimming and became so tired from not eating that he never woke up again. The adults were furious at the woman and they were hurt. They went to the old people to tell them what happened and how the little boy died in the water. The old people told her they reminded her three times of her responsibilities and that it would now be up to Shukwayaʔtísu to take care of this.

"The next morning, all the children went to find the woman. She was nowhere to be found, but they did find a cornhusk doll by her longhouse."[10]

Ernest told a different version of the story he heard. "Most people know about the three sisters," he began.

> There's the corn, beans, and squash, and they were to sustain the Indigenous people. They are like medicine to sustain us, to feed us. One day, the corn said, "I want to do something else besides sustaining our people." The corn

FIGURE 3. Ernest and Daniel Stevens looking at a photograph of Louisa Denny, their great-great-great-grandmother. The photograph was displayed at the Oneida Nation Museum. Photograph reprinted with permission of the Oneida Nation.

loved the people so much . . . So then the Creator said, "I will make a doll out of your husks." So one day, he made a beautiful doll so that the children could play with it. The children were saying that the doll was really beautiful, and every day the doll would just go to the river and look at herself over and over, admiring herself and how beautiful she was. Then one day, the Creator said for the doll to come to his lodge. She was sitting at the edge of the river looking at her reflection and didn't go to the lodge. The Creator said he was going to give her one warning. The next day, the Creator called her to his lodge, and she still didn't come because she was still admiring herself in the river. The next day, she woke up and she went to the river to look at herself, and when she looked at herself, she had no face. The Creator warned her, and she didn't listen, and so that is why the cornhusk doll does not have a face.[11]

As Brian explained it, the different versions of the cornhusk story remind us of our responsibilities and caution us to not be too conceited. If the individual is strong, then the family is strong. If the family is strong, then the community is strong. If the community is strong, then the nation is strong. If the nation is strong, then the confederacy is strong. Being conceited doesn't have a place in our community if we want to be strong. Even after the woman was turned into a cornhusk doll, she was still responsible for the children. The children played with cornhusk dolls. Also, as time went on and tourists came to Yukwanuhsyu·ní communities, the people made cornhusk dolls to sell to the tourists, making money during times of impoverishment. In a way, then, the cornhusk doll was still fulfilling her responsibilities to take care of the community.

Kim Nishimoto, daughter of the late Amelia Cornelius, shared a story about finding husks for making the dolls. Amelia Cornelius and her daughters were well known for their kanʌstóhale (cornbread) and their cornhusk dolls. Kim explained:

> There's no shortage of corn husk because every year my mother would make me go to Tsyunhéhkwʌ and harvest the corn with her.[12] We would get all of the husks, and we did this every year, so I always thought we needed more husks. But when she passed away, we found tons of corn husks in three or four really large plastic containers out in the garage. They were full of corn husks.[13]

Then there are the stories about the three sisters. Oneida Bear Clan Faithkeeper Randy Cornelius relayed a story that Amos Christjohn heard from a Seneca chief about people's symbiotic relationship with the three sisters.

> There was this young man who went out and hunted all the time for his family. He was a really good hunter. Then one day, when he was way deep in the forest where he had never been before, he saw these girls. One was tall. One was medium. One was a baby crawling along the ground. They were all in there playing, laughing, and having a good time. The hunter was watching

> them. This went on for some time. Then one day, that little baby came crawling right up to him and so he took her home. That was the bean. He took her to his longhouse. When he went back to the forest, those other two girls were distressed because they were looking high and low for that little one and they couldn't find her. They were really sad, and they were crying and calling for her . . . That middle child, squash, came up to him, and he said he could take her home because he had her sister there. So he took her home and they were united. Then he went back to the forest to find the oldest one, the corn. She was really sad, really crying. She didn't have that glow anymore in her face. He described her as being like this sunshine before, but now she was just sad. He approached her and told her that he took her sisters home and that he wanted to reunite them so that they could be all together again. So, he brought her home. Through the course of that winter, he took care of them. Because of that, they taught him the value of the corn and the beans and the squash. They taught him how to grow, harvest, process, and preserve the corn, beans, and squash. They taught him all of these ancient recipes. Then the people began to grow the corn, beans, and squash and use them for their main source of food along with the other things that the Creator provided.[14]

In telling me a similar version, Bob Brown explained how our stories often have multiple lessons. We have a responsibility to take care of the three sisters and they have a responsibility to provide sustenance for us. This story is good to tell small children so they see the importance of sticking together. They continue to hold symbiotic relationships that serve as a symbol for working together and relying on each other's strengths. The corn, the eldest sister, grows tall and strong and provides the main staple for Yukwanuhsyu·ní diets. The corn serves as a support system for the beans to climb up. The beans provide nitrogen to the soil. The squash spread out low, keeping moisture in the ground and suppressing weeds. Animals also don't like to cross through squash because of her prickly leaves and vines, protecting the corn and beans. This method of growing food made efficient use of space and provided a varied diet.[15] Curt Summers, an Oneida-language teacher, explained how the three sisters want to be planted together.

> The way we grow corn now today, a lot of times it's being grown by itself. . . . I think we have to remind each other that we have to grow the other two along with them. I don't mean we will have ten rows of corn here, and then next to them we will have ten rows of beans, then next to them we will have ten rows of squash. Well, no, you gotta grow them together! That would probably be one of the coolest things that I would ever see is when we get back to our traditional ways. I think you would see a difference in the way our food grows because one is always helping another out in some way.[16]

Seeing the three sisters growing together is a beautiful sight. They inspire me to create art. Often, my ideas come to me in a dream. As I was finishing up a very early draft of this book, before I was able to include the interviews from community members, I had a dream about a dress. The dress shape reminded me of the cut of the stereotypical nurse's dress, but it went all the way down to above the ankle. The dress was a black calico, with just a hint of gray in the floral designs. In the top center of the back was the moon. The bottom of the dress and the back of the dress were covered with gray, charcoal, and silvery appliqué designs of a three sisters garden. They didn't have any colors because it was nighttime. The moon was shining so bright that the flowers on the squash blossoms were still open, when normally they would close up during the nighttime. As I was taking a close look at this dress, she split away into three dresses, each dress taking one of the sisters with her. I woke up and sent a message to two of my friends and told them about this dream. We all agreed that we needed to make these dream dresses. Thinking back to this dream, I wonder if part of it was influenced by my guilt for singling out the corn in this book without paying enough attention to beans and squash. After all, the stories tell us that the three sisters were not meant to be separated, and yet my dream was pulling them apart. Maybe it means that my two friends and I need to get busy making these dresses and spend time together. Maybe it means I need to write books about beans and squash next. We'll see.

Husking Bees

Husking bees represent a contemporary progression of our storytelling. Harvest time was and continues to be a time for great celebration and storytelling. It was an occasion for everyone in the community to gather and to help each other. The late Arthur Parker, a Seneca from the Cattaraugus Reservation and a noted archaeologist, historian, and folklorist, published many works on Yukwanuhsyu·ní corn and culture. He provides a colorful description of a husking bee during harvest.

> Work was play in those days when mutual helpfulness made money unnecessary. It was not uncommon for men to engage in this work. They were lured to the scene by the promise of soup, song and the society of wise old matrons and shy maidens. The old women carefully noted the industry of their younger assistants and scheming parents were able to obtain information about prospective mates for their children.
>
> The older men did some work but not much. They aired their wisdom by making wise observations but soon lost their reserve in narrating exciting stories of personal adventure or by relating folk tales, gagää. They knew full well that a pail full of soup awaited them when the husking ceased whether they worked or not. Often the "bee" would be enlivened by a marching dance, and for this emergency the men brought their water drums and horn rattles and cleared their throats for singing. . . .
>
> The "bees" were often conducted out of doors under the white moonlight. A roaring fire of sumac brush or logs tempered the crisp air of the night but left it sufficiently invigorating to keep up spirit and keep the workers active. There was nothing unhealthful in these night carnivals where the smell of the corn plant, the breath of the pines blown by the autumn wind, the smoke of

> the fragrant burning wood and the pure merriment of the workers and the knowledge of good work furnished the sole exhilaration.[17]

During harvest, the people would pick the corn in the fields and use baskets to haul it to a spot where they made piles of corn. They would sit around the pile and pull the husks off the ears, leaving two or three husks on and lopping off the stem just above the remaining husks. This was also a time for the women to determine which cobs were suitable for keeping as seed for future planting. Yukwanuhsyu·ní varieties of corn typically have eight straight rows.

Today, because so many farmers grow GMO (genetically modified organism) corn near our corn, we need to watch for signs of cross-pollination. If there are any dents, dimples, or a lot of kernels of a different color than what we planted, that cob likely received pollen from a neighboring cornfield. We will keep that corn for food, but we will not keep it for seed. Not only do we feel it is culturally inappropriate to manipulate the genetics of our corn relative; once the modified genetics appear in a cob of corn, it has tainted that corn forever. After separating the cobs that we use for food from the cobs we keep for seed, we braid each type using the remaining husks into long braids and hang them up to dry. In Oneida, some of our families now make flowers out of the husks to decorate the tops of braids of seed corn to ensure that we can easily distinguish between corn meant for seed and corn meant for food.

In 2016, several Oneida families got together to form a co-operative to grow corn together. We named ourselves Ohe·láku. Two founding members, Laura Manthe and Don Charnon, had already experienced husking bees hosted by Tsyunhéhkwʌ, where the Oneida Nation grows traditional, heirloom white corn and other foods. Laura recounted:

> When I first moved here in 1993, Sugar Bear Paul Smith ran the Tsyunhéhkwʌ program. He would put on a festival in the fall to really invite the community members to Tsyunhéhkwʌ property and to have a party around harvesting the corn. They had all these little stations and these little booths for community members to make cornhusk dolls, and there were people cooking food and

> it was free. You could go pick a pumpkin. You could bob for apples. They had an art show. We did a little solar demonstration from our office at that event. You learned how to braid corn, and you left with a braid of corn because they really wanted you to have corn in your house. He knew we had to keep our community together, keep them healthy, and keep them comfortable growing the corn. That's my fondest memory is all the people together with the corn working for a common goal to put the corn away for winter.[18]

Don Charnon remembered the elementary students visiting Tsyunhéhkwʌ and told me this story:

> When all the students, first grade to fifth grade, would come to our farm, there was so many kids. They were just so tiny. They were like munchkins, but they couldn't follow the yellow brick road. They didn't know where to go, so they had to have buddies. I asked the principal about what he wanted us to talk about. He just wanted to talk about food that comes from the farm. That's enough because some of these kids are city slickers. They're not gonna get it. So if we just talk about that food comes from a farm, that's where it comes from. Then there was a circle of these young people, and as they were taking the husks off, we added an opportunity to not only reveal all the soup-grade corn but to actually find a seed-grade cob that is worth saving and putting aside and using for next year seed. I said, "If you do find a cob that is better than the rest, and I mean longer and it doesn't have any other colors in it, doesn't have any dents, and the rows are straight, and there's eight rows, then we need to save those. If you find one of those, let us know, and we will put them in the special box over here."
>
> So, this one kid, I could tell right away he was a competitor. He was anxious to find one of these special cobs. I saw him digging around, and he was still doing the job but he was cherry-picking certain cobs. He was trying to find the cob. He opened one up. He was sitting in the chair, and he was looking, and he says, "Oh!" He opened it up really slow, and then he stood up

> and he held the corn in the sky, and he said, "This cob is legendary!" Everybody was cheering and all his peers were cheering and saying they wanted to find one too. It was such a great moment I will never forget. Whenever I hear the word "legendary," I will always see him standing up with a cob in his hand like it's the sword in the stone and like he just pulled it up out of the stone and up into the sky. It was awesome. Those were some golden moments on sunny days under a big tent and a circle around a big pile of corn.[19]

Husking bees are a time for people of all ages to come help with the corn and participate in the celebration of harvest. Young children share their good medicine with the corn and with everyone around them. It can be a lot of work to chase kids around during harvest, but the lessons they learn and the memories they will have are priceless. So many Yukwanuhsyu·ní stories are meant to convey lessons and morals to our children. Husking bees and caring for the corn in general are an extension of those lessons in real-life practice. Bev Scow, another Ohe·láku founding member, brought her young grandson out to the cornfield to help weed. He accidentally bumped some corn over and learned an important lesson: "When my grandson was about two, we took him out to weed with my son. My little grandson was kind of like going wild in there and bumped over a stalk of corn, and we heard a crunch or something. So, my son talked to him about the corn and how it's a friend to us. In the end, there's my grandson hugging the corn and saying sorry to the corn. It meant a lot to me that he learned to recognize the corn was alive."[20]

Bev also brought her grandson and other grandchildren out during harvest time. She and her son, Kwnwahta Smith, helped watch the children and ensure they had a connection with the corn from an early age. Kwnwahta told me:

> We have a big household, and we have everyone help. My mom and I are the main ones that try our best to help out. My little sister is back from college and my older sister, Yonakwala, takes all the kids to help. The kids love to go out, but they are actually more work than help, but it's still good to get them

> out there, out in the corn. We get them connected with the culture and have fun. We carry this tradition forward so it's worth it, but sometimes we wish we could leave them behind so that we could get our work done, so we didn't have to run after them all the time.[21]

Bev acknowledges that the little ones are a lot of work as well, but she says, "I love how everyone is so patient when I bring my grandchildren. They are just all over and I have less time to do actual work, but I want them to have that experience, that joy of being with the corn. Everybody has been so encouraging and helping that have that good experience when they can come. When I ask 'Who wants to go to the barn?' they all say, 'I do! I do!' It just feels so good."[22]

After the husking bee, people hang their corn to dry for months at a time. After the corn is dry, the kernels can be removed for more compact storage or for processing into meals. Often, people keep the braids of corn hanging in their homes for a variety of reasons. Braxton Wisneski, young son of Jamie Betters and Kyle Wisneski, staff at the Oneida Cannery and Tsyunhéhkwʌ, excitedly explained how his parents have corn hanging in their home: "We have some in our living room. Sometimes I see our corn hanging from the top and going down, down, down. There's like four layers, I think."[23] Similarly, Eliza Skenandore, another founding member of Ohe·láku, explained how she keeps the braids in her home to remind people of their responsibility to be kind around the corn.

> We keep a braid of white corn and blue corn at the entrance of my house, and I would just take a cob off as I would need it. The reason why I have that corn right there is because they say the corn is pure like children, and you're not supposed to have any negative thoughts or use any bad language around it because our thoughts go into our food, and we don't want negativity in our food. When people walk in my house, they see that corn and they want to have that positive mind. It gives them a positive mindset when they come in the house.[24]

Schuyler Ryerse also keeps her corn on the braids because it is so precious. She knows people in her family will be less likely to help themselves to the corn if it remains on the braids until they need it. She explained:

> You got to understand, my dad's family is very big, and they walk through the garage and that's where he was keeping it. They would be like, "Oh! I'm gonna make some soup and stuff." Everyone would take some and he would ask what happened to his white corn. So, it's easier to keep it on the cob and in the braid. It's like a precious commodity. It's there for ceremonies and for gatherings. If I'm making a bowl of corn soup for work, then I'm just going to get dehydrated corn because there's a lot of work that goes into this. Then, if somebody asks me to make a Nesco for a funeral, I need to start today and get everything going, because that's what we do.[25]

After harvest, we make use of the different parts of the corn plant.[26] Historically, the Yukwanuhsyu·ní had many more uses for the plant than we do today, although we are learning to reconnect to those practices. Our ancestors hollowed out the stalks and used them as tubes for medicine. Hollowed out stalks could also be used as fishing line floats. The corn silk was used for tea as a medicine. The husks had many purposes, including weaving them into sleeping mats, baby hammocks, doormats, moccasins, trays, and baskets. Husks could also be used to start fires and to carry fire from one place to another. Our ancestors also used the husks to wrap up the cornbread wedding cakes described in chapter 1, and to make dolls. Braids of husks were strung between the rafters of houses to hang clothes on. They burned corncobs for smoking hides, meat, and fish. Ashes from burned corncobs were used as a medicine to induce vomiting and as seasoning for food. When used as a seasoning, the ashes killed stomach worms and prevented indigestion. Dried kernels of corn were strung up for jewelry or used in rattles. Pulverized parched corn was used as a compress on the navels of newborn babies to absorb blood and help the belly button skin heal. The corn plant also had uses before the harvest, while the plant was still green. The leaves during this time could be used for bandages, while the green stalks and roots were made into a lotion for cuts, bruises, and sores. The green corn stalks could also be boiled into syrup.

Conclusion

Our original instructions teach us to be mindful for all of creation and to give thanks for the world around us. Our stories are there to constantly remind us of these instructions and of our responsibilities to each other and to creation. We are all interconnected. Those connections and lessons come to life when we care for our corn and when we come together to help each other harvest. Husking bees are the embodiment of historical and modern storytelling and passing on lessons to the younger generations. They are a time for community to come together and celebrate and be thankful for all that creation has provided for us.

In addition to our instructions that tell us to be grateful, corn also shows us how we can be joyful. Even when we are learning hard lessons and engaging in the labor of planting and harvesting, these stories show us how our corn is weaving in smiles, laughter, humor, and love into each moment. Her ability to bring our people together to celebrate everyday duties in gardening and cooking is as timeless as she is.

CHAPTER 3

Kayanlásla?kowa

(Great Matters)

NE· YAKA LATUHÁKWE THE STORY OF THE FORMATION OF THE YUKWANUHSYU·NÍ as a confederacy of nations centers on how should sustain ourselves both through our foods and through our relationships with each other. Sustenance, and corn in particular, played a central role in the formation of the confederacy by first bringing individual communities together, then by bringing the tribes together to stand as a united front, all while being thankful for the gifts the Creator provides. During the Peacemaker's journey to Oneida territory, he made special note of three chiefs who had responsibilities for watching over and protecting the corn.[1] After the chiefs were assembled and all agreed to accept the Peacemaker's message, the chiefs feasted on beaver stew and corn. This chapter outlines these events that helped shape the formation of the confederacy and places this history in a context to help us better understand our long-standing relationship with corn.

In a time prior to European contact, the people suffered great conflicts with each other. Traveling between communities wasn't safe and no one trusted one another. The late John Gibson, Seneca chief from Six Nations, described the conditions and conflicts as follows: "What is going on is that they are killing one another, specifically, they are scalping one another; in fact, they are shedding each other's blood, people of their own kind, living here on earth."[2] A Huron/Wyandot by birth, the Peacemaker and his partner, Hayé·wateʔ, would bring the Seneca, Cayuga, Onondaga, Oneida, and Mohawk people together to form the Yukwanuhsyu·ní Confederacy under the Great Law. The story of how the Peacemaker and his partner ventured among the tribes to deliver their message and obtain agreement about how they would collectively govern themselves is a lengthy account. Mohawk elder Tom Porter explained that the recital can take ten days.[3] I heard a shorter version, lasting just five days. Gibson explained what the message of the Great Law of Peace entailed:

> Then [the Peacemaker] stood up in front of the whole group and said, "You shall listen well, for you wanted to ask questions so as to understand what it means, 'Good Message'; this is what it means: people respect each other as though they are one person; also everybody is related among the various nations, so that that now they will stop, the sins and activities of evil people; now everyone will repent, the old people and the young people; now everyone will respect one another among all of the nations; and just this is what will operate again, the good, and that is what the 'Good Message' means.
>
> Secondly, this is what 'Power' means: all of the nations will unite all their affairs, and the group of several nations will become just a single one, and their power is that they shall join hands. This, moreover, will be the basis upon which they will survive as a group, forming a single family, similar to being one person having one head and one life, surrounded by the Good Message. This is how peace will now come about among all of the nations, and power will arise for families to continue from here on in.
>
> Thirdly, this is what 'Peace' means: now it will stop, the massacre of humans and the scalping and bloodletting among themselves, specifically, among the people of the various nations. Now as to that, it will end, the

> human slaughter, because the Great Spirit never planned for humans to hurt one another nor to slaughter one another. So now it will end, the warpath, and everywhere it will become peaceful; the different nations' villages are as neighbors and as to the localized families their children, what will happen is that they will all be very close relatives; and it will come to pass that they will become just like one family which will encompass every nation and every language. And this: when everyone can travel from village to village, then it will end, the danger and terror, and then everything will be peaceful, and they will rejoice by day and by night as the family continues on, there being no end to peace; that is what it means, the Great Law of Peace, that everyone will be united; now I am finished."[4]

As with all stories based on oral tradition, many people share different variations of the story. The late Seneca historian Arthur Parker published a version of the Great Law that the chiefs of the Yukwanuhsyu·ní council compiled. Their version acknowledges that "books have been written by white men in the past, but that these have been found to be too voluminous and inaccurate in some instances."[5] The remainder of this chapter includes a few detailed excerpts from different variations of the story told by Yukwanuhsyu·ní people that address what Yukwanuhsyu·ní relationships with corn looked like at the time the confederacy was taking shape. In particular, this chapter covers how the Peacemaker's grandmother tried to kill him, how the Peacemaker asked the people to prepare meals before sharing his message, the Oneida chiefs who guarded the corn, and a reminder of the importance of the Thanksgiving Address.

Grandmother's Attempts to Kill the Peacemaker

Near the beginning of the story, the Peacemaker's mother becomes pregnant with him. His grandmother was very suspicious of her daughter because her daughter told her she had never been with a man. His grandmother felt betrayed by his mother. Either the Peacemaker was born as a result of a shameful lie, or he was brought by an evil spirit. Either way, the grandmother thought it necessary to try to kill him three different times. She tried to drop him through a hole in the ice, she tried to bury him, and she tried to burn him. After each attempt, she returned to the house she shared with her daughter to find her daughter and grandson alive and well.

As Tom Porter described:

> And so the grandmother, in her knowledge of the universe and its truths, thought that even if it was witchcraft and evil, it would really be no match for fire, and that fire would be able to destroy this baby. So, what she did was she gathered dried grasses and branches. And she gathered the fallen limbs from the trees, until they made about a five- or six-foot pile. Then, she began to kindle that and make a fire. And she waited until those branches and wood that she had piled started dancing with flames, and it was apparent that they wouldn't go out, that it would be a real fire.
>
> Then, she went into the house, and she grabbed her grandson away from her daughter. And she took this little baby, this little bundle that he was, and she placed his whole body upon the dancing flames of the big fire in the woods. And she stood there and she watched until that baby turned into black charcoal to make sure that he died. When there was nothing but a little charcoal left, she turned around and she went back into the house where she and her daughter lived.
>
> And when she went in there, again she heard the gurgling sounds of a little child. . . . There her daughter was on that fur mattress. And there in her arms was this little baby nursing from his mother, gurgling, making baby sounds.[6]

These three ways the grandmother attempted to kill the Peacemaker correlate to how we cook our corn. First, just as the grandma dunked the Peacemaker in ice-cold water, we use cold water to begin to hull our corn. Second, like the grandma tried to burn the Peacemaker, we heat the water over a fire. Third, like the grandma tried to bury the Peacemaker, we use ashes to hull and clean our corn and we use a kettle or clay pot to heat the water over a fire. The earth represents the ashes because everything comes from and returns to the earth in an endless recycling of life. Trees grow from the earth. When we burn the trees, we save the ashes to hull and clean our corn. We eat the corn. When we die, we return to the earth.

Jasmine Jimerson, a young mother and member of Ohe·láku, explained how she thinks of this part of the story when she hulls corn.

> My favorite story is from when the Peacemaker was born. My mentor told me that when he was little, he remembered every time his grandma made soup, she would tell the same story over and over again. She would tell the story of the Peacemaker and how we learned to clean our corn in the same way from those stories. It shows how interrelated and how rich our culture is. Everything is tied together, and the more you learn about it, the more you see how these things are tied together. . . . How all these different things work together is just beautiful to me.[7]

After the grandmother's third unsuccessful attempted to kill the Peacemaker, she had a dream and received a message from a man richly dressed with a haze around him.[8] She thought she was awake, but she was sleeping. He told her that her grandson had a significant role to play, and Shukwaya?tísu sent her grandson as a messenger. He told her that they saved him from what she did to him. He also told her that she must love him and watch over him to make sure nothing happens to him. When the day came, she must prepare to go home and relay this information to the chief.

Feasting on Corn to Build a Confederacy

Feasting was a critical piece of the Peacemaker's directions for how the nations should prepare for him to share his message. When Peacemaker wanted the people to eat when delivering his message and someone wanted him to just start talking, the Peacemaker instructed the people to gather food before he shared his message: "We have to have deer meat that we cook, and cornbread, corn soup, stuff like that. It has to be present; then I can talk. It goes with that."[9]

In Gibson's version, he told the people:

> As to that, first as to the duties of our mothers, that is to say, the women, they will bake bread, cornbread, which they will collect. Thereupon as to you [men], you will collect the flesh of game animals. These, then, will supply provisions of bread and meat. Then they should assemble, everyone, at the place provided; the inhabitants, all of them, will gather in the same place, and everyone will hear me tell about the matter you wish to know.[10]
>
> . . . After sharing his message, they distributed the cornbread and the meat of game animals and they shared among the whole group, and they feasted, they rejoiced, and they were grateful to [the Peacemaker].[11]

Mother of Nations Feeds the Warriors

During his journey, the Peacemaker came across a woman named Tsikusaseh. She would play an integral role in the formation of the confederacy. Prior to the Peacemaker visiting her, she would feed the warriors traveling through her territory, assisting in the efforts to promote warfare and bloodshed. Arthur Parker described Tsikusaseh's house being located at Oniagara, among the nation of the cultivators (those who had corn and tobacco).[12] While none of the accounts I heard or read specify that she fed the warriors or the Peacemaker dishes that included corn, she undoubtedly did feed them corn. Not only was corn still a staple among many Indigenous people in that part of the world, but Parker explained that Tsikusaseh came from a corn- and tobacco-growing nation. A familiarity with Tsikusaseh and her story will be helpful in the chapter that discusses the Revolutionary War.

Tsikusaseh lived at the crossroads of people from the north, south, west, and east. The Peacemaker told her that she shouldn't help the warriors carry on their bloodshed. Bob Brown told me how their encounter happened.

> The Peacemaker came to a trail that leads to the east and to the west. He noticed men coming from different directions at different times. There was a dwelling. The Peacemaker noticed a woman inside and she told him to come inside. The Peacemaker told her of his responsibility to spread the good message. He said it was never the intention that we would take one another's lives. He came to realize that Tsikusaseh was feeding the men to give them nourishment to carry on and a place to rest. The men were engaged in warfare, and she knew it. Then she offered him food. He looked at the food she served him and saw bugs inside. He knew she was trying to poison him. Thankfully, he had a reed in his shirt. He pretended to eat the food, but he actually put it into the reed and it went out of the dwelling. He confronted her after the meal. He told her it's not up to her to decide who should live and who should die. She felt remorseful and said she wouldn't feed the warriors anymore.[13]

Gibson relayed the conversation that occurred between the Peacemaker and Tsikusaseh.

> [The Peacemaker] said, "You indeed are the person who has done a lot of work in relation to the warpath. . . . when they [the warriors] finish eating, they go on to kill people and also to scalp them. And when these warriors return, they stop here again, and again you feed them, doing so repeatedly, and you help both sides, those living to the west and to the east. So now you will stop; now, indeed, it is coming, the Good Message, also the Power, and also the Peace. Now, moreover, you will depart and towards the east that is where you will go. On the third day, indeed, you will become a peace chief and a leader for the Good Message, the Power, and the Peace.[14] There, moreover, you will arrive, at the place where they will assemble, the chiefs; and you

> will all cooperate in working on the Great Law, so that all of the people will survive, because now everyone will become related; now there will be peace in days and nights to come; and it will stop, the bloodshed among human beings here on earth. Moreover, we two will meet again there at the place where they will assemble, where a number of nations will unite by accepting the Good Message, the Power, and the Peace." Thereupon, Tsikuhsaseʔ said, "I accept the various words you have said to me. It will happen that I will go to the place where we will all meet again on the third day."[15]

After the Peacemaker convinced Tsikusaseh to stop feeding the warriors who passed through her home, she agreed to help spread the Peacemaker's message. She even helped the Peacemaker convince Tehototálho (the evil sorcerer in the Kayanlásla?kowa, or Great Law) to accept the message. It was Tsikusaseh who placed the antlers on Tehototálho. She was also responsible for instructing the women who would install subsequent chiefs. These clan mothers would then be responsible for feeding the chiefs. When you feed people, you feed them what you want them to be. Peace and caring should be in the food.

Oneida Chiefs Who Guarded the Corn

The Peacemaker not only emphasizes the value of feasting together but also highlights the importance of corn as the people's sustenance when he selects the first three Oneida chiefs from those guarding the corn. When the Peacemaker and his partner, Hayé·wateʔ, entered Oneida territory, the Peacemaker asked a person responsible for guarding cornfields why he did so. The man responded, "No one should spoil the field; they roam about, people we don't know, and they may spoil it, or perhaps wild animals might spoil the corn field, and this is what will impoverish the people, the old people and the infants and children. Actually, it is our sustenance, the corn."[16] When the Peacemaker asked what he does when he tends the corn, the man answered, "I hold my bow, and in my quiver are my arrows, and there I carry on my back; further I always sit close by the great tree that is down."[17] Hayé·wate? then gave him a new name, Ho?tatshehte?, meaning "the great tree." Another version explained that this man was renamed Oh-dah-tshe-deh, meaning "quiver bearer."[18] The Peacemaker then explained that his role in the community changed because of the Great Law: "Your duty as a guardian of the cornfields is now changed because the Good News of Peace and Power has now come. Your duty hereafter shall now be to see that your children (instead of fields) shall live in peace."[19]

When the Peacemaker asked who helped the one who guarded the corn, another man replied that he also tended to the fields. When the Peacemaker asked this man how he tended to the fields, the man responded, "When it just dawns, I am roaming about all over the field; sometimes I find corn cobs lying on the ground and I pick up as many as I can find. Then I take them back to the chief's house, and that is how we do it through harvest. Actually everything is owned jointly, and when the task is done, the way our chief distributes it is in equal shares for them to receive it, all of the people in the settlement."[20] The Peacemaker then gave him a new name, Kanukwe?yotu?, meaning "growing corncobs." The Peacemaker explained, "It shall therefore now be your duty to propagate the Good Tidings of Peace and Power so that your children may live in peace."[21]

The presence of three chiefs among the cornfields offers us two important pieces of insight. First, corn was an integral part of Haudenosaunee daily life. It was commonplace for people to be involved with the corn. In fact, there are many passing references to cornfields and foods made with corn throughout the Kayanlásla?kowa. Second, corn was so precious to the Haudenosaunee people that they had security posted day and night to watch over their fields. They protected their corn from animal predators as well as from other people. With the acceptance of the Peacemaker's message across the new confederacy, the need to guard the fields transferred to finding ways to protect the corn from animal predators.

Kanehelatúksla (To Extend Greetings and Thankfulness)

In explaining the message of Kanehelatúksla to the people, the Peacemaker reminded them of their original instructions as prescribed in the creation story to be thankful for all of creation. Gibson tells it this way:

> We shall thank the Creator of the earth, that is, he who planted all the kinds of weeds and all the varieties of shrubs and all the kinds of trees; and springs, flowing water, such as rivers and large bodies of water, such as lakes; and the sun that keeps moving by day, and by night the moon, and where the sky is, the stars, which no one is able to count; moreover, the way it is on earth in relation to which no one is able to tell the extent to which it is to their benefit, that is the people whom he created and who will continue to live on earth. This, then is the reason we thank him, the one with great power, the one who is the Creator, for the which will not move forward, the Good Message and the Power and the Peace; the Great Law.[22]

Along with thanksgiving comes the responsibility and power of sharing. The Peacemaker explained the commitment the chiefs made by reciting, "We promise to have only one dish among us; in it will be beaver tail and no knife will be there."[23] Not having a knife means no one will get cut and cause bloodshed. The one dish means they will have equal rights to use their shared territory.[24] They need to be mindful of not harvesting too many wild animals, and any animals they do harvest should be shared among all the people. The same is true of harvests of fields. If one community had a blight or other disaster that impacted their crops, another community would be there to share their harvests with them. Similarly, when traveling among the various communities, each community had an obligation to care for their traveling guests.

Chef Arlie Doxtator told me a story about cooking beaver tail soup for a recital of the Great Law. He was cooking alongside Angela Ferguson, a well-known seed keeper and Onondaga Nation farm supervisor.

"There's a part of the Great Law where it talks about the chiefs eating beaver tail. Nobody knows when it stopped, but I think about two hundred years ago, and there is no recipe. Sometime later, I was planning on going to the Great Law recital and Angela called me and asked if I wanted to help cook. I was thinking 'I don't know,' but of course I have to. I talked to Sue [his wife], and she was like, 'Just go! You want to go, so go!' Moments later Angela called me back and said, 'You will never guess what happened. My cousin just gifted us two beavers.' I asked if they came with any recipes and Angela said they didn't. I told her that I haven't found any either. So, here's what I'm going to do: I am going to put some tobacco down, I am going to ask for some guidance, maybe kaye nihayukwetaku will instruct me because they are not only protectors but beings that will help you and will talk to you. So, I asked specifically when I burned my tobacco. About two days later, I called Angela and told her I got some instructions in a dream about what we are supposed to do.

"So, I originally brought my big pot out to Great Law. I was going to cook everything in this big pot, but there was only like maybe about eight or ten chiefs up there for the recital. So, I had brought my smaller one that I had with me, and we started with it. This clay pot has four effigies [faces] around the rim.

"In order to get the beaver tail meat, you have to sear the skin, and what that will do, it will pop up and that way it will separate from the meat. And we have to do that over maple wood. So, I did that. The next step is that we're supposed to smoke it with cedar and sage. The sage was not as important for us, but the cedar was very important for us. So, I smoked it with those two things for probably about an hour and a half, and then we took the meat off of the bone, and that went into the soup. Then I started in that clay pot. I started cooking cranberry beans in a white pine tea and water from the kanʌstóhale. Then I put the beaver tail back into it and I had to go back into the kitchen to get some stuff done.

"Angela was out there, and there was a young Tuscarora guy who was helping this other guy make soup, so he was watching the fire, so I gave him specific instructions. I told him there should be no flames, just good coals.

I told him to just keep the coals going to see how hard it's boiling. That's how I wanted to simmer. So, I am in the kitchen. Angela comes running, *running*, into the kitchen, and she said, 'Oh my God! You will never guess what's happened!' I'm thinking someone spilled the soup. As we're rushing to the soup, Angela told me to look at the pot. Remember, this clay pot has four effigies around it. Each one of those effigies turned a different color. They turned red, yellow, white, and a dark blue almost purple color. Angela explained that there were four of them watching and they all witnessed the colors changing. By the time I got out there, it was over with, but she said they were each a bright color.

"So, I'm walking, and I hear this behind me: 'Don't forget about me.' I turned around and expected to see Angela there, but I didn't notice anyone there. I went back into the kitchen, and I keep hearing this 'don't forget about me, don't forget about me' in my mind. When I got back in the kitchen, I was stirring the beans, and then I remembered that I forgot the squash. So, I pulled the squash out of the oven and cut it up and put it in the soup.

"The next thing I knew, I was in tears. I was bawling like a little baby. Angela came around the corner and she asked if I was okay. I told her to stir the soup. She said, 'Oh my God, Arlie!' I looked at Angela and she was bawling. The energy in this thing was just powerful. Normally, there were always about twenty people in the kitchen, but for some reason it was just the two of us. Slowly, people started to come in one at a time. Every time someone came in, we told them to be sure to stir the soup to get some of that energy. When it was time to serve the soup, we took it to the chiefs and told them the whole story of what happened. They were all so happy and appreciative. We told them that as long as we get beaver, we will continue to do this for every recital."[25]

Conclusion

In his infancy, the Peacemaker was giving us lessons about how we should trust, love, and respect our family as well as how we should care for our corn.

FIGURE 4. Chef Arlie Doxtator holding a clay pot he cooked in. He cooked in a similar pot for the Great Law Recital. Oneida artist Stephanie Muscavitch made the pot in this photo.

When the Peacemaker came across the individuals who would become our first Oneida chiefs, he saw them caring for our corn. He explained that if we accepted his message, we would not have to watch the corn for invaders and we could ensure our children lived in peace. The single act of accepting this message would later protect our children and our corn.

The formation of the confederacy demonstrates how the Peacemaker and his partner were able to strategically bring together communities and have them accept a common vision for how they would govern themselves and resolve conflicts. Together they formed a complex and fully functioning participatory democracy that continues to operate today. Corn played a significant role in bringing the people together and continues to play a role when the people convene. So enduring are the principles that brought our people together that we will look to our confederacy when we are in need while also promising to be there for others when they are in need.

CHAPTER 4

Wahutatya·thewéwe

(They Arrived)

NE· YAKΛ LATUHÁKWE THAT EXPLORATION IS THE FIRST STEP TO COLONIZATION. The early explorers that ventured into our ancestors' territory were reporting back to their European sponsors in the hopes of colonizing land that was new to them, but not new to the people who lived here since Sky Woman fell from the sky. These early colonizers were amazed at the strength of the Yukwanuhsyu·ní through their agricultural practices, knowledge, and respect. As a result, the colonizers soon targeted agriculture in the subsequent military conflicts. This chapter examines some of the writings from early explorers and colonizers to see how they documented Yukwanuhsyu·ní corn and agriculture and then attacked it.

Journals of the Explorers

Leif Erikson supposedly ventured into North America around 1000 AD and reported back about "self-sown wheat fields."[1] Some opined that the wheat field reference must have been wild rice, while others claimed it had to be corn.[2] It appears the debate is still not settled.[3] There is also debate about where these Norse explorers were venturing. Some say it was the present-day St. Lawrence region while others say they made it all the way to Massachusetts.[4] Nearly five hundred years later, Columbus journaled about corn the same year his lost ships landed on the Caribbean shore in 1492.[5] By 1498, the Spanish were growing corn in Castille, Spain. Many of the explorers that came after Columbus and traveled in the northeastern part of the continent documented their fascination with the ability of the Yukwanuhsyu·ní to grow and harvest massive amounts of a variety of foods.

In 1535, Jacques Cartier traveled up what is now called the St. Lawrence River and journaled about Yukwanuhsyu·ní people tending to large fields of corn and storing large quantities.[6] When Cartier arrived, he was already familiar with the three sisters due to the previous reports of explorers who came before him and the decades that Europeans had been growing food from the Americas in their homelands.[7]

Samuel de Champlain also recorded his exploration along the St. Lawrence River. On July 10, 1605, he wrote about Yukwanuhsyu·ní planting methods.

> They till and cultivate the soil, something which we have not hitherto observed. In place of ploughs, they use an instrument of hard wood, shaped like a spade. This river is called by the inhabitants of the country Chouacoet. The next day Sieur de Monts and I landed to observe their tillage on the banks of the river. We saw their Indian corn which they raise in gardens. Planting three or four kernels in one place they then heap up about it a quantity of earth with shells of the signoc before mentioned. Then three feet distant they plant as much more, and this in succession. With this corn they put in each hill three or four Brazilian beans which are of different colours. When they grow up they interlace with the corn which reaches to the height of from five to six feet; and they keep the ground very free from weeds. We saw many squashes and pumpkins and tobacco which they likewise cultivate . . . the Indian corn which we saw at that time was about two feet high and some as

> high as three. The beans were beginning to flower as also, the pumpkins and squashes. They plant their corn in May and gather it in September.[8]

On September 13, 1609, explorer Henry Hudson wrote in his log about the large quantities of the Yukwanuhsyu·ní-stored corn along with beans and squash: "I saw there a house well constructed of oak bark . . . a great quantity of maize or Indian corn and beans of last year's growth, and there lay near the house for the purpose of drying enough to load three ships, besides what was growing in the fields."[9]

From 1623 to 1624, Friar Gabriel Sagard served as a missionary among the Hurons. While the Hurons were a distinct people from the Yukwanuhsyu·ní, they were closely related and located near each other. Like the Yukwanuhsyu·ní, the Hurons were well known for growing corn. Sagard wrote a detailed account of the Huron ways of storing corn that warrants quoting in full.

> The wheat (Indian corn) being thus sown in the manner that we do beans, of a grain obtained only from a stalk or cane, the cane bears two or three spikes, and each spike yields a hundred, two hundred, sometimes 400 grains, and some yield even more. The cane grows to the height of a man and more, and is very large . . . in the Huron country. The grain ripens in four months and in some places three. After this they gather and bind the leaves (husks), turned up at the top and arrange it in sheaves (braids), which they hang all along the length of the cabin from top to bottom on poles, which they arrange in the form of a rack descending to the front edge of the bench. All this is so nicely done that it seems like a tapestry hung the whole length of the cabins. The grain being well dried and suitable to press (or pound) the women and girls take out the grains, clean them and put them in their large tubs (tonnes) made for this purpose, and placed in their porch or in one corner of the cabins.[10]

Harmen Meyndertsz van den Bogaert, a young explorer listed as a "barber-surgeon," kept a journal during his expedition into Mohawk and Oneida communities from December 11, 1634, to January 21, 1634.[11] He wrote about houses full of corn stored for the winter. "These houses were full of grain that they call ONESTI and we corn, indeed, some held 300 or 400 skipples [a Dutch measurement equivalent to about 0.764 bushels]."[12] Some houses were so full of grain and beans that the structures were dedicated solely for the purpose of storing food. Van den Bogaert also remarked on the customs of feeding guests: "This day we were invited to eat bear's meat. In the chief's house three or four meals were eaten everyday. Whatever was not cooked there was brought in from other houses in large kettles, because the council came here everyday to eat; and whosever is in the house, received a wooden bowl full of food, for it is the custom that every man who comes here, receives a bowl full. If bowls are lacking, then they bring their own bowls and spoons. They then sit down next to one another where the bowls are fetched and brought back full, because an invited guest does not stand up until he has eaten."[13]

In 1653, another explorer visited a Mohawk community and wrote about their farming practices.

> The women do all the farming and planting. The men are hardly concerned with it, unless they are very young or very old when they help the women under the latter's discretion. . . . [They] raise so much corn and beans that we purchase these from them in fully loaded yachts and sloops. They know nothing of manuring, fallow seasons, and proper tillage. The labor they devote to farming is all manual, using small adzes [cutting tool] that are sold to them for this purpose.[14]

Mary Jemison offered a different view of farming among the Yukwanuhsyu·ní. She was a white woman captured by the Senecas in 1755 when she was twelve years old.[15] She refused to leave when she had an opportunity, choosing to make a life for herself among the Senecas. She described the work in the fields as "leisurely." Forty to fifty women would meet up at a set time to work. "While hoeing weeds together, the women would carry bundles of short sticks, each with a personal sign and brightly decorated. These sticks were used to mark their workplace and to call attention to their work."[16] In

1790, one explorer described Oneida soils and farming as follows: "The land these Indians inhabit is one of the richest and most fertile on our globe. It is generally of open plains, cut from time to time only by small rivers and hills, and full of lakes abounding with fish and salubrious waters. But with the exception of small cultivated fields that are found close to their dwellings, all the rest is covered by thickest forests, in which about several species of quadrupeds and birds."[17]

JOURNALS OF MILITARY EXPEDITIONS

While the explorers were reporting back on their "discoveries," military officers were traveling with their troops through Yukwanuhsyu·ní territory, attacking the residents' fields and stored food. Arthur Parker explained these military tactics of the early 1600s as follows: "When the Iroquois took possession of the territory which we now know as New York State, they carried on corn culture on a large scale and so important an article of food and commerce was it that most of the European invaders of their territory burned their cornfields and destroyed their corncribs instead of shooting the Iroquois themselves."[18]

In 1615, Champlain led the first of many French expeditions into Yukwanuhsyu·ní territory in an effort to destroy the confederacy, employing tactics aimed at destroying corn.[19] These expeditions, known as the Beaver Wars, occurred through 1696, although they didn't succeed in destroying Yukwanuhsyu·ní power. In 1666, an expedition into a single Mohawk community resulted in the destruction of enough corn, beans, and squash "to nourish all Canada for two entire years."[20]

In 1687, during this series of expeditions, a French general named Jacques-René de Brisay de Denonville detailed similar efforts.

> I deemed it our best policy to employ ourselves laying the Indian corn which was in vast abundance in the fields, rather than to follow a flying enemy to a distance and excite our troops to catch only some straggling fugitives. . . . We

> remained at the four Seneca villages until the 24th; the two larger distant four leagues and the others two. All that time was spent in destroying the corn which was in such great abundance that the loss including old corn which was in cache which we burnt and that which was standing, was computed according to the estimate afterwards made at 400 thousand minots [1,200 bushels or 72,000 pounds] of Indian corn.[21]

After his attack, the Senecas dispersed with the warriors heading into the woods and the Seneca warriors sent the Seneca people to stay with the Cayugas and Onondagas, while the Mohawks went to stay among the Oneidas.[22]

Conclusion

The early explorers marveled at our corn and other crops, and the military generals targeted those same crops in an effort to defeat Yukwanuhsyu·ní people. When my oldest daughter, Grace Webster, learned of this period in time, she became very upset at the apparent betrayal. Grace lamented:

> We were perfectly fine before the explorers came. We all helped each other grow and hunt for food. We helped each other survive. The Haudenosaunee was one big family. When the explorers first came, they seemed friendly because they spoke positively about our ways and our crops. We fed them and opened up our homes to them. They were impressed with how much food we grew. They admired our agriculture and our ways, but it seemed they were just scheming on how to take it from us. When I learned about this part of our history, I was really upset. I wished there was something I could do, but there was nothing I could do. There was probably nothing they could have done either. There were too many colonists coming into our territory.[23]

Yukwanuhsyu·ní philosophy is to extend our rafters over all those who need protection and are willing to accept the Great Law. From Grace's perspective, and from the perspective of many Indigenous people, we welcomed the European explorers into our territory and they repaid us with bloodshed.

The act of destroying our life sustenance would crescendo with the Revolutionary War. The number of homes, corn, and other foods military campaigns destroyed prior to that war couldn't compare with the devastating losses the Yukwanuhsyu·ní suffered in the span of a few weeks in the fall of 1779. Countless Yukwanuhsyu·ní people succumbed to the elements and starved in the winter that followed.

CHAPTER 5

Wohotiliwahokénha

(They Tangled over Matters)

NE· YAKΛ LATUHÁKWE THE MID TO LATE 1700S WAS A DARK AND COMPLEX TIME in Yukwanuhsyu·ní history. The Beaver Wars officially ended in 1701, but peace would not last long. During the French and Indian Wars (1754–1763), the confederacy sided with the British to help them fight against the French.[1] A little over a decade after the wars, the American colonists revolted against British control and fought for independence. In the years that followed, the Oneida and Tuscarora would find themselves on one side of the conflict with the rest of the confederacy on the other side.[2] Even though they remained on opposite sides throughout the war, the Oneidas did everything they could to stop the colonists from attacking Yukwanuhsyu·ní villages.[3] This chapter's goal is to provide a brief overview of this period of time with an emphasis on the impact the Revolutionary War had on Yukwanuhsyu·ní relationships with each other and with corn.

Before getting into the details, it is important to note that numerous books and journal articles have been written on this complex and tragic period.

Historians report what happened to humans. They report on how much corn, beans, squash, and how many orchards were burned and destroyed during the Revolutionary War. But if you don't have a relationship with our food relatives, those numbers don't mean anything. It wasn't just food the Yukwanuhsyu·ní lost. Our relatives, our sisters—the corn, beans, and squash—were burned and destroyed. Treatment of food is synonymous with treatment of our relatives because these foods are our relatives.

No Yukwanuhsyu·ní Consensus

In late August 1775, at the beginning of the Revolutionary War, a delegation that included representatives from all the tribes in the Yukwanuhsyu·ní Confederacy went to Albany, New York, to meet with the Indian commissioners appointed by the Continental Congress.[4] The commissioners assured the Yukwanuhsyu·ní that they could remain neutral in the new revolutionary war and would not be compelled to take sides. The commissioners went so far as to request that the Yukwanuhsyu·ní remain neutral.[5]

Oneidas had more contact with the colonists than the other Yukwanuhsyu·ní tribes and perceived them as allies.[6] The Mohawks, on the other hand, lost their homelands to white colonists and thought that if they could defeat the colonists, they might be able to get their homelands back.[7] Beginning in 1775, some Oneidas served as spies for the colonists. Recognizing those long-standing relationships, when the Yukwanuhsyu·ní convened a grand council meeting in 1776, the rest of the confederacy did not provide a full account of their relationships with the British. During this meeting, the Yukwanuhsyu·ní recommitted to remaining neutral in the war. When confronted about passing information to the colonists, the Oneidas explained that they were helping their friends in minor ways but nonetheless agreed to resume acting with strict neutrality.

This commitment did not last long, and the tribes began to choose sides in the war. Joseph Brant, a Mohawk Christian missionary and British military officer, tried to convince the Yukwanuhsyu·ní to side with the British. The Senecas and Cayugas agreed, along with some Mohawks and some Tuscaroras. Many factors, including Oneida's relationship with Reverend Samuel Kirkland, eventually caused the Oneidas and their Tuscarora guests to side with the American colonists in the Revolutionary War.[8] Like many missionaries of his time, Kirkland preached the gospel of the plow and the Bible, encouraging his Oneida followers to abandon their traditional practices in favor of a European lifestyle. Kirkland was especially persuasive because he made an effort to learn the Oneida language and was able to preach in the language.

In an effort to remind the Yukwanuhsyu·ní of their commitments to each other, Oneida Chief Skenandoah had a wampum belt made that consisted of six diamond shapes and six square shapes to represent each of the tribes and council fires of the Six Nations within the Yukwanuhsyu·ní Confederacy. It has two white lines making a path along the diamonds to symbolize the peace and friendship among the nations. This belt is called the Oneida Tribal Belt. The purpose of the belt was to remind the Yukwanuhsyu·ní of the original message the Peacemaker brought with him and the reasons why the tribes agreed to form a confederacy of peace, protection, and unity.

Efforts to remind each other of their commitments under the Great Law of Peace could not hold the confederacy together as a unified front. The tumultuous relationships among the Yukwanuhsyu·ní were strained even further in the winter of 1776–1777. That winter brought an epidemic to Onondaga that killed ninety people, including three chiefs.[9] Some historians report that the Yukwanuhsyu·ní covered their council fire during this time, concluding that the confederacy had finally been defeated. However, this is not an accurate portrayal of what happened.[10] The way the Yukwanuhsyu·ní made decisions to try to reach a consensus was by sending issues back and forth among the tribes.[11] The issue of choosing sides in the war came to the Onondagas, and they understood the reasoning of each tribe to choose the side they chose. The Onondagas said that each nation should decide on their own what to do, with the understanding that no matter what choices anyone made, the war was going to impact them all. The Onondagas decided that the only thing to do would be to cover up the council fire to protect the peace they had among each other. Covering up the fire did not mean the Yukwanuhsyu·ní were defeated. They were protecting their ideal of what it meant to be a confederacy. What was going on outside their territory and outside their government would impact them individually, but it would not impact the confederacy as a whole.

In 1777, Oneidas fought alongside the colonists in both the Battle of Oriskany and the Battle of Saratoga.[12] In April 1778, the French, who were allied with the colonists, stayed in Oneida for a month to discuss building an American fort in Oneida territory for the Oneida's protection.[13] A French military officer wrote about the Oneida's hospitality in a letter to the commander at Fort Schuyler (also known as Fort Stanwix).[14] In the letter, he wrote, "We are at present plenty of Corn, which we receive from the Indians themselves, who made a prohibition to receive any money for it . . . and every day they Carry Corn much more than we want for fitting our horses."[15] The Oneidas delivering corn to the colonial troops during the war was a common occurrence during the Revolutionary War.

Polly Cooper, 1778

In the winter of 1778, Chief Shenandoah organized a relief mission to help feed George Washington's starving troops.[16] According to oral tradition, Oneida warriors walked hundreds of miles from central New York to Valley Forge and brought hundreds of bushels of white corn to share with the troops. An Oneida woman named Polly Cooper was among the delegation.

Upon their arrival in 1778, the warriors became acquainted with Washington's troops, and Polly Cooper got set up to prepare some corn.[17] While oral tradition explains that the Oneidas brought hundreds of bushels, other accounts state that the Oneidas lacked the corn and transportation capacity to feed the entire army. Regardless of the amounts, Washington and his troops welcomed the food. "Polly shelled the ears, ground the kernels into meal, boiled the corn soup, and mixed these items with available fruits and nuts, all with the intent of showing the soldiers how to improve the nutritional quality and taste of their sparse diets."[18] After the war, the Oneida warriors and Polly Cooper refused to accept payment for their services.[19] According to oral tradition, Polly explained that it was her duty to help friends in their time of need.[20] To express gratitude, Martha Washington sent her a shawl and bonnet, both of which are still in the care of Polly's descendants.

Today, when Oneida people talk about how their ancestors helped save Washington's starving army, some may be proud of those actions while others may be reminding the United States of one more debt they owe us. For me, when I think of Polly Cooper, I think of Tsikusaseh, the Mother of Nations, the woman who helped the Peacemaker and his partner form the Yukwanuhsyu·ní Confederacy. The Peacemaker had to convince Tsikusaseh that her actions in feeding the warriors who came to her home were wrong. She knew that by feeding the warriors, they would continue to spill each other's blood. Even though the confederacy's council fire was covered up during this time, I wonder what the Peacemaker would have thought about the Oneida people feeding an army they knew was coming for their relatives. Additionally, the only three chiefs the Peacemaker found tending to the cornfields were all Oneida chiefs. He instilled in them responsibilities for our foods. Generations later, those chiefs fed the enemies of our relatives with our sister corn. I can understand why other people in the confederacy may still have hard feelings for the actions of my ancestors.

In 2019, a group of Oneidas traveled to Cayuga territory in New York for a Braiding the Sacred event. This event was a gathering of corn growers to share ideas, stories, knowledge, seeds, and cooking methods. It was a great networking opportunity where we shared many corn-based meals. During one of the talking sessions, a man in Cayuga chastised our group for what Oneidas did during the Revolutionary War. Our whole group was humiliated and didn't quite know how to respond. So, we all put our heads down as he continued to talk about how the Oneidas betrayed the confederacy. I'm not commenting on whether he was right or wrong to do this. We all process trauma in different ways. I say this because within our confederacy, we still have a lot of healing to do. For me, one of the ways I am healing is by growing Oneida white flour corn, the same corn that Oneida people fed to Washington's starving army. This is different from the Tuscarora white corn that most people in our community grow. I am growing the Oneida corn to reestablish that relationship with this variety of corn so I can share her within our community. I want others to grow her, too, so they can nourish their bodies with her ancient healing properties. I want us to celebrate this corn in a time of peace and community building instead of only thinking about her role in a bloody war.

Sullivan's Campaign, 1779

In a war that was supposed to be between the colonists and the British, the Yukwanuhsyu·ní found themselves to be full-fledged participants. The Oneidas quickly became the object of resentment among the Yukwanuhsyu·ní due to the help they provided to the colonists.[21] However, in 1779, when George Washington ordered Major General John Sullivan to attack the four Yukwanuhsyu·ní nations that sided with the British, the Oneida hesitated to participate. Only a few Oneida warriors agreed to accompany Sullivan on his campaign, and there exists no evidence of any Yukwanuhsyu·ní engaging in the crop destruction that would infamously mark Sullivan's campaign.[22] As one historian explained it, "When Indian, rather than white, communities were the principal targets of Patriot military action, Oneida cooperation evaporated, and mitigation became their primary object."[23]

The journals of Sullivan and his officers provide insight into the breadth of their damage throughout Yukwanuhsyu·ní territory as well as the overall apparent lack of participation by the Oneidas. On July 11, 1779, one journal entry noted the promise of twenty-five Oneidas to join the effort: "a letter was received by express from General Clinton, dated head of Lake Otsego, announcing that twenty-five Oneida warriors had joined him."[24] It does not appear that twenty-five Oneidas ever showed up, because these sources include only a few sparse references to Oneidas helping. The following month, on August 22, the same journal noted that "with General Clinton came only two of the Oneidas."[25] On August 25, the journal noted the arrival of three more Oneidas.

Based on the contents of the journals of Sullivan and his officers, it does not appear as though Sullivan relied much on the assistance of the Oneidas as his nearly four thousand men carried out their brief yet destructive campaign.[26] Sullivan's campaign officially began on June 13, but his troops didn't attack the first village until August 12. The campaign ended on October 3; this time of year is when Yukwanuhsyu·ní people begin to harvest their corn. The series of attacks were strategic and brutal. Sullivan noted in his report that "the Indians shall see that there is malice enough in our hearts to destroy everything that contributes to their support."[27]

The journals detailed accounts of the devastation. In addition to the thousands of fruit trees uprooted and cut down, Sullivan and his men destroyed an unknown amount of beans, squash, and other vegetables, as well as an astounding 9.6 million pounds of corn.[28] They destroyed hundreds of homes in over forty Yukwanuhsyu·ní towns. The destruction was so commonplace in the journals, the men eventually began to make casual references to the quantities of corn and the number of homes they burned at each successive location. At each location, they ate their fill, packed a bit to supplement their rations, fed their animals, and destroyed the rest. When they came upon the towns, they commonly noted that the residents must have fled in a hurry because they often left behind their food cooking over a fire. Fleeing, or even a temporary truce, seemed to be preferable over the loss of life that would ensue if the residents chose to stay and fight.[29] Flight was possible because of the few Oneidas who accompanied Sullivan and ran ahead to warn the people in the villages that the troops were on their way.[30]

The Oneidas that joined Sullivan unsuccessfully tried to stop him from continuing his path of destruction through Yukwanuhsyu·ní territory. On September 18, the army was near Canandaigua Lake. One officer noted that they met an Oneida man who "brought a message from that Nation on behalf of the Cayuga Nation besides some other important despatches [*sic*]."[31] Another officer relayed the envoy's message: "the nation congratulated our chief on the success of his arms in this quarter, and begged that Cayuga settlement might be spared for the sake of the few righteous among them; that the corn would greatly alleviate the distresses of the friendly Onondagas, but the matrimonial connections of these tribes rendering the requisition suspicious, it was not granted. He likewise informed them that Marquis LaFayette had arrived; that New York was burned; with a number of stories calculated to gain their point; but all are supposed to be Indian tales."[32] It's clear from this entry that the officers knew the Yukwanuhsyu·ní bonds were strong. They understood that they may have chosen opposite sides of the war, but they did not choose to fight among each other. After all, this was a war between the colonists and the British. They surrounded Yukwanuhsyu·ní territory. It would have been nearly impossible for anyone to remain neutral in the conflict.

A couple days later, the Oneida tried again to get Sullivan to stop his campaign and accept the surrender of the Cayuga. On September 20, an officer wrote of Sullivan's rejection of the Oneida's proposal to stop burning corn and villages:

> the greater part of the day was employed at head-quarters in holding a council in consequence of the intercession made by some Oneida Indians, (our friends) in favour of the Cayuga tribe, who have been for some time past in alliance with the Senecas, and acted with them, and are now desirous to make peace with us. The council determined no treaty should be held with them, and a command of five hundred infantry, with Major Parr's rifle corps, were immediately detached and sent to Cayuga lake, on which their settlement lay, with orders to lay wait and destroy their towns, corn, &c., and receive none of them but in the characters of prisoners of war.[33]

Instead of accepting the Cayuga's surrender, the troops continued their path of destruction for two more weeks until Sullivan declared victory over the Yukwanuhsyu·ní Confederacy. His victory failed to recognize that the

Oneidas remained part of the Yukwanuhsyu·ní Confederacy and sided with the colonists throughout the entirety of the Revolutionary War. Perhaps the Oneidas who pleaded with him to stop his destruction or the apparent actions of the Oneidas to warn their fellow Yukwanuhsyu·ní of the incoming attacks caused Sullivan to claim victory over the entire confederacy.

Aftermath of the War

The aftermath of Sullivan's campaign was utterly devastating, and his claims of victory over the whole confederacy continue to permeate history books. One hundred years after the Sullivan campaign, Reverend David Craft gave several addresses celebrating Sullivan's historic victory. In one such paper from 1879 that was "carefully revised and amplified" prior to publication,[34] Craft declared that the Yukwanuhsyu·ní deserved the attacks: "They returned to their blackened homes and wasted cornfields, and looked with despair upon the waste and ruin before them . . . but the act was as justifiable as that which slays the assassin at your door, or the man who is applying the torch to your dwelling."[35]

In 1780, Seneca, Onondaga, Cayuga, and Mohawk war parties surrounded Oneida and Tuscarora villages, coercing village residents into leaving.[36] Many fled to Niagara where a total of five thousand Yukwanuhsyu·ní sought refuge.[37] In June, a Mohawk and Cayuga war party unsuccessfully pressured warriors from Oneida to join the British.[38] In July, Captain Joseph Brant led a war party that burned Oneida and Tuscarora settlements.[39] Four hundred Oneida and Tuscarora refugees sought aid and shelter at Fort Schuyler (a.k.a. Fort Stanwix). There were too many refugees for the fort to house, so General Schuyler sent them to Schenectady. The military hastily built them "miserable huts, scarcely fit for winter habitation."[40] Although many later moved into the barracks, Schuyler was unable to persuade Congress to send blankets. He eventually advanced the money on his own credit to purchase blankets, but they did not arrive in time. Many Oneida and Tuscarora refugees died from hunger, cold, and smallpox that winter. This is how the colonists repaid the Oneidas for their assistance in the colonists' war.

Shortly after the close of the Revolutionary War, the Yukwanuhsyu·ní relit their council fire at Onondaga to reunify the confederacy. They again brought out the Oneida tribal wampum belt to reaffirm their commitments to each other as a confederacy. In the 1830s, Turtle Clan Chief Elijah Skenandoah brought the belt to Wisconsin.[41] While on a trip to Albany, his acquaintances stole all his ceremonial clothing and possessions, including the Oneida Tribal Belt.[42] Today, the belt resides at the Field Museum in Chicago, pending repatriation efforts.[43] However, the three current and distinct Oneida communities are not in agreement as to which community should take possession of the belt, indefinitely stalling any repatriation efforts.[44]

The Corn Remembers the War

Sullivan's brief and destructive campaign might not have resulted in the immediate death of Yukwanuhsyu·ní people, but the remainder of the Revolutionary War cost lives on all sides of the conflict. Kwnwahta Smith, an Oneida youth and member of Ohe·láku, explained that an elder in New York told him:

> the red dots that show up on the white corn doesn't mean that it's bad. It's still good for you to eat. It has some of our history inside of that corn. Way back, we were sharing borders with George Washington's colonies. We made a treaty with George Washington and the thirteen colonies, but they didn't like us. They still thought we were brown savages. They encroached on our hunting lands, and they shot at us. They were trying to kill us, so we fought back, and we killed them. But then the colonies demanded George Washington handle the savages. So, he came to our villages, and he started messing with our people, raping our women, mutilating our people, burning our crops. That's why we call George Washington the village burner. Our people, we came out

> of the ashes. We were still able to preserve some of the corn. It was burned and ashed up, but we ate this survival food. It got us through the hard times and through the winter when we were very low on food. He told me the blood of our ancestors seeped into the soil, into the ground, into the dirt. It stayed there and it's connected to the corn. That blood of our ancestors is ingrained into the corn's DNA and it's a part of the history. When we get cobs with the shells of the corn that has red spots, it's a reminder that we need to remember our history and appreciate our resiliency.[45]

Similarly, chef Arlie Doxtator talked about the corn remembering its relatives.

> The corn is here to remind us so we don't forget where we came from. We had corn that had the pink in it. When I talked to some of the elders at Onondaga, they told me about how the Tuscaroras got that pink one called Tuscarora Rose. All of a sudden, it came back. So somewhere along that line, the Tuscarora Rose is making itself known again to remind us not to forget our relatives. Scientists will tell you there is a deficiency in the soil. Whatever. They can keep that. The corn is telling me a lot of our history.[46]

Conclusion

Of all the moments in history among the Yukwanuhsyu·ní, this one was the hardest for me to write about. Our original instructions tell us to be thankful for all of creation. They tell us we are all related and connected. We have responsibilities to the rest of creation, and they have responsibilities for us. The Kayanlásla?kowa̲ tells us that we need to seek out peace. I can't imagine what that must have been like for any Yukwanuhsyu·ní person, on either side of the conflict. I can't imagine what that must have been like to flee your home knowing that you would return to see everything demolished and gone. I can't imagine what that must have been like to be unable to protect our three sisters and other food relatives from being destroyed. The few Oneidas who accompanied Sullivan tried to get him to stop but were powerless to impart real change in the course of his destruction campaign.

The amounts of destroyed crops reported in the journals are enormous. People must have worked years to build up that much food in storage. The acreage of standing corn was likewise massive and hard to comprehend. They successfully grew acres and acres of our three sisters, all without the aid of modern farming equipment. They grew this food in community after community, working together. When we grow our small plots, we are so happy and thankful. I can't imagine how they would have reacted to how overjoyed we are with the relatively small amounts we grow in comparison to what they grew. I would hope they would rejoice that we are picking up our agricultural practices again, and that we are once again caring for our three sisters.

A way for me to process the trauma of reading these accounts came in the form of making a cornhusk doll. I took the words of Arthur Parker and wrote them on the husks before making the doll. His personal reflections as well as the historical accounts from these explorers and invaders in the 1600s and 1700s make up the "fabric" of the clothes this cornhusk doll wears. Colonization and federal assimilation policies stole much away from us. Despite that, the corn still survives, and she will continue to help us remember our history and our responsibilities. This cornhusk doll is my act of remembrance for this era.

Kaliwihyo

(Good Message)

NE· YAKΛ LATUHÁKWE THE KALIWIHYO (GOOD WORDS), MORE COMMONLY referred to as "The Code of Handsome Lake," attempted to bring the Yukwanuhsyu·ní people together after the Revolutionary War to remind us how to treat each other and be thankful for all of creation. In essence, it was an opportunity for the Yukwanuhsyu·ní people to recall their original instructions. During this time, both the corn and the people were suffering. Efforts to reunify the Yukwanuhsyu·ní came in the form of teachings from Skanatalihyo (Handsome Lake).

This chapter will take a closer look at the state of agriculture during this time as well as those sections of Skanatalihyo's teachings that pertain to food and agriculture.[1] In particular, this chapter contains lessons about sharing and stealing food, turning food into alcohol, and having too much pride in our gardens; a prophecy about short corn; lessons about giving thanks for the three sisters; and a story about the corn wanting to leave with Skanatalihyo. Like many of our stories and teachings, the Kaliwihyo can take days to tell, and different people have different variations on his story and his teachings.

Conditions after the Revolutionary War

In the years that followed the Revolutionary War, Yukwanuhsyu·ní communities faced many hardships. Cayuga Chief Jacob Thomas, working with Canadian author Terry Boyle, described the Yukwanuhsyu·ní during this bleak period:

> Towards the end of the 1700s, the Iroquois Confederacy began to deteriorate. Although the Confederacy had protected their territory from the Dutch, English, French, and the Thirteen Colonies (which later became the United States of America), their population was down to one-quarter of what it had been when white people had first arrived. Diseases to which they had no immunity—like measles, chicken pox, and smallpox—had swept through their villages. In 1779 the American General John Sullivan destroyed the basis of Iroquois power by burning their villages and cornfields and destroying a large number of the warehouses that held their supplies. The Hotinónshon:ni [Haudenosaunee] saw their territories decreasing and many of them turned to the fur trade for survival.[2]

The federal government placed the Oneida people on a reservation in their traditional territory in New York.[3] In 1794, Quaker William Savery wrote about the conditions there, with an emphasis on the overall goal of converting the Oneidas to Christianity. He observed that the Oneidas may have known the Bible but did not live up to his expectations of Christianized people.

> Ruminating on the state of the Oneida Indians, who are said to be more civilized than any others, it is natural to inquire what influence it has had on their manners and morals, which, from anything I can discover, has yet been very small. It is true, they generally cultivate a small portion of land, and for that reason are less exposed to absolute want than other Indians: they have also heard of Jesus Christ through their missionary, and have been taught to sing psalms and hymns . . . but it appears to me that the great body of

> the nation have received the Gospel in word only, and not in power. It has, therefore, had but little influence on their conduct.[4]

Similarly, Jedidiah Morse and Jeremy Belknap visited Oneida and Stockbridge territory in New York in June and July of 1796 for the purpose of reporting back to the board of commissioners of a Scottish missionary organization. They reported that not many Oneida families were growing gardens and instead they had to purchase corn and meat from their Stockbridge neighbors:

> Their agriculture is in its infancy, labor being performed almost wholly by the women. An Oneida chief, John Skanandogh excepted, would think himself degraded by driving a team or guiding a plough.
>
> Not more than 2 or 3 families procure a subsistence by agriculture and these have little encouragement to proceed, because their neighbors will live upon them as long as they have anything to eat. They may be said to procure a "subsistence" by fishing and fowling, and by raising some corn and beans and potatoes by the labor of their squaws, and by the help of what money they receive, hereafter to be mentioned; but what subsistence they get in these and all other ways would hardly be tho't "decent" by any people except themselves.
>
> The Oneidas affect to despise their neighbors of Stockbridge and Brothertown for their attention to agriculture, but they are obliged to buy their corn and meat of them. We saw several Oneida women bearing burdens of corn on their backs, which they had been thither to buy.[5]

In addition, their report noted that those few families that did have gardens shared what they could with other families in the community.

> They allow any of their people to fence and cultivate as much land as they please, and to take off the crops; but the land is the common property of the nation; and if one who has been at the pains to do this should have more corn or meat than is sufficient for his own use in the winter season, they will visit him, and expect to be fed as long as there is anything to be eaten. This is a

> great discouragement to those who are disposed to be industrious, of which the number is but small.[6]

This Western, liberal, individualist perspective ran counter to the ideals of sharing and hospitality that were central values for the Oneida people. Tensions ensued over these differences in values. To exacerbate the situation, there was a high number of murders occurring on the Oneida Reservation. Between November 1795 and June 1796, there were at least three murders, all involving alcohol.[7]

Skanatalihyo Falls Ill

During these tumultuous times, in 1799, after falling ill from alcoholism, a Seneca chief named Skanatalihyo (Handsome Lake) reported having visions and prophecies concerning the ways in which Yukwanuhsyu·ní people conducted themselves. During the four days in which Skanatalihyo laid unconscious in bed, Shukwayaʔtísu sent the Four Messengers to him. The Four Messengers explained how the Yukwanuhsyu·ní people had strayed from their original instructions and how they needed to change their behavior in order to make things right with creation. The Four Messengers also explained how the white people have been having a bad influence on Yukwanuhsyu·ní people, changing the way they lived their previously peaceful lives. When Skanatalihyo woke up, he began relaying the messages in the form of the Kaliwihyo. While the Kaliwihyo reaffirms the tradition and culture of the Great Law of Peace, not all Yukwanuhsyu·ní people embrace the teachings. Louis Williams Jr., former Oneida Cultural Heritage employee, wrote a summary of Skanatalihyo's teachings in the form of the Kaliwihyo.

> He said, "I have a message to deliver to you who are gathered. I have been told by the servants of the Creator that I should live upon the earth to teach the

> onkwehonwe [Haudenosaunee] the things that will please the Creator again. The Creator has seen that you have transgressed from the things that he taught you. He made you so that you could have good lives and not do harm to others. He sees that you have accepted the sins brought to you by Shawíhskla's Islanders. The worst thing that you have done is to take the fire water which you know to be the mind changer. The Creator says you have to stop this."
>
> He continued, "All this came about because your ancestors took it from the White man. You have suffered ever since because of it. Those that did this have never gotten to the Creator's world in the sky. This was not made for you. It was made for the White man as a medicine on his island. By drinking to excess, they too have violated the will of the Creator who blew life into all of you. The Creator says that to be drunk is forbidden, and he wants you to stop. In fact, he forbids you to continue this evil habit. If you leave it behind, much of your suffering will end, and your children will be happy once again. The Creator is sad that, because of it, there is so much crime and wickedness on the earth. There are some things that were never intended for his Red children."[8]

As previously mentioned, when we listen and tell stories, the interpretation is influenced by our own experiences. In order to have some understanding of Skanatalihyo, one must consider his lived experiences. He had some understanding of Christianity, he appeared to struggle with alcoholism, and he was involved with three different wars before he had visions of the Kaliwihyo. When people are under the influence, they are limited in their thinking. One may conclude that when Skanatalihyo had his visions, his interpretation of those visions may have been limited based upon his experiences.

Sharing Food

The Kaliwihyo teaches us about selfishness and generosity using food as an example. We shouldn't withhold food from our guests; rather, we must offer food to those who come into our homes. Also, when we visit people, we should not refuse the food they offer us. Parker's version of this section is as follows.

> Sometimes a mother is ready to feed her family. When she is ready to bid them sit down, she glances out and sees someone coming and straightway hides the food. A woman visitor comes in. Now after some conversation the visitor says she is unwell and goes out. Then the family commences to eat. And the Creator says that whoever follows such tricks must repent as soon as they hear this message, for such practices are most wicked.
>
> Now the messengers said this: "Now the Creator made food for all creatures and it must be free for all. He ordained that people should live in communities. Now when visitors enter a lodge the woman must always say, 'Sedékoni,' come eat. Now it is not right to refuse what is offered. The visitor must take two or three bites at least and say, 'Niawe.' Tell this to all your people."[9]

Another version of the Kaliwihyo ends each section with the need to repent for committing these sins: "So now you will relate this message to your relatives. When they hear of these wrongdoings, they will repent of all their sins for as long as they live here on Earth."[10] This section on repenting sounds a lot like a Catholic confession. However, another way to interpret it is for the Yukwanuhsyu·ní people to make it new between themselves and Shukwayaʔtísu. Nicholas Reynolds, Oneida community member and former Cultural Heritage employee, explained how his upbringing embodied the teachings in the Kaliwihyo with respect to sharing food.

> I can remember as a kid at times my parents being worried about food. I don't think we ever went hungry, but I can remember them having conversations about it. That made an impression on me. Traditionally, food in our culture wasn't personal property. It wasn't culturally or socially acceptable to allow somebody near you to starve. Some might have a little bit or maybe they

> should've planned better, but we wouldn't have allowed people to starve. Food is a basic human right. If there's food, we should all be eating.[11]

Stealing Food

The Kaliwihyo teaches us that stealing is wrong, again using food as an example. The following version from the North American Indian Travelling College is quite graphic in explaining the dangers and penalties for stealing food.

> This woman who also has a large family comes out of her house one day and finds that her neighbours have a food garden. So she goes without permission and takes some food for her family to eat. The messengers now tell us that this is wrong. They say that the food that this woman took and by feeding it to her family, she is giving them fire and it's burning their insides. Now we will tell you that in the future whenever anybody sees another person's garden, they should ask permission if they want or need food from that garden or ask if they can trade until their crop ripens and at that time they will return the food borrowed. We are not to go and take the crops without the owner's permission.[12]

When discussing this section of the Kaliwihyo, Parker explains the practice of marking gardens: "One of the old methods of gardening was to clear a small patch in the woods by girdling the trees and planting in the mellow forest mold. The name and totem of the owner of the garden was painted on a post, signifying that the ground was private property. The clan totem gave permission to any hard-pressed clansman to take what he wished in emergency but only in such a case. These isolated gardens in the forests were objects of temptation sometimes, as the prophet intimates."[13]

Thomas and Boyle expand on the trade discussion by clarifying that people shouldn't set a price for their food but rather should be open to exchange.

They also mention generosity: "the gardener should not set a price but should give the woman whatever she wants from the garden. If she accepts as a trade whatever the woman brought with her, she should give her more from the garden than the woman wanted."[14]

Turning Food into Alcohol

Aside from the perceived wastefulness of turning healthy foods into alcohol, the Kaliwihyo warns of the dangers of consuming too much alcohol. Recall that Skanatalihyo was likely an alcoholic and witnessed many of the devastating impacts that alcoholism can bring to a family and a community. It's no surprise, then, that his message about alcohol comes with a drastic anecdote about men murdering a friend. Parker tells the story:

> Good food is turned into evil drink. Now some have said that there is no harm in partaking of fermented liquids. Then let this plan be followed: let men gather in two parties, one having a feast of food, apples and corn, and the other have cider and whiskey. Let the parties be equally divided and matched and let them commence their feasting at the same time. When the feast is finished you will see those who drank the fermented juices murder one of their own party but not so with those who ate food only.[15]

Another version advises giving one side of a room alcohol and the other side cornbread: "Again, you say, 'Oh! the whiskey is not bad. It touches our food. It is made of our corn.' Go to the council house. Put half the people on one side, and give them whiskey. Put half the people on the other side, and give them bread. You will notice the difference. Those who drink will fight. Those who eat the cornbread will go peaceably away."[16]

Parker's version also contains a specific warning about drinking alcohol when planting corn: "We, the messengers of our Creator, see strong drink used during the season when corn is planted. Now let those who use this evil drink know that it consumes the elements of life. They must repent."[17] Randy Cornelius, Oneida Bear Clan Faithkeeper, explained what was going on in Yukwanuhsyu·ní communities during this period with respect to the destructive impacts of alcoholism and how it affected our relationship with corn, beans, and squash.

> There was a time in history where there was so much alcoholism going on and all this dysfunction, and people didn't have that respect anymore with the natural world or themselves. People were growing their gardens while they were intoxicated. When they were handling those seeds to start their growth, it burned the spirit of that seed so they can't reach their potential. People were going out with good intentions and planting and everything and then not coming back to weed. That choked out the plants, and I seen that in this community where people come out to garden and come back one or two times and you never see them again. All those weeds come in and it just chokes them. You just see little bitty plants, they don't even bear fruit. So, people didn't have that relationship there. The spirit of the corn came to Handsome Lake. He had that gift to be able to communicate with the natural world. They knew that he was going to the Creator's land, and they wanted to go with him because of all these things that the people weren't doing. Even the ceremonies were dying out. So Handsome Lake got the three sisters to think about what that world would be like if they were to leave. The children and elders would suffer and there would be famine. Handsome Lake said he would tell the people to revitalize the ceremonies and ceremonial songs to honor the three sisters who are the leaders of our sustenance of life. So, the three sisters decided that they would stay.[18]

Corn Wanting to Leave

Parker relayed a similar version of the story of when the corn wanted to leave with Skanatalihyo.

> The day was bright when I went into the planted field and alone I wandered in the planted field and it was the time of the second hoeing. Suddenly a damsel appeared and threw her arms about my neck and as she clasped me she spoke saying, "When you leave this earth for the new world above, it is our wish to follow you." I looked for the damsel but saw only the long leaves of corn twining round my shoulders. And then I understood that it was the spirit of the corn who had spoken, she the sustainer of life. So I replied, "O spirit of the corn, follow not me but abide still upon the earth and be strong and be faithful to your purpose. Ever endure and do not fail the children of women. It is not time for you to follow for Gaíwiio [Kaliwihyo] is only in its beginning."[19]

Thomas and Boyle add to this story by explaining that Skanatalihyo also told the corn, "What I will do to encourage you is to honour all of you at the ceremonies."[20]

Pride and Punishment

The Kaliwihyo warns us about pride, using gardens as an example. "If any of your people have cultivated ground let them not be proud on that account. If one is proud there is sin within him but if there be no pride there is no sin."[21] The North American Indian Travelling College version explains that "we are not to boast about our gardens, for these gardens will be feeding our families. Should anything happen to the head of the family, his family will not starve."[22] Thomas and Boyle's account talks about the need for gardens to be neat and well maintained and sheds light on the reasoning for not having too much pride in our gardens: jealousy. They explain that avoiding pride will bring community unity back. "Whenever a man works the land, his work should be neat and well done. His work should be right so it will produce things for his family to enjoy for much time to come."[23] It is important to note that this version also refers to men working in the garden. Traditionally, women held the responsibility for agriculture. For the Europeans, men were responsible for agriculture. After contact, and with the pressures of assimilation, Yukwanuhsyu·ní men began to help more with growing food. After the dysfunction and turmoil from the Revolutionary War, Skanatalihyo likely encouraged men to take up farming as a survival response.[24]

In the Kaliwihyo, those who commit sinful deeds in life will face the consequences after death. One version warns: "Lazy women would be employed in pulling up weeds in a large field of corn, which would immediately grow again."[25]

Short Corn Prophecy

Along with the lessons of morality, the Messengers shared prophesies with Skanatalihyo. Some of these prophesies have already come to pass, including horseless carriages, boarding schools, and the loss of wild strawberries. One prophesy predicted a time when our corn would not grow tall anymore. I personally experienced this in my own gardens, likely the result of our changing climate. The sections dealing with the prophecy of the short corn also contain information about different medicines we could use to remedy the situation and grow tall corn again in subsequent years. The North American Indian Travelling College tells the story this way: "Our corn plants and other plants that we eat will soon cease growing to their normal height, but Sonkwaiatison [Shukwayaʔtísu] has given us medicine to help them grow [iakoshienne]. This is what we are to use and are to burn tobacco before we use it. This will help our plants to grow big and healthy."[26]

Parker's version also includes reference to medicines: "Now it is understood that Dióhéko^{n} [the corn, bean, and squash spirits], have a secret medicine, ósagańâ and ósdîśdani. So soak your seed corn in these two medicines before you plant your fields. The medicines grow on the flat lands near streams."[27] Ósagańâ (also spelled gahságę:dá) is marsh reed, a plant that grows in the swamps. Ósdîśdani (also spelled osdeisda:ne) is wild bottle brush.

Parker published "The Code of Handsome Lake" in 1913. His *Iroquois Uses of Maize and Other Food Plants* was published in 1910. In this earlier publication, he described soaking corn in a medicinal tea. He also explained the purpose of these medicines and how they affected birds that might try to eat the newly planted seeds. Parker explained: "While the ground is being prepared for sowing, the seed corn is soaked in warm water or in a decoction made of helebore root and some other herb which the writer has not yet identified. These roots are said to be a medicine for the corn but in reality, the medicine is a poison for crows and other field pests which might eat the seed corn. A bird eating this doctored corn becomes dizzy and flutters about the field in a way which frightens the others."[28]

Similarly, the Thomas and Boyle version describes a medicine that will help the corn.

> The Creator has given you corn for food to live on. Someday the corn may not grow, or it may begin to grow but look sickly. So, your relations must know there is medicine for them, which should be gathered just before planting. The medicine is called gosdisdén:ni, and it is gathered fresh from the forest. The seed corn should be soaked in this solution before planting so that it will be free from disease and will grow well. So, this is the kind of medicine He has planted for you to use. He has given us a medicine to cure disease, and He has given the corn, beans, and squash a medicine because they have a living spirit.[29]

Thomas and Boyle go on to explain what gosdisdén:ni is, along with another medicine traditionally used, and how Yukwanuhsyu·ní people used those medicines: "Years ago, the people always soaked the seeds for two days in a container before planting. The medicine, gosdisdén:ni, used for the plant's seeds, is known as phragmites in English. Another medicine, oságén:dab (Hystrix patula), or bottle-brush grass, was also used at times. The roots of this plant were boiled and then put into the container of seeds."[30] These are the same two medicines that Parker mentioned in his version of this section.

In all these versions, Shukwayaʔtísu is providing these medicines for our use. It is critical to understand that everything in creation has a responsibility. The medicines rejoice when they are able to fulfill their responsibility. They are responsible for helping people and animals be well and thrive. Corn, a cultivated crop, cannot survive and thrive without people. Similarly, people cannot survive and thrive without corn. Animals and bugs also thrive on corn because everything is interconnected and everything has a responsibility.

Giving Thanks to the Three Sisters

Historically, Yukwanuhsyu·ní people didn't keep a calendar the way we do today. They relied on the world around them to give them clues about the timing of their activities. In this regard, Parker explained the timing of planting season: "When the leaf of the dogwood is the size of a squirrel's ear, the planting season has come."[31] Similarly, Thomas and Boyle explain, "When the leaf of the hickory is the size of a squirrels' ear, the planting season has come."[32]

The Kaliwihyo explains how people need to give thanks when planting their gardens. Parker's version of this section states: "It is a custom for thanksgiving to be made over the hills of planted corn. Let the head one of the family make an invocation over the planted hills that the corn may continue to support life. Now this will be a right thing and whosoever asks the help of the Creator will receive it."[33] Parker explained how giving thanks over planted corn was an old tradition that Skanatalihyo endorsed in his teachings: "the ceremony of invoking the Creator over the hills of corn was an old one and like many other old customs was endorsed by the prophet. This custom is still continued among some of the Iroquois."[34] Similarly, Thomas and Boyle explain the importance of wearing traditional clothing while giving thanks. "When planting is finished, the whole family will go to the field dressed in their traditional clothes. They will all stand in the middle of the cornfield, and the elder will speak on behalf of his family. He will say, 'We hope everything is all and good so we may see the Three Sisters ripen again, which will be our food.'"[35]

The Kaliwihyo also encourages people to include the three sisters when giving thanks to Shukwayaʔtísu. The North American Indian Travelling College's section on this states that we need to include the three sisters because "they are the main foods which give us life."[36] Thomas and Boyle explained the three sisters' need to be honored: "the way we see things, when you honour the supporters of life (the corn, beans, and squash spirits), they want to be a part of the ceremonies, as they play a great role every day in your lives. The corn, bean, and squash spirits wish to be honoured in the same way that you honour the Creator when there is a ceremony for Him."[37]

Conclusion

From this period of time, we see how corn teaches us about our roles and responsibilities. Our stories are there to remind us of our responsibilities to our community as well as to our non-human relatives that make up all of creation. Through Skanatalihyo's teachings, we learn again to respect all of creation and allow our plant relatives to fulfill their responsibilities. Stealing food, monetizing food, turning food into alcohol, and being boastful in our success are all acts that do not allow our plant relatives to fulfill their responsibilities. If we do those things, we take that power away from them and deny them the very gifts Shukwayaʔtísu gave to them. Skanatalihyo's responsibility was, in part, to remind us of how to allow our plant relatives to fulfill their responsibilities.

Skanatalihyo's teachings were also a direct response to what was happening in the aftermath of the Revolutionary war. Yukwanuhsyu·ní were scattered about, suffering from land loss, alcoholism, and the deaths of so many of their people. They were in survival mode. They were not growing their foods the way they had before the war. They no longer gave thanks through ceremony. They did not follow their original instructions. It's no wonder the corn wanted to follow Skanatalihyo to the Sky World. The Yukwanuhsyu·ní were not allowing her to fulfill her responsibility to take care of the people. Fortunately, the corn remained here on earth and the people began to care for her once again. The Kaliwihyo continues to remind us to grow our foods, allow our foods to fulfill their responsibilities, give thanks through ceremony, and follow our original instructions.

CHAPTER 7

WayukhinukulhaʔteOkhale Wayukhinató·li·

(They Dismissed Our Thinking and They Disrupted Our Towns)

NE· YAKΛ LATUHÁKWE THAT BEING THANKFUL FOR ALL OF CREATION AND caring for others became very difficult when the Oneidas retained less than ten thousand acres of their homelands by 1811.[1] There are a number of factors that prompted most of the Oneidas to abandon their homelands for a new home out west in the early 1800s. One of the most significant reasons involved the staggering loss of over five million acres of land as a result of twenty-six illegal treaties with the state of New York beginning in 1785 and continuing until 1842.[2] Despite the promises of the federal government, they did nothing to prevent, stop, or remedy the loss of land. Even though the Oneidas fought for the Americans in the War of 1812, the federal government was pressuring them to move westward.[3] Ultimately, the Oneidas did not appear to see any other choice but to abandon their homelands and move west.

CONDITIONS AT ONEIDA

Before getting into the details about moving west, it is important to consider the agricultural conditions at the Oneida Reservation in New York at that time. Author Julia Bloomfield wrote about the conditions in Oneida in 1818 when Bishop John Henry Hobart visited: "There are said to have been about a thousand Indians, who held the land in common. A small portion was under cultivation for their tobacco, potatoes, maize, beans and pumpkins, a part for pasture land for their sheep and cows, but the greater portion was a forest wilderness. Through the woods there were no roads, but simply Indian trails. Their houses of logs, or wigwams of bark, were scattered about in wild irregularity on the hill-sides or near the cultivated fields."[4] Jasper Parrish, a U.S. agent and interpreter, sent a letter to Secretary of War John C. Calhoun on November 3, 1819. The letter discussed his observations, including a note about impressive agriculture accomplishments that, as he explained, were the result of white influence and a rapidly decreasing hunting territory. His observations are self-serving and historically inaccurate considering that the continent's original inhabitants taught the colonists everything they knew about growing corn. An excerpt of the letter is as follows.

> The only advantages they have had for improvement in agriculture, have been the examples of the white people around their reservations. The Six Nations of Indians, residing within my agency, have, within the last season, raised more corn, wheat, oats, potatoes, &c. than they have before in any one season for thirty-five years. This change among them, from an indolent, hunting, fishing life, to that of useful industry, is to be ascribed, under Providence, not only to the means which have been employed for that purpose, but in part to their necessities, for the support of themselves and families. Their hunting grounds being small, and game becoming scarce, have operated as a powerful stimulus to this change in their habits.[5]

As a result of their conversion to Christianity, the Oneidas divided into factions of Christians, known as the First Christian Party, Second Christian Party, and those who followed the traditional Oneida ways, the Pagan Party. In 1816, Reverend Eleazer Williams converted some of the traditionalists and some Presbyterians, and they became known as the Second Christian

Party. A year later, he proposed the idea of moving the Oneidas and others westward.[6] Oneida tribal member Guy Elm relayed the situation in New York prior to removal.

> The Oneida Castle and the valley of the Mohawk was owned by the Oneidas and their adopted tribes, the Brothertons and the Stockbridges . . . the New York Land Company had a tract of land adjacent to this Mohawk Valley. And so the company's incorporator Thomas W. Ogden negotiated a deal for the removal of the Indian tribes of the Mohawk Valley to a distant western reservation. Mostly through Eleazer William's influence over the Indians. Sometime in 1816 Eleazer Williams was sent as a Missionary to the Oneidas at Oneida Castle. Being handsome and he could speak the Indian dialects, he at once became their favorite and he gained their respect for him.[7]

While it seems the Oneida people were still growing their traditional foods, their land base was quickly disappearing during this time. Combined with the negative influences of alcohol, Christianity, and the growing population of white settlers around them, the idea of moving westward had become quite appealing to many Oneidas.

Negotiating for a New Home

In the summer of 1820, the Oneida people chose Daniel Bread, an informal community leader, to travel to Green Bay in the Michigan territory (later to become the state of Wisconsin) to meet with the Menominee to discuss their possible relocation.[8] Eleazer Williams, a Mohawk descendant, and two other Oneidas were sent with Bread to serve as the negotiation team. While they were preparing to set out, they learned that John Bowyer, the Indian agent at Green Bay, negotiated a treaty for the same land the delegation was coming to discuss. They turned back to New York and were relieved to hear that the treaty Bower negotiated had not been approved. It was during this trip that Bread and the others realized Eleazar Williams wanted to use the entire Yukwanuhsyu·ní Confederacy relocation to scare the French away from Michigan territory, effectively positioning the confederacy into a war zone as a buffer. When they returned, they relayed how Williams deceived the Yukwanuhsyu·ní, causing many Yukwanuhsyu·ní communities to change their mind about possibly relocating.

The following year, on August 5, 1821, Eleazar Williams's boat landed in the Fox River in Green Bay in the hopes of finally negotiating with the Menominees and the HoChunks for a new home.[9] While Daniel Bread didn't join Williams on this trip, the missionary was accompanied by John Anthony, John Skenandoah, Cornelius Baird, Neddy Archiquette, and other Oneida leaders of the First Christian Party.[10] They eventually secured two treaties with the Menominees and HoChunks, one in 1821 and one in 1822. Pursuant to these treaties, the Menominees and HoChunks agreed to allow the Oneidas to jointly occupy 6,720,000 acres of land west of the Fox River and Green Bay in exchange for a total of $5,450 in cash and goods. There was some dispute over what this transaction entailed. The Oneida people believed they purchased the land.[11] The Menominee and HoChunk people believed they "agreed to let the landless Oneida and Stockbridge Indians from New York state settle on land they shared in eastern Wisconsin."[12] This dispute also caused factions to emerge among the Menominee people, with some supporting the sale of land to the Oneida and Stockbridge and others challenging the terms of the transaction.[13]

Oneida storyteller Guy Elm explained the negotiations for land from the Menominee and HoChunk, as well as the conditions upon arrival: "In July 1821, the first delegation of the New York Indians famous Iroquois confederacy came west in few of seeking a suitable tract of land to be bought by them, from the Winnebago [HoChunk] and Menominee Tribe of Indians." He continued:

> The Oneidas knew how to select their new home. Because today they are right in the best farming land in the State of Wisconsin . . . the older people still tell about the hard times they had those that first settled here, although the

> country was full of different kinds of wild game, the creeks and rivers were full of fish. but they managed to survive the first winter, and from that time on they got along fairly good, at least that's what I been told.[14]

Bloomfield, writing from a Eurocentric perspective, described the land the Oneidas purchased near Green Bay and the steps they took to survive in their new homeland.

> The land they had purchased was an unbroken forest and the streams which threaded this wilderness had worn for themselves deep channels, from which the timber land rose in easy elevation on either bank, assuming here and there the dignity of hills. The forest was chiefly composed of pine, oak, chestnut and maple. The Oneidas were busy people in getting settled on their Reservation. The first step of the red people was to build wigwams of bark along the banks of the streams; then came the clearing of a small space in the forest for the little fields of maize. beans and potatoes.
>
> The toll of the first year was severe, and it fell chiefly upon the women. The Oneida men, at heart, still despised field labor. However they supplied the families well with game, venison, wild turkeys, duck and fish. Matters went on quietly and steadily in the new country. The bark wigwams disappeared; cabins of unhewn logs took their place. The size of the little fields was enlarged. The number of cattle and sheep increased. After a time, the men went to work more in earnest; cows, and oxen, and swine were purchased; the plough was set in motion; a few horses appeared on the largest farms. Still the people were very poor and had many hardships to contend with. They mourned for the old gardens and orchards, and fruit trees they had left behind them.[15]

Soon after securing the land and until 1836, three major waves of Oneida people began emigrating to Michigan territory.[16] When the federal government entered into the treaty with the Oneida in 1838 to secure a reservation around the main settlements around Duck Creek, there were 654 Oneidas.[17] Unlike other treaties that contained descriptions of territory, this treaty called for a reservation to be drawn that consisted of one hundred acres per Oneida. Immediately following the ratification of the 1838 Treaty with the Oneida, the federal government created a 65,400-acre reservation. During this time, roughly two hundred Oneidas remained in New York.[18]

Invitation to Join the Oneidas

The removal of the Oneidas west was never meant to include only Oneida, the Stockbridge, and the Brothertown. The initial idea was that all Yukwanuhsyu·ní people would abandon their homes for the newly secured land in Michigan territory.[19] Removal would undoubtedly benefit the Ogden Land Company, which lobbied for and secured purchasing rights for much of Yukwanuhsyu·ní territory in New York upon their removal. On December 11, 1822, Secretary of War John C. Calhoun wrote a letter to Eleazar Williams informing him that any Yukwanuhsyu·ní people were welcome to relocate in the vicinity of Green Bay on land the Oneidas purchased from the Menominee. His letter stated that he received instructions "to give the Indians of the Six Nations who may choose to emigrate to the country acquired by the Treaty every facility in establishing themselves there, in his power, without incurring any additional expense."[20] On October 27, 1823, Calhoun sent a similar letter to the Onondagas, Senecas, Tuscaroras, Oneidas, and Stockbridge, reminding them that they were welcome to come to settle on the land purchased from the Menominee. The letter stated, in part: "I take this occasion to repeat to you the assurance, that all who may choose to change their residence will continue to receive the same friendship and protection from the Government as they did while they resided in New York and that their removal will in nowise change the relation in which they previously stood to the Government."[21] It seems the other tribes were not interested in the same "friendship and protection" from the federal government; the Oneida, Stockbridge, and Brothertown were the only nations that ended up relocating to Wisconsin.

Making a New Home at Duck Creek

When the Oneidas arrived in Wisconsin, they quickly began efforts to rebuild a new permanent homeland. I can't imagine what that must have been like to leave everything you knew behind and venture out into a whole new world, bringing minimal possessions with you. Fortunately, they had the foresight to bring seeds with them to plant soon after arrival. Mr. and Mrs. Tom Elm explained the conditions their grandparents faced upon arrival in their new home. Mrs. Elm said:

> When I was a child, my grandmother used to tell stories about the time Oneidas came here from Onudake. She said that the Oneidas each received three hundred dollars to move away from New York. At that time it was all woods here [in Wisconsin] and there were all kinds of wild animals. The GadmΛn [government] used to send food stuffs by boat and they used to go on foot after it from the boat. And all what they got they would lug it on their backs. This was done ever so often. On their way back they would always stop to rest over night and they would make a big fire as there were so many wolves which they could see circling around them as far as the light from the fire would reach. At that time their homes or houses were made of bark from trees. But the thing they did have was good rich ground to plant; they used to raise potatoes that were so big clean and white, and they would raise good Indian corn and beans.[22]

Her husband, Tom Elm, added, "The landing or stopping place was where the city of Green Bay is now located. They brought with them what tools there were such as axes, saws, and other tools. They also brought with them seed corn, which they planted as soon as they had some clearings broke up for gardens."[23]

Similarly, Laura Manthe, Ohe·láku founding member, explained the difficult decisions between eating the corn they brought with them or waiting to plant the corn in the spring.

> We started growing corn in Wisconsin when we moved here in the early 1800s. Our ancestors brought the corn to Wisconsin because they had to have some food to eat. When they came here, they were hungry. They had to decide to eat the seeds or eat something else and grow the seeds in the springtime. They knew the value of the corn and the corn seed. They decided to wait and plant it in the springtime so they would always have food. We have to give them a lot of credit because they knew what to do and they came here with the right tools to care for themselves. They didn't have government programs. They didn't have grocery stores. They had to be completely self-sufficient in an unfamiliar wilderness. We need to give our ancestors a lot of credit for our survival.[24]

Many of these stories were preserved because of an oral history initiative during the Great Depression. In the late 1930s and the early 1940s, the federal government funded the Works Progress Administration (WPA), which among other things paid Oneida people to collect stories from other Oneida people in an effort to preserve their language and history. A number of WPA storytellers talked about the Oneidas' new home. Aaron House explained the conditions when the Oneida began to settle and the different locations people settled in.

> Oneidas landed between Green Bay and Depere on the East bank of Fox River. They settled there until Oneidas finished blazing division lines for 3 groups; when this was done, Oneidas settled on it. Each group were related some way and some were of same clan. Those settled on the south end of reservation were all Methodist. The central or the Duck [Creek] group were Episcopalians, and those settled on the north end were mixed some Methodist, [some] Episcopalian, and some did not belong to either. The south group helped each other by building a temporary shed composed of pine logs for walls and basswood bark for roof, plastered with clay and ashes mixed, between logs. When this was done, they cleared a garden spot from 1 to 5 acres. Everybody helped regardless of relationship or clan as long as they

> were members of same religious denomination; next thing they done was to plant. Their main food was corn, beans, pumpkin and greens when they can get it. When they came here from New York they had with them cows, pigs, and ponies. I will say about the second year the Oneidas were a little better fixed. They started building log houses (the other 2 groups helped each other same as the south group) . . . they had milk, butter, eggs, pork, beef and all the berries they want in the summer time, and fish of all kinds. Fish was cured in three ways, salted, dried and smoked. Berries was also dried and some put in cans and put away for winter.[25]

Similarly, Rachel Swamp described the work that Oneidas did when they first arrived. "When the Oneidas arrived here, they did all kinds of work. Some sold wood, logs, furs, and others found work in Green Bay. They went to shell corn that was in boats, and they were also paid in corn for their work. The women had baskets that they would load with groceries that they earned."[26]

When my youngest daughter, Amelia Webster, learned about the Oneidas' removal to Wisconsin, she was curious about what seeds our ancestors brought with them and what seeds they may have planted when they began to settle in their new homeland. She was thirteen years old when she shared this story with me.

> We shouldn't have had to move in the first place. The colonizers brought over diseases and alcohol. Our bodies were not ready for that. The colonizers made illegal treaties knowing they were not fair. They took all the land that we used to grow and harvest our food on. They put us through a lot of danger in moving us west to a land that we were not familiar with. We had to start new, which wasn't easy. They underestimated us. We were able to rebuild and establish a lifestyle in our new land. We were able to grow enough food again for all of us. One thing that I want to know more about is what kinds of seeds they brought with them. I know it was corn, beans, and squash, but what varieties? And what varieties did we have to leave behind? I also want

> to know what seeds we may have started growing from our new Menominee and Ho Chunk neighbors. Today, we grow a lot of varieties of corn, beans, and squash, and they might be new to our reservation because my mom got them from people in New York. Maybe our ancestors did grow them here, but those varieties might have died out. Maybe there are people in our community that are still growing them, and we don't know about it. I'm interested in learning about more varieties.[27]

Amelia's ponderings did not need to last long, at least with respect to beans. Less than a year after this conversation, a friend came over to share four varieties of beans that his family had been growing since the Oneida people were removed to Wisconsin. We also learned that one variety of beans we had been growing for several years was another variety Oneida people had continuously been growing in our new homeland. Our family now helps grow and care for these beans as well as other Oneida beans from our Yukwanuhsyu·ní relatives out east. We are still searching for other varieties of our foods historically cared for by Oneida people.

By 1830, the Oneidas cleared 237 acres predominantly for corn, potatoes, and turnips.[28] In 1834, a total of 400 acres were cleared for crops. The Oneidas in Wisconsin were laying the foundation for a viable farming community, an opportunity not afforded to the Oneidas who remained on a dwindling land base in New York.[29] Alfred Cope, a Quaker shipping magistrate from Philadelphia, wrote in 1849 about the Oneidas in Wisconsin: "It was asserted that these people formed the most important part of the agricultural population of this vicinity, were quite superior as farms in industry and productiveness to the farmers of French descent, and, in fact, brought to market more corn and beef than anyone else."[30]

The Oneidas remained subsistence farmers in their new home. For the most part, men had taken over farming, with one notable exception: corn. One author described the relationship as follows: "There was one task, however, that wives and mothers would not give up; they always worked in the corn-fields with the men, planting, hoeing, and harvesting the maize. This they considered their privilege of birthright, a holiday task bequeathed to them by their Konoshioni [Haudenosaunee] mothers of bygone days. The maize, that beautiful plant and sweet grain, had always held a very important place with the red man, and the Iroquois are said to have 12 different ways of preparing it for food."[31]

In 1866, Ellen Goodnough, wife of a missionary to the Oneidas, wrote in her diary about how the women were gathering corn husks in the fall to save money for a proper altar for the Hobart Church.[32]

> It is a busy time with the women now; they gather and husk the corn, having planted and hoed it in the spring and summer. They also dig the potatoes. They do not, however, work in the fields nearly so much as a few years ago. Many of them are depending on the corn-husks for their contribution towards the new Altar. They are carefully stored away in the house, and winter evenings are braided into mats which sell for 8 or 10 cents apiece. Some of the husks are very nicely prepared for mattresses. They are carefully dried and split in fine strands with a wire, then carried in bundles on the backs of the women to the Bay, a distance of 10 miles, where they sell from 4 to 6 cents a pound, according to their quality.[33]

This entry is interesting because it relays the continued importance of corn in the Oneida community, the continued role of women in corn agriculture, and the incorporation of Christianity into both of these practices.

By 1880, the Oneidas were transitioning away from subsistence farming to market agriculture.[34] During this time, much of the reservation was still uncultivated. In 1887, there were 1,732 Oneidas and approximately 2,700 acres of the reservation were under cultivation. More drastic changes would be coming as the federal government would break its promises to keep the Oneidas' new reservation secure and protected less than fifty years after entering into the 1838 Treaty.

Conclusion

It can be difficult for many of us to place ourselves in the situation the Yukwanuhsyu·ní people were in when they discussed leaving their homelands. War, catastrophic land loss, and alcoholism were among the factors that drove the Oneidas westward. They packed up the possessions they could travel with and set out for a new beginning. They carried with them precious seeds to plant upon their arrival. Those seeds represented a new start, the continual cycle of life, and a continued connection to Yukwanuhsyu·ní history going all the way back to creation. They were able to plant new roots even if they were now disconnected from the rest of the confederacy. Both the seeds and the people carried our knowledge, history, stories, language, and ceremonies. The non-Indigenous neighbors that would soon move alongside the Oneidas may not have recognized our deep cultural connection to our seeds and food relatives. To those neighbors, it may have simply looked like we were good farmers, using our corn for food and commerce. but we were communicating with this new land through the way we knew best: reciprocity. We entrusted the land with something most precious: our seeds. Our seeds and the people were once again relying on each other for survival. We planted ourselves in this new land, infusing our culture into the soil, creating our own place for generations to come.

Wayukwahutsyákwa Okhale Wayukhiwiláhkwa

(They Have Taken Our Land Away and They Have Taken Our Children Away)

NE· YAKΛ LATUHÁKWE THE ONEIDA PEOPLE HAD JUST BEEN SETTLING IN THEIR new home along Duck Creek when the federal government once again changed its policy toward Indigenous people. It was no longer enough to push them westward out of sight; the federal government now wanted to assimilate them into mainstream society. It did this in a number of ways. Two such ways had devastating impacts on the Oneida people's relationship with corn and other traditional foods. This chapter will look at the impacts of the boarding school era in Oneida (1884–1918) and the General Allotment Act (1887).[1] Day schools and boarding schools were a means of erasing Oneida cultural identity, and allotment crippled the Oneida people's ability to grow their own foods.[2] In many ways, growing our foods is synonymous with growing our children. It becomes increasingly evident that the corn reflects the condition of our people.

Not unlike any other period, during this time period the non-Indian people were constantly comparing Indigenous people to themselves to see

FIGURE 5. Writers on the Works Progress Administration Oneida Language and Folklore Project. From left: David Skenandore, Floyd Lounsbury (supervisor), Lester Skenandore, Stadler King, Alex Metoxen, Louis Webster, Dennison Hill, Guy Elm, Andrew Beechtree, Ida Blackhawk, Oscar Archiquette, Rachel Smith Miller, John Skenandore, Tilly Baird. Photograph reprinted with permission of the Milwaukee Public Museum.

whether the Indigenous people measured up. For example, United States Indian agent Inspector McLaughlin commented on his visits throughout the Oneida Reservation: "I was delighted to find on this reservation something I haven't found on any other reservation. We have found homes as though they were expecting us, everything clean and floors—well, almost polished, laundry on the line, fields well cultivated, no weeds in the gardens, gardens growing potatoes, corn, onions, cabbage and everything kept up. No white person in this country could have done any better."[3] It's this last sentence that is especially troubling. It's not enough that the Oneida people had clean homes; rather, as

McLaughlin demonstrated, "white people" set the bar to measure all others to determine their level of civility.

A primary source for understanding the impacts of day schools, boarding schools, and allotment on the Oneida people came from the people themselves. As I mentioned in the previous chapter, between 1938 and 1942 Oneida people collected stories from other Oneida people as part of the New Deal work relief effort called the Works Progress Administration (WPA).[4] Stories included topics such as religion, witchcraft, jokes, boarding schools, government, removal, language, and medicine. These stories, along with other primary sources, reveal that non-Indian people often lacked any meaningful education about the efficiency and productivity of the Oneida people's well-established agricultural practices. Instead, they often felt a need to come into our communities and teach us the "proper" way of doing things. After the federal government used allotment as a tool to take our land away from us, outsiders continued to teach us their agricultural practices on land we lost through allotment. The WPA stories demonstrate how Oneida people held on to advanced Indigenous knowledge even while non-Indian people used boarding schools and allotment to try to replace that knowledge with their own notions of civilization.

Kill the Indian, Save the Man

Boarding schools took children away from their parents and took language, culture, foods, and family ties away from the children. Despite the United States' supposed commitment to keeping the church separate from the government, churches often ran these government-funded boarding schools. The goal was supposedly to help "civilize" Indigenous people. However, the types of education delivered at these schools signaled a clear intent to erase Indigenous identity and culture and replace it with Christian values. The intent was not to teach students to become contributing members of society, but to teach them to become good servants to non-Indian people.

The church missionaries viewed their role among Indigenous people as one of continuing to civilize them. As one missionary put it:

> the Church's work among these Indians is the double one of helping them in their advancing civilization, and educating them into greater self-reliance and self-support. It also seeks to prepare them to exercise intelligently their full rights of approaching citizenship, and to develop that spiritual and moral Christian character that elevates work into duty and pours its blessed sunshine into every department of life.[5]

In talking about Carlisle Indian Industrial School, Andrew Beechtree, WPA storyteller and employee, shared his perspectives on boarding schools in general. "The school is the fruit of the imaginations of one Major R.H. Pratt, U.S.A. Retired and it was also because of his military training that he, as the first director, was able to make it a successful undertaking," he wrote. "It is said that stern measures were used to subdue the students from the more independent western tribes. It is my contention that the words uncivilized and savage as a distinction between a white human and a red human does not apply . . . I believe it is only a cultural difference."[6]

Construction of a boarding school on the Oneida Reservation began in 1892.[7] The Oneida Industrial School opened on March 27, 1893, and had far more applicants than the school's capacity. Many parents were under the impression that a Western education was essential for their children to succeed in life. In addition, if they sent their children to the boarding school, the government would feed their children and provide them with clothing. In a book published by the Church of the Holy Apostles, William Stetson Merril described the school and its nearby farm:

> the school is beautifully located on a high ridge across the Duck Creek from the Hobart Mission, near the railroad station. It can be seen from all directions, and its fine brick buildings, over which floats the American flag, present a beautiful as well as patriotic scene. The Indian children are taken

> from their homes at the age of six years, and during ten months of the year are kept at the school where they are educated, clothed and cared for by the government without expense to the parents.
>
> . . . A farm is connected with the school and the boys, under the direction of the farm instructor, are required to perform the work of planting, cultivating, and harvesting of the crops.[8]

In Oneida, young children were sent to day schools and boarding schools on the Oneida Reservation as well as schools just outside the reservation's boundaries. By 1917, one half of all Oneida people had between one and two years of schooling.[9] As they got older, the children were sent to other schools in Wisconsin, including those in Tomah, Wittenberg, and Keshena. They also were sent to Hampton in Virginia, Carlisle in Pennsylvania, Flandreau in South Dakota, Haskell in Kansas, and Chilocco in Oklahoma—all widely known Indian boarding schools. As of 1902, over four hundred Oneida children were attending the larger training schools.[10] These schools would attempt to take their language, replace their food, sever their family ties, and brainwash them into thinking boarding schools were for their own good.

Our original instructions teach us about the importance of how everything in creation is connected. So much of the meaning behind the natural world gets lost in translation from Oneida to English. Our vocabulary is beautiful, descriptive, and full of meaning. Looking back, it is no surprise that one of the first things boarding school survivors talk about is how they were punished for speaking their language. The non-Indians who founded the boarding schools knew that they had to take that away from the children if they were going to transform the children into obedient servants.

In the WPA stories, there are over a dozen accounts that tragically describe how children only spoke Oneida when they were forced to go to boarding schools, how they were punished for speaking their language, how difficult it was to learn to speak English, and how they realized they had forgotten their Oneida language when they came home. Anderson Cornelius and Mr. Powless are among these accounts. Cornelius explained,

"I had a hard time at first, because I couldn't speak a word in English. I was punished almost every day for almost a month until I was able to say yes or no, but then sometimes I make bad mistakes, I say yes when I should have said no and the other way around, no when its yes. I finally was able to speak broken English. I used to scrub the floors in the hallway for talking in Oneida language."[11] Similarly, Mr. Powless said, "I had a dickens of a time to learn it for some reason I can not explain. But once I got to talking English, I forgot all about the Oneida language. When I came home to Oneida, I couldn't speak the Oneida language to save my neck."[12]

When the children went to boarding schools, the schools did not feed them their traditional diets and certainly did not feed them corn soup or cornbread. Instead, they fed the children processed food that they could make and serve on a large scale. Andrew Beechtree compared the school meals to the foods Oneidas traditionally ate. He wrote:

> We, the government school children had nearly all of our food cooked in water or boiled. . . . Even the bread we got we soaked by pouring gravy on it. The gravy, by the way, was at times dished out to us three meals a day. It is no wonder that these schools were referred to as gravy schools. Although conditions were ideal otherwise at these schools yet its human products were below stature and strength and virility of those who went to school for only a short period or those who stayed at home and ate fried salt pork, fried game meat, potatoes lubricated with grease or pounded cornbread also lubricated with grease. What weaklings we are compared to the hard battling constitution of our grand-fathers.[13]

Beechtree also noted the threat the new cooking methods posed to traditional ways of preparing food.

> A government institution will furnish food for its people at the least proper expense and for the Indian schools, this food is cooked in large lots and as

> plain as possible. Cooking ability of the girl is therefore made latent, and when it behooves her to cook for the family, she is at a loss. The material and ways of cooking as practiced by the older Oneida women, acquired by long experiences becomes a lost art. The grandmother no longer has her grandchild in whom to confide her innermost secrets of life and medicine.[14]

William Metoxen explained that when he was sent away to the Tomah Indian School, it was the first time he was so far from home. He was so lonesome for home that he stole corn to cook it the way he knew how from home. "We used to steal corn from the farmer and then parch the corn in the woods. We would fill our pockets up to eat. One night a mouse got into my pocket and ate the corn also chewed my pocket up, make a big hole in it."[15]

Similarly, Anderson Cornelius, who attended a school closer to home than Metoxen, told a story about the food his mom brought for him. "The grub they put on the table wasn't fit for pigs, but sometimes they fed pretty good, I suppose when they knew the inspectors were coming around. My folks used to visit us every Sunday. My mother used to bring lots of good eats. And oh boy! The way we used to eat the food she brought. She would tell us to be good and not try to run away from school."[16]

Without a doubt, the children sent to these schools missed the food their parents prepared for them. As Andrew Beechtree pointed out, in cutting off the grandmothers' abilities to teach their grandchildren how to cook, the boarding schools both changed the diets of the children and also severed precious family ties.

Boarding schools removed children from their parents to be raised by teachers and clergy. When the children returned home and had children of their own, they didn't know how to raise them. Tom Porter discussed the generational trauma that boarding schools caused.[17] He explained how his grandfather had been taken to Carlisle Indian School when he was four or five years old and didn't return home to the Mohawk Reservation until he was twenty-one years old. His mother and father died while he was away, and he didn't have any other family. He could no longer speak Mohawk. When he had children of his own, he treated them how he had been treated at boarding school, with orders to do chores and no affection given. "And my grandfather never held his daughters or his sons, any of the twelve of them, on his lap. He'd never shake his leg and bounce them around. He never put his arm around them. Because sergeants don't do this to the people in their army."[18] Beechtree wrote about a similar lack of love and affection caused by being raised in a boarding school. He explained, "at these schools, the children lost much of the natural love of an offspring for the parents. They were subjected to severe discipline and punishment. They acquired the supposition that childish spirits must be broken and lead in channels prescribed by society."[19]

The WPA stories seemed to echo the same themes. It seemed many Oneida people didn't know how to raise their children other than to send them to boarding school. They themselves were raised in a boarding school, so when it came time for them to raise their children, they often didn't hesitate to do the same with their own children. Coupled with a declining economy, sending children to boarding school with the financial help of the government seemed an obvious course of action. Beechtree explained that even when the older generations questioned the validity of sending their children away to boarding schools, they did so anyway because of tough economic times.

> I attended this [Oneida] school for maybe two years but as I see it now what we learn during the school term, most of it we forgot during vacation . . . and in view of past experiences, some of the elder Oneidas were doubtful of the virtues of education. And again, a large number of the Oneida people sent their children to this school for no other reason than to get out of supporting them. This support in many cases would be absorbed by the liquor sellers. This lack of enthusiasm and encouragement of the parents for their children, naturally obstructed and in some instances stopped or killed any interest an employee [of the school] may have had in the welfare of the Oneida youth.[20]

One of the most disturbing revelations in the WPA stories about day schools and boarding schools was the staggering number of stories where the storyteller recalled fond memories of their school experiences, how they were proud of their education, how they looked up to the people who came home speaking only English, and how they looked down on people who did not attend school. These people had been indoctrinated to believe that day schools and boarding schools were a good thing and did not realize the valuable knowledge they had lost in the process. As with the practice of boarding school survivors sending their own children on to boarding schools, the practice of measuring success by non-Indian education quickly became prevalent in the community. Guy Elm explained how boarding schools encouraged people to be obedient and clean. "I don't remember ever having any trouble with my teachers or the students at any of the schools that I attended both Indian and white schools," he wrote. "The first teacher that I had used to tell the class, that obedience, perseverance, honesty, cleanliness were the stepping stones for building a person's character. I have followed the golden rule, as much as possible, and I have no regrets or am I ashamed my character even today. I make friends where ever I go, both men and women."[21]

Similarly, Stadler King measured people in the Oneida community based on the level of education they had. As he rationalized it, only educated people knew how to be clean and decent.

> The lower class are those without any learning and therefore do not take pride to be decent . . . [They] have no schooling and when people do not go to some school they do not have a chance to learn what all people should know and that is to be clean and decent and respectable to themselves and to others. This class also are of all ages and all do nothing but common labor. Some work on the W.P.A. and some are employed by farmers. These also are scattered all over in the Towns of Oneida and Hobart. These people do not seem to have much regard for any church so they hardly ever go to church, only at some funeral. These people are seen more at taverns on Sundays. They stay around all day and some times they get drunk and many times they get

> into trouble with one another so there is a scrap and many times they get arrested and put in jail.[22]

These descriptions illustrate the colonial success of boarding schools. They show how the church and federal government worked together to brainwash our children into thinking that the only way to be a good and decent human being was to essentially do everything the non-Indian people did and discard all Indigenous knowledge.

Mohawk elder Tom Porter summarized the problems our communities continue to face today as a result of how our children were brainwashed in boarding schools.

> But the Indian people were not born to be failures. We were survivors. We were people of dignity and honor. We were not born to be the most likely to be alcoholic people in the world. That is a new development in the last 150 years, this negativeness among my people.
>
> There are reasons for this. And one of those reasons is because our great-grandfather and grandfathers and grandmothers were forced to go to this government school, which stripped them of their language, their beliefs, their culture, and their spirituality.
>
> And so it is that without identity and without dignity, the Indian is walking the earth, almost in a state of numbness. And almost without a goal, without the feeling of being wanted by anyone, even within our own society. Because our whole society has been broken. That is why we have the highest rate of alcoholism, why the highest rate of drug activities is among the Indian nations, and why there is so much hopelessness.[23]

As Porter pointed out, boarding schools stripped Indigenous people of their language, their beliefs, their culture, and their spirituality. In its place was Christianity. The lessons at the boarding schools focused on the trades. Clearly, these institutions were never intended to teach Indigenous children anything other than how to work for non-Indian people. Indigenous children were not taught to be leaders, scholars, or doctors at these boarding schools. They were also not taught how to come out of allotment still owing their own land.

Allotment

While the government was removing children from their homes, the government was also scheming for other ways to assimilate Indigenous people and take their land. In 1887, Congress passed the General Allotment Act with the explicit purpose of breaking up tribal landholdings and assimilating Indigenous people into mainstream society.[24] In Oneida, the federal government realized some of their goals. Oneida people lost the title to 90 percent of their land by the mid-1920s.[25] With such a devastating loss of land, most Oneida people were no longer able to grow corn and other traditional Indigenous foods.

Allotment started off seemingly in favor of the Oneida people. It transferred communal ownership of land to individual people. The land was supposed to be held in trust for a period of twenty-five years, after which point the land would become taxable and could be mortgaged or sold. However, land speculators couldn't wait the twenty-five years to get their hands on Indian lands, so Congress responded by passing the Burke Act in 1906.[26] Under this law, if a federal competency commission deemed a tribal member competent to handle their own affairs, the tribal member could own their land outright through a fee patent. This form of ownership meant that the land would then be subject to taxes, mortgages, and sales. This change sped up the process of removing ownership of land from Oneida people because Oneida people did not fully understand the responsibilities that came with owning the land through a fee patient. Even in cases where the Oneida people didn't want fee patents to their land, the federal government forced this transfer.

During one of the hearings in 1917 to determine whether Oneida people should get the title to their land right away, inspector James McLaughlin noted that "we have granted a great many patents in fee to Indians who objected to applying for the patents. They are granted arbitrarily upon the reports that we have made that they are fully competent and well provided with worldly goods."[27] McLaughlin also compared receiving the allotments and fee title to non-Indians that inherit property and squander their inheritance: "the white man has accumulated a great deal of property. When he dies, the property is inherited by his heirs. The property never cost them any effort. They dissipate and squander it in a short time because they inherited it. And the same is true of you people. You received an allotment from the government. They came without any effort on your part and the young people, getting hold of that property, are apt to be very reckless."[28] Aside from the fact that this statement clearly ignored Oneidas' worldview, allotment and its obvious goals to dispossess Oneidas of their land was a violation of treaty promises to protect the land base.

During the hearings, it was clear the Oneida people were afraid of the continued conversion of their trust land into fee status. John Archiquette responded to the philosophy of issuing fee patents to dispossess Oneida people of their lands and explained that no one actually cared about the struggles of the Oneida people. "Now, it seems to me—for an illustration, there are a few black stars in on this reservation," he told those attending the hearing on the matter. He continued:

> Call it black stars to represent these trust patent lands and for these black stars to appear here and there it makes the others feel that they ought to not be there. It makes them sore. It makes an eye-sore to see them. Now, the government knows just about exactly what's going on here out on the Oneida Reservation. They know just about how the people live but there is these few here that don't like to see these black stars. They want to wipe them out and call it clean. It will never be clean until it is wiped out. That is the idea of the people and these few others who are holding the fee simple, they don't care what will become of us when we get our land deeded. We will say, what are we going to do? They will say, do what you can. If you can swim with your head above water, stay above water; if not, go down to the bottom and drown.[29]

Sampson Stevens clearly stated he was afraid the land speculators would swindle his land away from him. "I am competent to become a citizen, but I want to say that I am afraid of the speculators. As I am now [living on trust land], they have no chance to get the best of me. If I was to get a deed to my land, then the chances would be good."[30] Thomas N. Cornelius explained how all the recent improvements on the reservation only benefited white people because they were quickly buying up the land. "Gentleman says the greatest thing we have is roads; before we have mud holes before our door." Thomas told those in attendance: "It may be that way, but here when you come to good roads, improvements, barns and nice houses, good roads, I don't deny that. Who owns that? Does it belong to the Indian? No. New settlers just come in; they are the ones who own that. Those that took patent deed; they are gone and scattered today. They ain't got no pillow to lay down to rest. So I don't call it a great improvement."[31]

Unsurprisingly, the Oneidas' pleas were met with no sympathy from the federal government. Superintendent of the Oneida Indian School Joseph C. Hart responded by essentially stating that the federal government did all it could to help the Oneidas: "We can't stop progress. We are going ahead as a child has got to take his chance. The government has done as well as it could in the furnishing of schools and the giving of instruction. We haven't any complaint to make."[32] Essentially, federal officials said they were doing the Oneidas a favor by educating them and giving them individual ownership to property, when in actuality they were finding ways to turn Oneidas into obedient workers and get ownership of Oneida land.

Oscar Archiquette explained, "This act caused the complete destruction of Oneida Indian wealth. Lands were mortgaged for 1/4 of its value and never redeemed. Lands was also lost through delinquent taxes."[33] In addition, often the parcels in an allotment and in a single family were scattered throughout the reservation, making the maintenance of the scattered property inconvenient at best. The WPA stories captured a number of heartbreaking accounts of how quickly this turnover in land occurred, often under fraudulent circumstances and occasionally with the help of fellow Oneida people. Archiquette explained that boarding schools educated the Oneida people with "education to read and write, some just enough to be fools, while some turned out to be respectable and of some use, and some were real double crossers who helped the local real estate man to get Oneida lands for little or nothing some for whiskey."[34]

Joel Reed told a story about how he believed a fellow Oneida swindled him out of four acres of land.

> I was allotted 23 acres in Outagamie County Town of Oneida. My allotment was in three different places, one piece was 15 acres, [the others] 4 acres and 4 acres. Since the land was located in a swamp, I could not use it. I was single at the time which was 28 years ago or 1913. I decided to sell it, I had our agent Mr. J.C. Hart, Oneida to transact business for me, I sold 19 acres to P.W. Silverwood of Oneida for 18.50 per acre. He paid me in cash. The other four acres I kept for future use. I thought maybe some day I will build a house on it. One day I met XX in Green Bay, and he said, "I am going to tell you something which will make you happy." I said, "What is it?" "You have four acres of land that you can sell, if you wish I can sell it for you." I ask him how much would he charge me to transact business for me. "Well," he said, "Just a cigar a piece, I will sell it for half." I told him we better not smoke cigars, it cost too much. Sometime later I heard my four acres of land was sold by XX. I didn't believe it, because I never signed any kind of documents pertaining to my four acres. I asked an official about it, some two years ago. He said, "It happen so long ago it may be outlawed by this time, besides, the owners now are rich people and they would put up a fight before they would let it go." So I never got a cent for my four acres of land.[35]

There were also instances of using alcohol to persuade individuals to sign away their rights to their land. An anonymous Oneida told a story about their parents being swindled out of land by getting the father intoxicated.

> My father and mother had a 26 acre piece and a man from De Pere came to say he wanted to buy it. They told him they didn't have a patent yet and he said that for $200 he could get them one. In the meantime, the Indian Bureau had already issued the patent but the Agent held it up and told this fellow about the land. Well, after a couple of weeks they came to get my folks in a carriage and said the papers were all ready and they would have to go to DePere to get them. They got in the wagon and went off. My mother didn't know they were buying the land—she thought they were going for the papers—when they got there she went for some shopping and they got my father drunk and he signed the papers, taking out the $200. So he would end up with an old pony and a cow and a wagon. My mother got him home and in a few days some whites moved on the land and we couldn't use it. They showed papers where we had sold it to them. That was about it.[36]

Even in cases where Oneida people were not outright swindled out of their land, their inability to pay taxes or repay mortgages caused a significant amount of land to fall into the hands of non-Oneidas. Jonas Hill used Henry Doxtator as an example of how an individual lost everything without having a say in the matter.

> Take Henry Doxtator for one, he did not want to become a citizen or a taxpayer, because he was not capable of making enough money to pay taxes and for that reason he never approved of becoming a citizen and never signed his name to any kind of paper or an agreement approving of such, but the Gov. went right ahead and issued a patent in fee (deed) to his allotment of land. Mr. Doxtater lost his land through delinquent taxes; if the Gov. did not force Mr. Doxtater to become a taxpayer, he would have a home yet and be self supporting.[37]

Martin Hill described how he lost all but half an acre of land in a series of successive transactions.

> When we were permitted to sell or mortgage our land, I mortgaged 40 acres of my land; but then when time came to pay for the mortgage, I did not have any money to pay for the mortgage; so I lost it. Then later on I mortgaged some land where the house stood and again the same thing happened. Time came to pay mortgage and there was no money to be paid towards it. Finally we only had one acre left. We mortgaged half of that, too. So today all we have left is 1/2 acre and our home.[38]

Our community has countless stories just like these. I can't imagine how such a transition could happen to a community so fast. Within one generation, Oneida people lost so much of their land for a variety of different reasons. As these stories demonstrate, taxes, mortgages, and unscrupulous land sales all led to the catastrophic loss of land. As the federal government planned, non-Indian people were the ones to acquire ownership of these lands and began to operate their own farms on the Oneida Reservation.

In less than twenty-five years, the Oneida people went from a communal lifestyle, sharing their traditional and modern garden produce with their neighbors, to an almost landless people, forced to find work on land that white farmers acquired from Oneida families. Several of the WPA stories describe how when the Oneida people came home from the schools, they worked for white farmers who now owned land that used to belong to the Oneida people. Frank Danforth stated, "When I came home [from boarding school,] I started to work out around the white farmers near the reservation."[39] Ida Blackhawk described how non-Indian people bought land from the Oneidas, drained the excess water, and started to farm the land. "When the white businessmen of Green Bay took over the swamp land, they had a ditch put through and drained the land, then the land was sold to farmers, and is now under cultivation."[40] Similarly, Tom Elm explained how white people were buying up a lot of the land the Oneidas lost after allotment. "The Oneidas began to feel the heft of taxes and after three or four years some lost their homes and land," he said. "I knew that I was not anymore able than these people who have lost their homes. So I could not pay either, so I went and sold mine right out, and only kept a small place. The Oneidas lost their homes one after another and white people were coming in all this time."[41]

The speed at which land transferred from Oneida hands to non-Indian hands is astonishing. The entire reservation consists of approximately 65,400 acres of land. In a 1917 report on allotment, inspector James McLaughlin noted that the Oneida people were cultivating approximately ten thousand acres of land and a large part of that acreage was owned by the original allottees or their heirs.[42] The remainder had passed to non-Indians. By the mid-1920s, Oneida people lost approximately half of their remaining land, leaving the total land loss at about 90 percent of the land on the reservation.[43] As of 1941, Stadler King estimated the number of Oneida homesteads remaining on the eastern half of the reservation: "There were about twelve homesteads left in Town of Hobart and which are still owned by Oneidas today."[44] Without land, it would have been very difficult to grow traditional, heirloom foods.

With Oneida farmers rapidly becoming the minority on their own reservation, the church seemed even more emboldened to comment on Oneidas' lack of agricultural skills and the Oneidas' desperate need for the church's instruction. One representative of the church described the state of agriculture during the early 1900s: "Farming methods have for the most part been primitive, and as a consequence the lands which have been long in use have been cropped with wheat and corn until they have lost much of their original fertility and need intelligent methods to restore them."[45] Of course, the church and government schools thought it their duty to help the "primitive" Oneidas catch up to modern agricultural methods. The church representative continued: "There is also a large area still uncultivated that only needs to be cleared of brush and broken up to be immediately productive. It is to these lands that the small army of young men and women that the Government has been training for self help can prove that their education has been of advantage to them so that they may keep up with the onward march of agricultural improvement."[46]

Andrew Beechtree commented on this sentiment that Indigenous farmers used primitive and less productive technologies and that the white farmers needed to teach them how to farm. He explained how many of the old Oneida farmers were not educated but nonetheless knew more about farming than the educated white farmers. "Most of [the Oneidas] do not know of the existence of the Agricultural school and none asks for or get advice from the County Agricultural Agents," Andrew wrote about Oneida farmers.

> He goes on farming in the manner that their fathers have taught them. As a result, their way of farming and their equipment are not very modern . . . the big Larson Farms use fertilizers, rotation of crops and other modern discoveries and I grant they have good crops. I asked an Oneida neighbor man of the big farm why he didn't follow the example of his neighbors and use fertilizers. He answered me curtly, "Fertilizers nothing. Once I spent a lot of money to buy fertilizer to put on part of my field. I got just as good a crop on the part that I did not fertilize." If we have good weather and the time and ability to keep the weeds down and stir up the ground, the ground will pay us good with good crops, said the late Hyson John. Just where the last generation of farmers got their knowledge of farming I do not know. They certainly knew more about raising crops than we so called educated people.[47]

It can be difficult to focus on the positive when the negative is so overwhelming. As devastating as the loss of land was, as Andrew Beechtree noted, there were Oneida people that continued to maintain traditional agricultural practices and held traditional knowledge. That knowledge would serve to help Oneida people survive into the future.

After allotment, many people lost their land and had to move away to find work. Shortly after, the Depression hit, and many people lost those jobs and had to move back home to Oneida. Ida Blackhawk, WPA storyteller and employee, moved back to Oneida at the beginning of the depression and explained the situation there: "As the Depression became more acute, the Oneidas returned to Oneida, and some rented and others lived with their parents or other relatives. In a short time all the vacant houses were occupied. By 1933, a great many of the Oneidas, who had previously found employment away from home had returned to Oneida, because they could not continue to live in the city without work of some kind."[48] Wilson Cornelius described how he coped with the tough economic times by growing corn: "We have plenty of [Indian] corn so we can make cornbread. We make lot of cornbread and sell it all around, this is a good way to make cash money because everybody will buy good cornbread. We have went out selling cornbread and make as much as five dollars. I have planted as much corn as I usually do this year so that I will have corn next winter."[49] While growing their own corn was a luxury that few Oneidas were able to enjoy after such a devastating loss in land, it demonstrates that people in the Oneida community still found a way to rely on corn for survival.

Conclusion

During the late 1800s, the federal government tried to get Oneida people to meld into mainstream society. The government implemented laws and policies that made it easier for churches to take Oneida children from their homes in an attempt to erase Oneida people's language and culture. They found ways to break up Oneida community landholdings knowing that ownership of reservation lands would quickly pass into non-Indian hands. All of these changes had devastating impacts on our ability to grow our own foods and take care of each other. This was always part of their plan. They understood that they were replacing the ways we cared for our children and our foods. They tried to take both skills away from us. They tried to make it impossible for Oneida people to pass on traditional teachings and knowledge.

This was a difficult chapter to write. This era was filled with so much pain and loss. Oneida people's very identities were being ripped away from them. It's important to note that this pain didn't just end with those stolen children. We are still suffering every day because of these actions the federal government and churches took. Yet we are still expected to behave in a certain way while we are out in society. We are expected to fit their standards of cleanliness and appropriateness to be accepted or taken seriously.

Fortunately, enough Oneida people held fast to Oneida language, culture, and agricultural practices during this period of time. When others were ready to pick those practices back up again, those who held on could help others learn. And while we are caring for our corn and other plant relatives in our gardens, we are healing from past losses. We are rekindling those relationships that we did not grow up with because our parents and grandparents were part of the assimilationist experiment. While many people in our community still feel the impacts from this era of time, more and more of us are rejecting the expectations that mainstream society places on us. We are heading to the gardens, to the fields, to the woods, to the prairies, to the water—to reconnect to creation and give thanks to Shukwayaʔtísu for all he created. Through all this return, corn is taking up her role as the leader of the plants and is leading the way forward.

CHAPTER 9

Wayukhinikuhlá?kháshyi

(They Have Separated Our Minds)

NE· YAKΛ LATUHÁKWE TOWARD THE END OF THE GREAT DEPRESSION, THE Oneida people would again see more changes. President Franklin Roosevelt's New Deal brought two changes to Oneida. First, Congress passed the Indian Reorganization Act (IRA) in 1934. This legislation had both positive and negative impacts. It further factionalized the community but it set in place a mechanism for Oneida to reacquire land so they could build homes and grow food, including white corn. Second, beginning in 1938, the federal government funded the Works Progress Administration (WPA) to bring work relief to the reservation by paying Oneida people to gather stories from other Oneida people. The stories gathered under the WPA project form a significant basis for understanding the Oneida people's factionalization and relationship with the land and corn during this period of time. These oral histories are documents recorded by and from the Oneidas themselves rather than from people outside of the Oneida community. This historical record illustrates their perspective on their political divisions and continued relationship with the land and corn.

The Meriam Report and Roosevelt's New Deal

In 1934, Congress passed two key pieces of New Deal legislation in response to the impacts allotment had on Indian people and Indian reservations: the Johnson O'Malley Act and the IRA.[1] These pieces of legislation responded to a report published in 1928 by Lewis Meriam and Hubert Work titled "The Problem of Indian Administration."[2] Later known as the Meriam Report, this document noted that allotment was successful in breaking up tribal landholdings, but that Indigenous people had become poorer and more desolate than ever. The people were in survival mode and in most cases did not have the land nor community support to maintain their traditional agricultural practices. The Meriam Report argued that improving the conditions on Indian reservations required restoring management of tribal affairs to tribal governments. As WPA storyteller Oscar Archiquette perceived it: "When the White man got everything the Indian had, then he found out that the Indian was just an expense to the tax payers."[3] The solution was to push the problem back on tribal government to fix for themselves.

The Johnson O'Malley Act provided for direct financial relief on Indian reservations, and the IRA allowed tribes to reorganize their governments and to begin to reacquire land lost through allotment with federal assistance. Oscar Archiquette noted that under the IRA, people would be able to resume their farming practices: "The object of this act is to give the Indian his land back, and let him cultivate his land and be self supporting."[4] Pursuant to the IRA, tribes voted on whether to accept its provisions and reorganize their governments under a new constitution. Tribes that accepted the provisions received help from the federal government to write new constitutions, often based on a boilerplate document from the Bureau of Indian Affairs, and received federal funding to begin to reacquire land on their reservations that had been lost through allotment.

Support and Opposition of the IRA

The IRA received mixed support in Oneida.[5] There were a number of different factions with their own perspectives on whether Oneida should accept the provisions of the law. Francis Skenandore, a retired Oneida attorney, identified four different factions led by William "Willie Fat" Skenandore, Laura Cornelius "Minnie" Kellogg, Oscar Smith, and Morris Wheelock, respectively. According to Francis,

> Skenandore opposed adoption of the IRA on the grounds that it would affect treaty guarantees, take from the Oneidas the last bit of land they were still holding, and leave Oneidas worse off than ever. He further argued that the IRA was vicious, detrimental, and injurious to the Oneidas, and that it gave the Bureau of Indian Affairs absolute and arbitrary power of over the Oneidas. The Kellogg and Smith groups also opposed the IRA in order to reaffirm Oneida sovereignty and the sanctity of treaties. The Wheelock group supported the IRA because of its tribal rehabilitative features: the restoration of a tribal land base, community betterment, and self-sufficiency.[6]

Andrew Beechtree described the factions falling into two main parties: those who supported the IRA and those who opposed it. "The major political parties at that time was the Oneida Tribe of Indians of Wisconsin, a federal incorporated organization which was usurping the bargaining power of the tribe, and which had assumed the nickname of New Deal Party. Its opposition was the Oneida Indians of the Oneida Reservation, Wisconsin. This party had long been in existence and was mutually called the Injun Party."[7]

These competing factions made the federal government's task of contacting the Oneida people to set up meetings complicated. Federal officials intended to set up meetings to talk about the IRA and answer questions. In doing so, they refused to acknowledge the fully functioning traditional government that had been governing prior to European contact. As a result, they had to choose some other group or person, as Oscar Archiquette explained. "Since the Oneida chiefs were not recognized as legal representatives for the Wisconsin Oneida tribe, the Ashland Indian agency did not know just whom to contact for a meeting in regard to the Reorganization Act," Oscar wrote. "But they started out with the self-appointed chief"—his term for William "Willie Fat" Skenandore, who initially supported the IRA but changed his position and ended up leading one of the factions that opposed it. Oscar continued, "I finally did get a copy of the act, and I read it. I thought it was a good thing for my people, and I started talking about it to friends, and we had a number of Oneidas who had fair education and were not followers of the self-appointed chief; they also favored the act."[8]

Andrew Beechtree was a part of the Injun Party. Along with William Skenandore, he preferred to rely on the traditional chiefs and clan system for governance and fought for the Oneidas' treaty rights, the federal government's promise to protect their land base, a promise violated when the allotment acts were passed. According to Ida Blackhawk, the Injun Party organized to get the Oneidas' taxable land back.[9] When the group tried to gather to discuss their opposition to the New Deal Party, their opposition tried to stop them, and on at least one occasion, tried to stop them with violence. Beechtree told his WPA interviewer the story.

> The New Dealers had been holding sessions first in one church hall and then another. So one time we decided to hold a meeting in a public hall also. on the morning of the evening that we had scheduled our meeting, we got word that the New Dealers were going to break up our meeting. So, we requested of the county officials for a protection. When we got to the Parish Hall, our entrance was blocked by three of the New Dealers. A few minutes of

arguments and there were several blows struck. Another little scuffle and the speed cop arrived. He persuaded the meeting busters to leave. After several days of blaspheming and threatening us, we decided to give them a lesson. We got out a warrant for them and they fought on and on to their utmost, but to no avail. Mr. Baird, a member of the New Deal Party, was found guilty of assaulting Wm. Skenandore of the Old Injun Party, by a jury of six men. There was no repercussions from this trial either. But it took nerve and much logic to attack a federal enterprise. But if we had not checked them or if they had won the case, their egotism would have known no bounds.[10]

In the WPA stories, Guy Cornelius told a funny account about one of these meetings where an older man was asking his grandson about the IRA.

We were all waiting for the meeting to open, and so we were telling stories, and talking about this New Deal, and trying to explain to one another just what was all about in regards to provisions and benefits to the tribe. The old man said to the younger man, "Grandson, what do you think is the looks of this New Deal if a person could see what it looks like," he said it in Oneida. The younger Oneida took a long breath and look at the old Oneida square in the face. He said, "Grandpa, you wouldn't get mad if I was to tell you what it looks like?" Well, the young Oneida said to his grandpa, "You know," he said, "how the bear's hind end looks like, the New Deal as far as I can make out looks something like it." Some of the men folks that were listening started to laugh, besides the old man got mad at his grandson. He said to his grandson, "at your age if you saw a bear you wouldn't take the time to find out what his hind end looks like, you would be running away from there as fast as your legs could carry you." The grandpa and his grandson almost got into a fight before they stopped slurring with one another. It was the best joke that I have heard about the New Deal.

The older people were hard to make them understand about this New Deal. They just couldn't believe it was possible for the government to give them all these advantages lots of them died before they could get any of this

> help from the United States government. Some of the Oneidas have been waiting or wishing that the day would come when they could get some land and have their own homes again.[11]

The different factions continued to advocate for their positions throughout the community. They continued to gather and hold meetings to debate on the pros and cons of accepting the IRA in Oneida. In the end, the factions that showed up to vote chose to accept the IRA.

Voting on the IRA

When the federal government offered to help tribes reorganize their governments, it wanted tribes to do so in a way that the United States approved. Instead of memorializing the Oneidas' traditional government in a written constitution, the federal government required that the Oneida people adopt a boilerplate constitution it provided, with minimal modifications. Most tribes that accepted the IRA continue to operate under this standard boilerplate constitution today. Among the Oneidas, the Injun Party refused to participate in the vote, but many others decided to do so. Guy Elm explained, "The Oneidas, they are practically landless, therefore had everything to gain and nothing to lose."[12]

Not everyone showed up to vote, as Andrew Beechtree reported. "Our advice to our still-loyal backers was to stay away from the polls if they didn't believe in the act," Beechtree wrote. "We figured the New Deal Party would win anyway, so why waste time and risk getting crowned unceremoniously. At about the time of the counting of the ballots, I screwed up my courage to go and hear the results of the election. I hired a white man to drive me down there because I thought if anything happened, I could have him as a witness. I also did not care to create a young war."[13] Those who did vote voted to accept the IRA. By 1937, the Oneida people had reorganized under a new constitution. The government set up by this new constitution did not resemble the traditional form of government the Oneida people operated under as part of the Yukwanuhsyu·ní.

Benefits of the New Deal

Without a doubt, the New Deal did bring many benefits to the Oneida people. However, these benefits might not have been necessary if the federal government hadn't carried out its plan to dispossess the Oneidas and countless other tribes of their land bases. Guy Cornelius closely followed the progress of the New Deal and commented on the advantages it ultimately brought to the Oneida community. "Some of the provisions were self form of government amongst the Indians in their communities or reservations," Guy said, and listed several more:

> Government to buy land for landless Indians, and government to hold in trust all the Indian land owned by the tribes. A revolving fund to be advanced to the tribes for loans for members of the tribe. A rehabilitation fund for building homes and other improvements. Loans to young Indians that want to continue their education after completing the high school. Free hospitalization and medical treatment for the poor Indian that are on relief or W.P.A. projects. Clothing for the school children. The Oneidas have received all these advantages.[14]

Similarly, WPA storyteller Nick Denny was one of the individuals who received direct benefit from the IRA. As a result of receiving a land assignment, his family was again able to grow their own foods, including corn. Nick explained:

> I happened to be a strong supporter of this New Deal, therefore I was one of the first Oneidas to be granted land assignment of ten acres. They also built me a small three room house to live in. I can't express myself how glad I was, when they told me I could move in. I have been making my payments up to

> now. I think the U.S. government should buy more land for the Oneidas. My wife and I live fairly good. We raise all our vegetables such as potatoes, beans, carrots, onions, beets, corn, cabbage, radish, lettuce, spinach, cucumbers, and melons.[15]

The Oneida people elected Guy Elm to serve on the Land Committee, the body responsible for determining which families received a land assignment, and whose decision would be ratified by the Executive Committee. Elm commented, "I was elected by the vote of Indians last election in July as a chairman of land assignment committee. I find the work very interesting and some times very hard to decide which party should be assigned the land first, because there are more people seeking land assignments than what is available at the present time."[16] Oscar Archiquette summarized the land reacquisition under the IRA as follows: "Since the Indian Reorganization Act came into being, the Oneidas of to-day are now planning for the future, the U.S. government has bought back 1300 acres of land once owned by the Oneidas, and the executive committee of the Oneida Indians of Wisconsin Incorporated have assigned same to some 30 Oneida families."[17] This reclamation of land allowed more Oneida families to resume their agricultural lifestyles and begin to grow their own foods again, including white corn.

WPA Project

Part of the New Deal was the funding of the WPA, mentioned earlier because of the oral history project it supported. It also provided employment opportunities to help people recover from the Depression. There were two distinct projects in Oneida. The first was the Oneida Language and Folklore Project, which focused on preserving the Oneida language. The second was the Oneida Ethnological Study, whose focus was history, ethnography, and autobiography. Both left records that offer a wealth of information about the daily lives of the Oneida people during 1938–1942.

The Oneida Language and Folklore Project was part of the larger Federal Writers' Project, which was established in 1935 to subsidize the income of professional writers and enhance the nation's culture by funding socioethnic studies.[18] The goal of the Oneida project was to teach Oneidas to write in their language. It had a number of other positive impacts as well, including the preservation of Oneida history and folklore, the creation of a hymnal in the Oneida language, and the employment of numerous Oneida people who had lost their jobs during the Great Depression. In 1930, 77 percent of Oneida people were receiving some form of public assistance.[19] By 1939, that number jumped to 86 percent.[20]

During this time, the Oneida language was declining.[21] The older generation was speaking the Oneida language, but the younger generations were increasingly relying on English. Oneidas who attended boarding schools were punished for speaking their languages. In addition, many Oneida people moved to the cities to find work, exacerbating the loss of their language.

The beginnings of the language project can be traced back to professor Morris Swadesh, a linguist who took a position as an assistant professor of linguistics at the University of Wisconsin–Madison in 1937. He wanted to work on an Iroquois language, and the university's proximity to the Oneida Reservation made working with the Oneida community an ideal opportunity. Swadesh traveled there and became acquainted with some Oneida people. Oneida tribal member Earl Webster returned to Madison with Swadesh to serve as a Native speaker. Swadesh had his students practice writing the Oneida language phonetically and try to decipher the system underlying the language.[22]

In 1938, the University of Wisconsin–Madison submitted a number of project proposals to the WPA, including Swadesh's "Project Sub-Unit 7, a Phonetic Vocabulary of the Oneida Indian Language and the Accumulation of Native folklore."[23] His project was awarded $10,728 and set to begin in January 1939. In 1938, as Swadesh was reaching out to the Oneida community to prepare for the project, he found out that his employment contract with the university was not going to be renewed.[24] He accepted a position in Mexico to head the

Tarascan Literacy Project. Prior to his departure, he selected Floyd Lounsbury to carry out the Oneida project. At the time, Lounsbury was an undergraduate mathematics major interested in structural linguistics and had taken Swadesh's classes. The two men then met with Oneida people to become more familiar with the Oneida language. Swadesh and Lounsbury decided to depart from the orthography previously used with the Oneida language and the closely related Mohawk language that dated back to 1532.[25]

In January 1939, the Oneida Language and Folklore Project officially began.[26] About twenty-four Oneidas participated in a two-week training session lasting eight hours a day to learn how to phonetically spell words in the Oneida language. After this training, Lounsbury tested the workers until they were 98 percent accurate. Oneidas working on the project earned fifty cents per hour, totaling forty-five dollars per month.[27] Lounsbury selected thirteen Oneidas to continue with the project. Eight speakers remained throughout the whole project.

The Oneidas went into the community to conduct interviews of Oneida elders and collect brief stories.[28] During the interviews, the worker would take notes. The worker would return to the WPA office in Oneida and write out the stories in Oneida with an English translation. A typist in the WPA office in Green Bay would type up the stories varying in length from a paragraph to a page.[29] The topics varied and included religion, politics, witchcraft, jokes, recipes, medicine, boarding school, removal to Wisconsin, and more. Funding for the Oneida Language and Folklore Project ended in 1940.

The stories collected through the Oneida Language and Folklore Project were used as the basis for an Oneida-language program in the 1970s.[30] The written transcripts in Oneida with an English translation provided insight into the mechanics of the Oneida language. The collection was also later used in the Oneida newspaper as well as made into booklets for the community in the 1970s. Furthermore, the stories helped Maria Hinton and Amos Christjohn, two Oneida first-language speakers, to develop an Oneida dictionary. Though the collections remain invaluable, Lounsbury later noted that it could have contained more stories: "We had no magnetic recordings, no tape recorders, no photocopying machines, no computers, no data processing. Had these machines been available, we would have accomplished much, much more . . . It is incredible to think of what we could have done if we had had computers and photocopy machines."[31] While the Oneida Language and Folklore Study became an important resource for language revitalization efforts in the 1970s, the remainder of the WPA project remained hidden for several decades before being discovered in 1998.

As the Oneida Language and Folklore Project wrapped up, the Oneida Ethnological Study began as a continuation of that first project and also relied on WPA funds. Begun in late 1940 under the direction of Harry Basehart, a graduate student in anthropology at the University of Chicago, it continued until 1942.[32] Basehart changed the focus from language to history, ethnography, and autobiography, but like the earlier study, he employed Oneida people to interview community members. However, this new project also included the observations, recollections, and opinions of the Oneida writers. They were also often collected in English and the pieces ran much longer, a single story often continuing for several pages. The collection consists of 167 spiral steno pads running more than 18,000 pages filled with handwritten texts.

This Oneida Ethnological Study had been inadvertently separated from the earlier collection, and for reasons that aren't clear, it remained lost for decades. It wasn't until 1998 that the University of Wisconsin–Madison rediscovered it.[33] Herbert S. Lewis and L. Gordon McLester then selected some of the stories and published this "untapped resource" in a 2005 book titled *Oneida Lives*. Even today, these stories remain largely untapped.

Tom Elm, one of the WPA storytellers, explained the benefits of gathering the stories as part of the WPA project.

> [The government] also knows that now is the only time left that it could ever get information about Oneidas because we old fellows are passing away, and it will not be long when those of my age will all have passed away, and the

> younger ones that will take our place do not know anything of those older days. If they waited twenty years or so they would not have been able to find anyone that knows and be interested in telling of this life of Indians. Those who have gone to school have their minds on something different from these so they are not interested and would not know.[34]

Oscar Archiquette talked about how the WPA project helped revive the Oneida language. "Years ago say up to 1920 we had good speakers, this died out until 1936 when the Indian Reorganization Act took action here, today we again have a few good speakers," Archiquette explained. "In closing my history, about Oneidas, I wish to thank those who was so kind and interested about us Oneidas, to give us a chance to tell about ourselves and to get a true picture of Oneidas as a whole. I trust that we Oneidas benefit from our true Oneida Indian history some time in future."[35]

Many stories in the WPA collection offer recollections of the Oneidas' recent and distant past and of their historic relationship with corn. While corn remained a normal and integral component of daily life, the storytellers were concerned about the Oneidas' changing relationship with it as a result of assimilationist policies and the loss of land to grow it on because of allotment. Read collectively, these stories also reveal a decline in traditional farming practices, in community work, in drying foods for winter, in consuming traditional foods, and in their health.[36]

The storytellers described an overall change in the way they cared for their gardens. In the past, they would use their traditional tools and implements and go from garden to garden in the community and help each other out. During the twentieth century, the storytellers noticed that the work became more individualized and the farmers made use of modern tractors and other farm equipment. Many lamented that people no longer helped each other out the way they used to. "Back in my boyhood days . . . I can well remember well how the neighbors used to help each other," Hyson Doxtator, WPA employee and storyteller, began.

> Starting early in the spring . . . Now for dinner they give the best they can afford, meat, usually a young pig is butchered for roast. They never forget old fashioned cornbread and corn soup with dried vegetables, pies, and cakes. They are all well fed, both women, men, and children. After dinner they sit down for a while to settle their heavy dinner. Some telling stories, joking as it is the custom with the Indians when there are a few together.
>
> The work starts again in the afternoon they work harder and try and do more than they did in the forenoon. They usually work until about half past four o clock, then supper . . . That extended at the Bee as it was called. [the farmer] also announced which neighbour they are going to help next. This was kept up until spring work starts.
>
> Corn was their main crop, two to four acres is what is usually planted. After the crops are up, they would begin to help with their hoeing and clean the fields of weeds. The ones that could afford had grain, corn, potatoes, and gardens of vegetables . . . As times is changing so is customs amongst the Indian race. The young have put away the customs of older generation. There are no more community work anymore by the Oneida Indians. If a man wants anything done, he has either to do it himself or hire it done by someone, just as times changes, so it is with all race of people . . . All this cooperation work has been declining. Around about 1900 to 1910 some of the cooperation work was done but very little of it . . . I from my boyhood days have seen this all, that our traditional organization is slowly dying out of the Oneida Indian tribe.[37]

Similarly, Andrew Beechtree explained how a word previously used to describe husking bees transformed into a new meaning. Andrew wrote, "He [the farmer] used to hold a wadʌnha.u. This was an Oneida word for benefit, more lethargically called a bee . . . it shows the early existence of community group work. This wadʌnha.u was once very popular among the Oneida people. but now that word means to hire. I suppose it is because that now when you ask a person to help, you the first thing they ask is what is going to be their pay."[38]

The WPA storytellers also talked about not drying food for the winter. For a point of reference, Rachel Denny provided a vivid description of her childhood home with plenty of dried foods for the winter.

> I still remember when I was five years old. Our house did not have any floor, only a fireplace made out of field stones. We had a table and shelves nailed onto the wall. We had one window and one door, but we had lots of food that we had stored up: dried corn, dried fruit, dried meat, dried fish, beans, and dried pumpkin. Spring time we would have maple syrup and maple sugar. Upstairs there were shelves and that's where the maple sugar was stacked up.[39]

Mrs. Nelson B. Cornelius then explained how people no longer prepared foods for winter. It is likely that people began to rely more on stores to purchase goods during the winter instead of preparing food for themselves. "It may be that Oneidas of these times are not so ambitious, in comparison with the old timers in storing up provisions for themselves," she explained. "No doubt if you went into anyone's home, there would be bundles of dried pumpkin hanging here and there, also they would have several hundreds both dried and salted fish. They would also have several bags full of dried corn and beans of all kinds. They used to dry apples and also blackberries. By that they used to have a lot of food stored up when cold weather set in, in the fall of the year."[40]

The storytellers also noted a decline in eating traditional foods and, as a likely result, a decline in their health. Jessie Peters said, "When I was ten years old I used to hear old people say that our health would change if we eat what the white people eat. They eat so much of fine cakes and sweet stuff. The best foods are the old time Indian Corn Soup and Indian Cornbread, and now as I don't eat much of that at my age, I look to be about eighty years old and I am unable to work much."[41]

The movement to once again rebuild ourselves and our culture often centers on language and food. I was not familiar with a lot of the ways of cooking and preserving our foods referenced in the WPA stories. It made me wonder how many methods are still out there, waiting to be dusted off and celebrated as part of our connection to our culture and our foods.

WPA Short Stories about Corn

The stories in the WPA collection do not all contain warnings for the future or laments for a long-lost past. There are a number of jokes and funny tales as well as stories about good times, including weddings, births, sports, music, and community gatherings. Some of the short stories about corn give us a glimpse into the Oneida people's sense of humor in the early part of the twentieth century. A handful of these stories are relayed in this section.

The first story was about what happened when someone found a red cob among the white ones during a husking bee. WPA storyteller Lucy Rose explained, "Long ago the Oneidas had a custom that usually in the fall, they would start to hire corn-shuckers. At their houses they would just do things around the bee. And when a man finds a red ear of corn, then he will look around to see who he likes, and on the sly he will go where a young girl is sitting and give her a kiss. And for the young girls it is the same when they find a red ear of corn. They will kiss the ones they like."[42]

The theme of working to shell corn was common in the stories. Ida Blackhawk told a quick, funny story about a man too lazy to shell any corn: "One time in Oneida there was a man lazy about working. Those that lived there said, 'Let's bury this guy who is so lazy.' So then they made a coffin and put him in there. One man pitied him, so he said, 'I have some corn to give him to eat.' They say he sat up and looked around and said, 'Is the corn shelled?' They said, 'No, you have to shell it yourself.' He said, 'Never mind, put the cover on and continue to bury me.'"[43] WPA storyteller Celecia Hill told another story about a man wanting to shell the corn, but he couldn't because it was Sunday and he was Christian.

> An old man used to be always shelling corn they say. He used to keep a basket of corn by his bed. Just as soon as he got up he would start to shell corn. It happened that it was on a Sunday morning, but he wanted to shell corn, so his granddaughter told him that it was Sunday, this particular day, and therefore not to do any work. So the old man laid down, and fell asleep again just a little while, and he awoke again and got up and started to shell corn again. His granddaughter again stopped him, so he went back to bed again. When he awoke, he pulled his basket of corn again, so his granddaughter stopped him again. Then the old man said, "Is everyday Sunday?"[44]

Another short story came from WPA employee and storyteller Dennison Hill. He told a story about a car accident and some loaves of cornbread.

> One time some Oneidas were hired to go pick blueberries somewhere up north, probably Munising. [The farmer] got a vehicle here, a big car and they got in the automobile, those who were hired. They were riding somewhere and it tipped over on them. Some white people pretty soon made a crowd and they helped these Oneidas. Some who were hurt let off in town at a hospital. Others they say they just cleaned them up and they recovered. Around where they had their accident, they say there were various loaves of cornbread since they were carrying their lunch. These white people thought they saw some kind of stone lying around.[45]

This last story is a humorous account of what happened when a husband and wife tasked their daughter with making corn soup with what ended up being insufficient instructions. Tom Elm told this story.

"This happened a while back now. There was a man who used to be called He-hired-himself and he had a child, a step-daughter, by the name of Melinda. On this Sunday morning Melinda's mother told her, 'Make a little corn soup. The kettle will be on and we will eat when we return from going to church.'

"So she began to make the corn soup, but she realized they did not have any meat. 'What will I add in when I make the corn soup,' she asked her mother, 'to make it taste good?'

"'Just look around,' her mother said, 'Look for something you can throw in to make it taste good.'

"When her parents left to go to church, she sharpened her knife for herself and she looked around for something, some sort of meat to throw in the soup. And she noticed a large group of piglets penned in the pigpen. So she cut off the ears from those piglets and added them to the soup.

"When they returned from having gone to church, there was a kettle on the stove and the soup was really boiling and it smelled really good. Melinda's mother uncovered the kettle on the stove and she started to stir the soup, but it wasn't long before she was surprised that she saw something floating there. She realized they were pig ears. She said, 'Melinda, what did you do now?'

"'Now, now, Mom,' Melinda responded, 'You yourself told me to look for meat.'

"He-hired-himself started to suspect something funny was going on so he peeked into the pigpen and he noticed the bodies of his animals—they were running around with no ears."[46]

These stories share a lighter side to daily life in Oneida during the early 1900s. They show that not only did Oneida people maintain a deep connection with corn, but that they were willing to freely share their sense of humor.

Conclusion

The New Deal era in the 1930s and 1940s had positive and negative impacts on the Oneida community. The IRA exacerbated the factionalism within the community and disregarded the traditional governing structure that was already in place. The government pit families against each other by giving gifts to some families and making others jealous. During this time, some people were clinging to their original form of government. They were desolate and living a meager life. The government told them that the only way to have a better life would be to do things their way.

Despite this, it implemented a mechanism for the Oneida people to begin to reacquire land lost through the General Allotment Act. Families were able to build new homes and resume their agricultural practices. Once again, families were able to grow their traditional, heirloom corn along with beans, squash, and other garden foods to sustain themselves.

The New Deal also funded the Works Progress Administration, which funded projects that collected numerous stories from Oneida people. These stories served as an invaluable resource to understand what Oneidas' relationship with corn looked like during the storytellers' lifetimes. People at this time showed great concern for the continuity of Oneida identity and traditional aspects of their lives, including growing, harvesting, cooking, and consuming traditional, heirloom corn. Our relationship with corn and the healing aspects of cooking our foods comes through the humor within the WPA stories. The WPA stories are glimpses into our pasts, many of which may have been completely forgotten. These stories tell us of our past generations and their ability to maintain their humor in the most trying times. These stories tell us of how our corn relative evoked the humor and joy of being a people. She still does this today; as we gather for the bee, we smile, laugh, and enjoy each moment with intention because we are still here healing our minds as Yukwanuhsyu·ní.

CHAPTER 10

Ohutsyo·kú· Wahatiha·wíhte

(They Took It to under the Earth)

NE· YAKʌ LATUHÁKWE THAT THE 1940S TO THE 1970S MARKED MORE CHANGES for the Oneida community and their declining relationship with corn. During this period of time, we saw tribes being terminated, Native Americans being relocated off their reservations to cities, and increasing consumption of commodity foods that failed to resemble our traditional diets. Near the end of this time period, we start to see hope in what the future might bring. Terminated tribes were being restored and the Oneida government began to increase its efforts to look for funding to support tribal agricultural programs. However, it wouldn't be until the 1980s that the tribal government would have enough funding to operate them.[1]

Despite the changes happening during these decades, several families held fast to the tradition of growing corn and sharing with the community raw corn as well as cornbread and corn soup. They continued to care for our sister, the corn, when other people were unable to. Like so many other periods of time, most of the people in the Oneida community were the children or grandchildren of those who were forced to lay down their agricultural practices in order to survive. It is because of the perseverance of the people who continued to care for our corn during these years that we are able to pick those practices back up today.

Renewed Assimilation Efforts: 1940s to 1950s

In the late 1940s and early 1950s, federal policy turned away from tribal self-determination toward a goal of terminating tribes.[2] The goal was to sever the relationship between tribes and the federal government—once again an attempt to assimilate Native Americans into mainstream society. While Oneida escaped outright termination, many tribal members left the reservation as part of the 1950s relocation programs that may have been a blind step toward termination but in a much different way.[3]

Those who remained struggled to survive in a world that continued to exert assimilationist pressures. In a 1953 newspaper article, the *Milwaukee Journal* reported on the conditions of poverty on the Oneida Reservation, quoting Oscar Archiquette, Oneida Chairman, who said that the solutions were better jobs and more land. "Archiquette said one of the needs at Oneida was more land to be purchased by the federal government for settlement by Oneida Indians. Not all Oneidas, however, care for farming, and a survey is needed to determine how many want to farm and how much land is needed."[4]

An increase in the amount of government-issued foods sent to Indian reservations also marked this period of time.[5] These commodities were often prepackaged, processed, and high-calorie foods that failed to resemble the traditional diets of Native American people. Commodity foods are often to blame as a contributing factor in disproportionate health problems Native American people face when compared to other races.

Amid these renewed assimilation efforts and the increase in poor-quality food, the elders I interviewed turned their focus to recalling fond childhood memories of corn. These stories reveal a continuing connection to Indigenous corn in the Oneida community. Some of the names of corn growers that commonly came up in the stories included Sherman (Shorty) and Sarah Skenandore; Ed and Electa Skenandore; David Skenandore; Hank Skenandore; Loomis John and his wife, Norbert Skenandore; Lydia Denny; and Anderson Cornelius. Oneida elders Julie Barton, Stan Webster, and Gerald Danforth talked about how these people helped provide food to the community. Julie Barton recalled how she and Sarah Skenandore became fast friends and how Sarah taught her all about growing and cooking corn.

> My sister would get corn soup from Sarah and Sherman Skenandore. I got to be really good friends with them. Sherman would always tell Bob [my husband] about how to grow corn and I would always be listening. Sarah would be preparing it. Gradually I got interested in how they were making it. They had their own little factory in the garage. They had an iron stove and they were always feeding it. Sherman had a motor and then he took an old-fashioned hand grinder and he connected it to the motor. He would pour the corn in there and he would turn on the motor. It would grind it and then Sarah would sift it in this big sifter. Then she would put it in again and then she would sift it again. I think about three times, that was for the cornbread. Somebody was always coming and going at the house to buy corn, corn soup, or cornbread. A lot of times I would be there when these people came, and they would stop to visit . . .
>
> I couldn't afford to keep buying corn soup and cornbread, so then I said, "Well, I'll buy the dried stuff from them." Corn got to be precious to me because in those days you had to worry about where every dollar came from. I had to scrape up enough money to go down and get enough corn for soup. By the time Sarah and Sherman got older, I knew all of everything that they could teach me. It was nice to have known them because they were like old-fashioned traditional. They always spoke Oneida always to each other and sometimes they would slip in a phrase or two when they were talking to me.[6]

Stan Webster recalled how Sarah always sent him home with samp for his father.

> When Sarah was going to make corn soup or kanʌstóhale, we knew all the way down in Milwaukee. If you didn't get here early, you didn't get any kanʌstóhale. She used to make those big loaves. When I was walking to her house, I could smell the kanʌstóhale all the way from the driveway. Everybody would come out with a big smile with kanʌstóhale because it was a big event. I remember so well how we would all gravitate to the corn soup. They had turkey and ham and all this fancy food set up on the table, but everybody was standing in line to get the corn soup until it was all gone . . . When I was younger, my dad always asked me to go over there late to get samp. When you make the kanʌstóhale, the water gets real thick after you put so many loaves in there. When you take that last loaf out, they call that "samp." My dad always wanted a great big half gallon of that. So, I used to go there, and the first time I said that, she asked me who my dad was. I said "Stanley." She said, "Oh! Okay." Then she would give me a great big container of it. My dad drank that whole thing.[7]

Gerald Danforth told me about a childhood memory of Ed and Electa Skenandore driving down the road, going from house to house selling cornbread.

> I remember the car coming down the road. There was a half a dozen houses between a mile distance between where we lived and where Chicago Corners[8] was. They would be coming down the road. Those older cars had these big wide running boards on the side. They had their cornbread in the car. Somebody would be hanging with their arms through the window and standing on the running board so they wouldn't have to be getting in and out of the car they as they were pulling to various driveways. They would just pull into the driveway and come to the house with some cornbread. Depending on what each family wanted, they would buy the cornbread. I don't know what the price was, but it wasn't a lot of money. It was maybe fifty cents or a dollar

> a loaf or something like that. Ed and Electa Skenandore was one family that sold cornbread like that. Shorty and Sarah Skenandore did also, and of course Loomis John and his wife. More recently, Amelia Cornelius was the go-to person for cornbread. Finally, I started learning to make it for myself.[9]

These three stories show us that in the 1940s and 1950s, Oneida people were still growing and cooking corn as well as sharing their harvest and their meals with community members. Other storytellers also mentioned these people in passing, making note of how popular the cornbread and corn soup sales always were.

A handful of other short stories from this time period reveal that even if a family didn't grow their own corn, they had access to raw corn from someone else in the community and cooked it fairly often. Elders Stan and Loretta Webster, Julie Barton, and Carol Elm all shared stories about their families storing and cooking white corn. Stan Webster fondly recalled his grandfather having a feud with the mice to keep them away from his raw corn. "My grandfather, Richard Metoxen, lived down Seymour Road," Stan told me. "He would get white corn and braid it and hang it up. He always had to fight the mice because he would hang it up outside and the mice would come out there along the fence line. Then he put it inside a shed he built, but the mice eventually get in there too. So, he put it into a crock with a big wooden cover that fit tight. So that's what I remember. God, that was the early '40s."[10]

Loretta Webster spoke about how her mother had braids of corn hanging in the kitchen.

> My parents grew corn, beans, cucumbers, squash, pumpkins, and I think we planted maybe five acres. We didn't grow any white corn that I remember, but we always would buy a braid of white corn that would be hanging in the kitchen. My mother adored it. It was sort of precious. It was gone in the spring. We would have maybe one thing of braids and that would have to last us all winter long. The corn was dried in the kitchen, so whenever she was

> going to make soup, we had to do the work. We had to take the corn off the cob, and sometimes it was a family affair. My cousins lived down the hill and they would have to come up. It was going to be a family meal or something, so all of the kids had to get involved and do the corn.[11]

Julie Barton shared how she and her siblings would pay the people who owned a tavern to use their running water to wash her family's corn.

> I was about twelve when my mom remarried and then we moved to Black Creek. Then we had electricity. We still had an outhouse. We had a water pump and my mom used to pay the tavern people fifty cents a month to haul water. Fifty cents was a lot of money in those days. Corn soup took a lot of water. We always had to make sure we got all this water. I had a time my sister Charlene and I had to haul it on a sled, like this time of year when there was enough snow outside. Otherwise we had a wagon, and sometimes we just had to take turns carrying these old milk cans [full] of water. So, anyway, that's what Sarah always said, because she didn't have running water. She had a pump and she would say, "Well, you know you gotta start out with a lot of water."[12]

Julie also told a story about how her mother would cook corn soup and feed it to guests for days. "My mom always had a kettle of corn soup on that big old cast-iron stove," She reminisced.

> It was simmering on the stove. We didn't have any fridge, so she kept it on the burner. There was always someone coming and going, always neighbors, relatives and people would walk in. They would stay for a couple days. We would have that corn soup. She would have homemade bread. That was usually a meal for two or three days. I remember stirring it. I don't remember actually cooking it, but I watched her. Sometimes, I ran away from the hard work when I was a little kid. If she said "Go and stir the corn soup," that's what I would do. I didn't participate in that whole process when I was little.[13]

Carol Elm recalled how her mother made cornbread using a type of large, purplish bean called a Bear Bean. "We used a meat grinder for the cornbread. I remember how good it was. She made it with kidney beans and maybe it was only one or two loaves, but they made them big, probably two-pound loaves. Also, the purple bean, the Bear Bean. My mother and I got them one time and I planted them. She said, 'Oh, I remember using this in the cornbread and corn soup years ago.'"[14]

These stories illustrate a number of things. The Oneida community wasn't relying on just a handful of people for corn—and even if people didn't grow their own corn, they knew how to cook it. As so many stories during this time show, corn was relatively commonplace. Although it was readily available, many people in the community still considered it precious. We also get to see a glimpse of how technology has changed over time. It gives us a whole new appreciation for modern conveniences, as well as a deep respect for past generations that survived and thrived without them. They continued to build and preserve the community through sharing resources.

Hanging in There: 1960s to 1970s

This period of time marked the buildup toward positive changes throughout Indian Country. While the federal policies of tribal self-determination in the 1970s would lead to great changes, including more resources and autonomy for tribal governments, they often took a long time to have impacts on Indian reservations. As the storytellers reveal, this time period hinted at the changes that would be coming. More people in the community were growing corn and helping others grow and cook it as well. Notably, a number of the corn growers previously mentioned continued to grow and share their corn with the community. Young elders Artley Skenandore, Chaz Wheelock, and Linn Cornelius talked about sharing skills in growing and cooking corn. Artley's grandfather was ahead of his time when he turned an old bus into a greenhouse for his corn. "My one grandfather, David Skenadore, his specialty was white corn," Artley began.

> I spent a lot of time with him. He had an old bus that he had pulled up next to his barn. Everybody was looking at him like, "Oh, what is he doing with it?" It was a little short bus. The bus had windows, so that was the solar dryer for the white corn. He always had three cats. They were his sentries to take care of the mice problems with the corn. He had a little stove on one end and not much of a fire, but in January, that's when I would go sit with him in there. He would do his seed selection and he would shell. Outside it was 20 below zero. Inside the bus it was probably 40 degrees. You didn't have to wear a coat and you had a little fire in there. It was a little bitty stove like a camp stove. It was mostly the corncobs after shelling that he used to heat it.[15]

Chaz Wheelock told a similar solar story about a community corn grower and a solar shed.

> Back in the day, we ran out of white corn, and we knew an elder who grew white corn—Anderson Cornelius. So we went over to see him. We went into his appropriate technology shed, and there was every kind of wood there was. It was kind of like a maze and where he stored the white corn. It was in the middle of the winter. It was cold and snowing. We noticed that it was pretty warm in there and we asked Anderson if his fire was on. He said it wasn't cold enough yet. Then we noticed he had fifteen different windows facing south. He had a solar system! He knew that if he had the windows facing that way then he wouldn't have to have a fire during the day. Eventually we applied for a grant to build a solar system on the farm and the intent was to grow vegetables. We always thought we were the first solar farm, but Anderson was the first solar guy we ever knew.[16]

Linn Cornelius talked about the different women who taught community members how to make cornbread, including her mother, Amelia Cornelius.

Amelia Cornelius was well known in the community for her contributions to the tribal government as well as her cornbread and cornhusk doll making. “Sarah Skenandore and my grandmother Lydia Denny were the cornbread ladies,” Linn began.

> They both made cornbread and my mama learned from them. I remember going to Sarah Skenandore’s house and helping her out with grinding the corn. With Grandma Lydia, we just went over there for the holidays, and we would have cornbread to eat. That’s where my mom learned, from those two ladies. You take two cornbread ladies, and you get my mom becoming the cornbread lady. My mom believed that the tradition needs to be passed on, so she had no problems teaching anyone that wanted to learn. She would teach in Maxine Thomas’s class at the Oneida Elementary School. They would make cornbread prior to Thanksgiving. She taught cooking the corn, drying the corn, grinding the corn, making the flour, and making the bread itself. She was very careful with that because of the age of the kids. When you make cornbread, you use boiling water. She didn’t want anybody to get burned. She also taught about using the cornbread paddle and how to use it so that when you put it into the water, you’re not burning up. She would have people come to the house and we would make cornbread too. . . . I’m trying to pass it on and teach others how to make it so that it doesn’t die. That was something that my mom felt should not die. It should live on.[17]

Elder Gerald Danforth and young elders Brian Doxtator and Linn Cornelius shared more stories about their work with corn. Brian told a story about my uncle Gerald Doxtator when he was a young boy and what happened to him one day when he decided he didn’t want to help out in the garden.

> Gerald came to his dad one day and it was hotter than heck, and he said, “I don’t feel like weeding.” He was a young teenage boy. You know teenage boys. He asked if he could not weed that day. His dad said he didn’t have to weed. Gerald went off and played. Suppertime comes along and they all sit down

FIGURE 6. Laura H. Denny Smith pounding corn. She passed away in 1941 at age eighty-two. Photograph reprinted with permission of the Oneida Nation.

to eat, and Gerald sits down at the table. Chicken [Gerald's dad] says, "I don't know what you're doing at this table, but you don't belong here. Only people that work to put food on the table. You did not. You played. There's no food here for you, so leave the table." Gerald left the table because that's what his dad told him. He couldn't eat that night. He got up the next morning and that's the first thing he did was weeded his row.[18]

Gerald Danforth recalled a time when he was on leave from serving in the Navy, and his family was quick to put him to work helping them husk and shell white corn.

> I was in my late teens, early twenties. I was home on leave, and at the time, harvesting was taking place. At my younger age, we helped dry it and shell it. It was my parents and my aunt and uncle; they were going to husk and braid the corn. We used to just hang it to dry in a small garage on a string liner. There would be maybe a dozen braids of corn hanging. We wouldn't braid it in those big, long braids. Typically, we would just have maybe two dozen cobs in a braid hanging on this clothesline to dry. During the course of the wintertime, that would be the time to shell it. We probably had maybe a five-gallon pail of shelled corn kernels, so it wasn't a big amount.[19]

Brian Doxtator explained how an elder would painstakingly sort for seed, bread, and soup. "Norbert Skenandore harvested his own corn, and he would go through each kernel and say, 'This is for bread. This is for seed. This is for soup,'" Brian explained. "The large ones were for bread because we used the flour inside them. The nice, straight ones were for seed. The small ones were for soup. Holy smokes, it just boggles my mind because I think of all that work. I don't even do that, and so he probably learned from his parents or his grandparents."[20]

Similarly, Linn and her sister Kim Nishimoto both talked about the lengthy process to grind corn for an astonishing fifty to a hundred large loaves of cornbread. "When we were kids, we had a hand grinder for the corn," Linn recalled.

> We literally had to use muscles and grind it, and you didn't do it just one time. Our mom made us do it a couple times because she wanted the corn to be really good. Eventually, my dad hooked it up to the truck and then it ground it faster. We always made between fifty and a hundred loaves. That meant grinding all the corn. It takes a quart of corn to make a loaf of bread.

> My mom didn't believe in making small loaves. She wanted people to know what it's really like. Knowing how to make it now is precious, and the fact that I know, my sister and I, we still teach when we have the opportunity. It's cute because people always thought my mom made all this cornbread, and we would laugh really hard because whoever got the cornbread, you didn't know if mom made it, Kim made it, or I made it.[21]

Kim also shared her recollections of this cornbread-making process. "Ever since I can remember, since we were really young, my mother would make cornbread," Kim told me. "I remember as a small child, we were always grinding corn. We used to have this old grinder that we had to hand grind the corn with. We would just take turns. We would do the sifting and she would just make the bread. Eventually, my mom bought a coffee grinder, and that's what we use now."[22]

Young elders Arlie and Brian Doxtator shared sad memories about the corn. Arlie regretfully talked about how he missed out on the stories he heard from his ex-wife's grandmother when she was teaching him how to make corn soup because he was too focused on the technical aspects of cooking and not at all on the stories she was sharing. "I learned to make corn soup from my daughter's great-grandmother, Margaret Skenandore," Arlie began.

> She was my ex-wife's grandmother. I was nineteen years old, wanting to be a chef. She heard I wanted to learn to make soup. She had me come over and stay with her for three days and to learn to make corn soup. I was very analytical. I had my notebooks all ready. We cooked outside in her little kennel, and I was writing down the whole process. I was taking corn out of the pot as it was cooking and analyzing it. I had this whole notebook full of all of these notes. But, dum-dum over here, I didn't pay attention to the most important part of this whole process, and that was the stories and the teachings that went along with it. I didn't listen. I didn't hear. That was one of my biggest lessons I learned as a young man. I needed to pay attention, not just what's in front of you, that you forget to pay attention to what's around you. Years

FIGURE 7. Three elders drying corn on a rack. Racks are still used to dry corn at different stages of harvesting and processing, including the process to dry the corn to make cornbread. Photograph reprinted with permission of the Milwaukee Public Museum.

> later, I still kick myself because I don't know the stories and the teachings. I wasn't listening. She told me, but I wasn't listening.[23]

Brian told a heart-wrenching story about how his grandmother would make cornbread to sell to help make ends meet. One time, the corn soured overnight when he was helping her make it, and the loss made her physically ill. "We worked two days in December because of Christmas," He recalled.

> Because [of] the high electric bill, my grandmother would run out of money. She would always do a huge cornbread order to help pay the electric bill and get us through until February. All she had to do was tell one or two people, and people would come flocking to come buy her loaves. There was a batch that spoiled overnight, I suppose because of the humidity. The next morning, when my grandmother realized it was spoiled, she actually got sick. She was in bed for three or four days because it was a lot of waste. It made her sick to

> see all that flour. For me, not being raised during the Depression or the wars or poverty or anything, I am even one step removed from how much those people looked at corn.[24]

The corn has remained with us during our saddest moments as well as moments filled with joy and laughter. Young elders Deborah Heckel and my mother, Michele Doxtator, both shared funny stories about corn during this period of time. Deborah recalled a time when she traveled with her mother and grandfather to deliver corn to a nearby town and the laughs they shared along the way.

> When I was going through a difficult time in my life, my mother was taking a big tub of corn up north. She had some people that would buy a lot of corn, like maybe a hundred quarts. My grandma had passed already, so my grandpa and my mother and I took a road trip and went to deliver this corn. My grandpa always had such a sense of humor. We went to this house. She was an older lady and it was a very old house. She bought all the corn. Well, on the way to her house, the road was kind of rough. My grandpa said we were bouncing around so much that he was going to have a miscarriage! (laughter) Oh gosh. I guess those times, those moments that you share with family that aren't here anymore, they are precious. I remember the things that my mother would do and my grandpa and grandma, and I think sometimes in life we don't take the time to stop and think about those things. Life is always so busy.[25]

My mom shared a hilarious story about how Stan Webster's father, Stanley Webster Sr., lost his eyebrows making corn soup during a family gathering.

> During my grandma's later years, she lived with Stan Webster Sr. Stan's whole backyard was a giant, long garden. He grew all kinds of vegetables, including white corn. During Thanksgiving one year, my husband went hunting. So, I took my daughter to Stan and my grandma's house to eat. My Auntie Faye, Uncle Jim, and Auntie Lyons were also there. When we got there, my grandma

> was telling everyone about an incident with the corn soup. While she was cooking in the house, Stan was cooking over a stove in the breezeway between the garage and house. When he went to light the stove, he turned the knob before he had the match ready and there was a gas buildup. The flame went up so high and fast, he burnt off his eyebrows. Grandma must have been upset and worried afterward because whenever she walked past him during dinner, she would remind him to be more careful and lightly smack him upside the head.[26]

These stories about corn during the 1960s and 1970s show us again that a growing number of community members were raising, cooking, sharing, and teaching about our corn. Despite all the pressures of assimilation, poverty, and buying convenient foods from grocery stores, time and again, the community came to support efforts to grow and consume our traditional foods. As time progressed and more resources would become available, the Oneida people would see even more increases in the amount of corn that became available within the community.

Revitalization of Culture: 1970s

The late 1970s were a time when more Oneida people in our community became interested in learning about our history and culture. This era marked a period of rediscovery. Native Americans were fighting back and reclaiming their rights. Our neighbors, the Menominees, were restored in 1975 after having been terminated, fueling the momentum created by groups like the American Indian Movement.[27] As Oneida elder Julie Barton explained, "People were getting more involved in their education, and people were starting to work back in the early '70s to keep the traditions. People still wanted to eat corn, except they weren't making it at all. Sarah and Shorty were getting up in age, but they still had their old factory going and they even grew their own corn."[28]

During these years, Oneida people were traveling to and from Canada and New York with increased regularity to learn and teach more about our traditional ceremonies. Bob Brown, Oneida Bear Clan Chief, originally from the Oneida community in Thames, Ontario, came and stayed with us in Wisconsin to assist in our learning, then relocated here as he married into our community. He described the decline in interest in culture right before the late 1970s, as well as the current renewed interest.

> People are beginning to listen to us talk about those things. We are at a point now where people are listening more so than what it was like in the '60s and the '70s, where things started to dwindle for a lot of our communities back at that time. People would talk about what's going to happen. They were in a desperate mode. They were continuously giving that information and understanding to those of us who would listen to be able to continue that on. There are those of us that did listen and are still continuing to do the best that we can to make that information out there for our people.[29]

Randy Cornelius, Oneida Bear Clan Faithkeeper, talked about his own personal journey to learn more about Oneida language and culture.

"Even as adults, you can change behaviors. You can change eating habits and change your attitude about these gifts that the Creator has given us. The more that we do that, we are going to see the positive effect that has on our children. That is going to continue to get better and better and better in each generation. To me, the key component is the cultural component because those are the things that I didn't grow up with. Nobody grew up with it in my generation anyhow. There was a little bit that came here in 1820s and 1830s in terms of the culture teachings, but by the time I came around, everything was pretty much gone in our community. It wasn't any different than any other community, other than we had Indian corn, we had cornbread. I didn't even know we had mush.

"Those elders that I worked with got excited when I brought in a braid of Indian corn because most of those elders that I worked with grew that as kids. That was a highlight, for me to see that. They remember that as babies, as little kids, eating that corn mush for breakfast. It was a morning meal. To see that in those elders before they passed on, that was something I remembered. What we are doing here is a good thing and encouraging people to get back to a more Indigenous diet. There is so much diabetes and obesity. Becoming more active and being out there out in the woods or out in the garden is all a part of that getting back in touch with mother nature. She responds, and I see it in our community with all the wildlife that is coming back, all these different kinds of plants that are coming back, and birds . . .

"When we started having ceremonies and learning the language, I started to understand the things being said in the ceremonies and in the songs and how and why we do them. That gave me a different perspective, because I didn't really look at it as a spiritual relationship before. Gardening was work, that's what it was. When I started learning about the culture in the language and those teachings, it gave me a whole different perspective. Maybe I didn't have respect towards any food or any sustenance. Through ceremony, the songs that we do in there are about honoring them through dance, through songs, and through speeches and stories. We have stories about of them wanting to leave because our people were so disrupted by alcoholism, and they went through all that chaos . . .

"I am still learning about those things. It makes me look at the world different and to understand that I have a responsibility to ensure that the things that are here from my ancestors are going to be here seven generations down the road. That's a perspective that I didn't grow up with and didn't know nothing about. I didn't start learning about it until I was in my late twenties, and I created a shift in my psyche about self-sufficiency, food sovereignty, and looking back at our history. We were growing food as kids, but it wasn't the same as it is today in terms of the mindset and the cultural component that was brought in here back in the early '80s when we started doing ceremonies. It's not easy. There's so many distractions and other things that go on in daily life that we have to take time out to remind ourselves of how we are to be thinking and feeling and acting, especially when we're interacting with the natural world. They can sense what's going on up here and what we're feeling. Something they talk about when you go into the longhouse is that you leave the garbage outside. You don't bring it in. You try to be there with a good mind and that's a really hard thing to do sometimes. Our teachings are forcing us to do that every day, not just when we have ceremonies."[30]

Leander Danforth, Oneida Wolf Clan Faithkeeper, told a story about how he was fortunate to learn how to cook corn soup on one of his trips out east.

> We traveled with an entourage over to Onondaga for a Grand Council meeting. It was in the springtime. Norman Doxtator was living in Onondaga on the corner there and he was making maple syrup at that time. It was just after the meeting. There was a blizzard coming in at that time and we ended up getting snowed in. We couldn't go anywhere. We didn't want to be out on the road, so we stayed there in Onondaga. There was a bunch of us staying there. We were all just sitting around talking about making corn soup and making cornbread, and I guess somebody made mention that he would like to learn how to do that sometime. Bruce Elijah was there, and he said he knew how. I said, "Look around. Maybe we can do that. Maybe we can make some right now." So, we looked around. We had the ashes and the corn and a basket. His girlfriend at the time said she had a venison roast. She pulled that out to put in the oven. We went and traded this Doxtator fella for some maple syrup. Bruce started showing us how to sift the hardwood ashes. Then we put on the kettle, and it started boiling and we put the corn in there. We stirred it with a wooden paddle, adding ashes in. I don't even know how much we used. There was no measurement. We put enough ashes in so that it turned bright orange. So that's when we knew we had enough. When we boiled and cooked it for a certain length of time, we washed it. And we ended up making cornbread. We started in the evening; I don't know what time it was. We got done somewhere around midnight and then our roast was done. We had our maple syrup, and we had our loaves of cornbread. We had a big feast. It took us about fifteen minutes for us to eat it all.[31]

Our chiefs and faithkeepers have so much to share with our community. As Bob explained, there have been Oneida people who tried to share their message, but few people were there to hear it. Fortunately, we have people in our community like Randy and Leander that did eventually hear that message. It is easy to forget that not all of them grew up with the Oneida language and culture being the norm in their homes. They may have grown up with corn in the community, but some of her connections to language, culture, and our original instructions had not always been followed here throughout the years. Those who now hold the knowledge in our community continue to help the rest of us pick up those practices our ancestors had to lay down.

Conclusion

Collectively, these stories describe an active community food system with corn still playing a significant role. I was incredibly honored that members of our community agreed to share their stories with me. Time is relative and it is easy to forget that the elders in our community witnessed an entirely different period of time and hold a lot of our history through lived experiences. For example, Oneida elder Julie Barton's mother came to Wisconsin in the migration from New York as an infant. Our elders are a piece of living history. Our original instructions teach us that we all have reciprocal responsibilities to all of creation. These elders enjoyed sharing their stories about their relationships with corn, knowing they would be passed down to future generations. The younger generation has a responsibility to hear these stories and treat them with great care. In hearing these stories, I noticed there was a type of healing and comfort many of the people I interviewed continue to find in corn that reminds them of their love for their relatives that have passed on. Those who spent time with the corn growers during this time period would be the ones to usher the Oneida community into a time when the Oneida government would be able to help teach people about growing, processing, and increasing the supply of corn for the community.

Ona Waekwatahtaskenhá

(Now We Have the Means to Help Ourselves)

NE· YAKΛ LATUHÁKWE THAT THE LATE 1970S USHERED IN A NEW ERA OF self-governance and cultural awareness. With state and federal government grants and later with Indian gaming dollars, the Oneida Nation created then expanded operations to honor and celebrate our agricultural roots. Several projects came from these initiatives, including Iroquois Farms, Oneida Cannery, Tsyunhéhkwʌ, the Oneida Market, Oneida Nation Farm, and Oneida Community Integrated Food System (OCIFS).

The projects started off small and grew into large-scale operations. When the Oneida government was developing its comprehensive plans in 1973, 1979, and 1987, it relied on surveys of the community to determine what they wanted to see for the future of the reservation. In 1979, the Oneida Nation set the following economic development goals within the comprehensive plan.

- Provide a level of industrial, commercial, and agricultural development that promotes a minimum level of unemployment among the Oneida people and produces goods and services required by area residents; and to develop a stable revenue source for the Oneida Nation.

- Develop a viable agricultural operation on the Oneida Reservation together with an educational program relating agriculture to the Oneida culture and traditional land ethic.
- Vertically integrate the Oneida agricultural operation to include production and processing of foods, while making products available at lower than market prices.[1]

Iroquois Farms

The first of these tribal initiatives to revive our traditional agricultural practices was the Iroquois Farms. It began operation in 1978 on two properties consisting of an approximate total of one hundred fifty acres and twenty-five head of cattle.[2] The primary purpose of the farm was to grow vegetables for the community and raise enough crops to feed the cattle. The establishment of the Iroquois Farms signaled a return to our agricultural roots and the search for ways to incorporate traditional and contemporary farming practices. Chaz Wheelock, one of the founding members of Iroquois Farms, and Artley Skenandore, young Oneida elder, described the purpose of the project and how it was an awakening for the Oneida community.

> After the '60s, there was a lot of questioning about who I am, where do I fit, and what are the roles and responsibilities of men and women. All of this was a key part of our fitting together in a relationship to the future. Certainly, we all need food every day. Where do we get the food? Do we have a relationship to the food? Do we have a relationship to money to get our food? There's a different experiential part of the connection to that relationship if you're involved with growing and harvesting it, processing it, cooking it. I think Iroquois Farms was a part of that social awareness about who we are and what our purpose and place is in what we call life . . . I think that is a nice statement

> that we consciously are advocating for what happened and was like magic. Iroquois Farms was a learning experience for all of us in the community here. We started to realize the importance of sovereignty, security, self-sufficiency, sustainability, and stewardship. It was a seed at the time. A seed for thinking about a lot about what we're doing now. I think the white corn growing group is a good example. People are organizing and getting together and effecting change in the community in a positive way . . .
>
> I think we were kind of a demonstration without knowing it at the time. We had our hands full just trying to figure out what the hell we were doing then. It was a statement about ourselves as a community going through getting our Indian names and understanding we come from New York and we are immigrants here next to the Menominees. We were trying to be aware of that in a good way. It was kind of a demonstration site for a lot of things. I think there was a bit of a catalyst, an awakening, an advocacy for trying to discover who we are and what our responsibilities are once we discover who we are. It raised an awareness about a lot of things. Some people didn't know we were a part of the Iroquois Confederacy, the Haudenosaunee. I didn't know that. They just thought they were Oneidas. That was a long time ago.[3]

Artley also talked about the Iroquois Farms. "The Iroquois Farms was an effort that was ahead of its time because it was about a co-operative, it was about food sharing," he told me.

> When Iroquois Farms was initiated, it represented more than planting. It represented a renewing of doing things ourselves. We were going to start a co-operative so people can learn how to plant food. We were looking at it in that context of extended family. A lot of people were trying to do things on their own. We gotta be able to grow our food. That's the main part in an economy. It was about what kind of jobs we were going to create and making sure there was food for families. Iroquois Farms was kind of like the marquee for cultural revival. We were trying to learn social songs and renewing the ceremonies. Our challenge was to link all those stories together so there is

> an appreciation for what the original stories represent. We should be very proud of what we have done as a nation. There's very few nations that can look back and say that we reversed one hundred fifty years of history in less than forty years of time. We were able to take all those things that occurred to our community and culturally addressed them in such a way that the language grows, growing food grows, and relationships grow.[4]

While Iroquois Farms as an entity did not last more than a few years, the concepts that the founders wanted to instill in our community eventually transferred to Tsyunhéhkwʌ and the Oneida Nation Farm. Their drive and determination to help our community reconnect to our culture and our foods helped lay the foundation for future tribal programs.

The Cannery and Tsyunhéhkwʌ

The Oneida Cannery and Tsyunhéhkwʌ have a long history of helping the Oneida community learn how to grow, harvest, cook, and preserve our traditional Indigenous foods. With a focus on white corn, they have helped countless families gain the confidence to try these practices at home, including our family. By taking classes at the cannery and helping Tsyunhéhkwʌ with their harvests, our family eventually began to grow, harvest, cook, and preserve our own foods. We are now able to pay it forward and are helping other community members do the same, all because the cannery and Tsyunhéhkwʌ were there to help teach us.

The history of these two institutions dates back to 1973 when the Oneida Nation began plans for a cannery.[5] The original idea came from Caroline Smith under the direction of Loretta Webster, who was the Director of the Community Action Program.[6] In 1977, Ruby White negotiated with and earned approval from the local Catholic Diocese to rent a room locker in its Norbert Hill Center to set up the cannery.

After several years of planning, securing grant funding, allocating tribal contributions, and setting up the facility, the Nation began operating the Oneida Cannery with the support of the Oneida General Tribal Council in 1978. One of its first initiatives was to prepare fresh, traditional, heirloom white corn and sell it to the community. This project came to fruition in 1980. Below are three stories about growing corn and learning how to process it.

During Carol Elm's twenty-five years of working in the cannery, she was able to refine the process of storing and selling white corn. She eventually developed dehydrated corn, which remains the cannery's most popular product. She explained how the staff had to first find people who grew white corn and then learn how to make cornbread.

> When I started working at the cannery, we were doing mostly vegetables and somehow or another the corn got in there. I'm not quite sure how exactly if we were talking about the corn and what we could do. I guess we just said we could buy it from this person or that person and we will see if we can learn if we can do it. The corn had become quite precious to me at that time . . . When I first started out, we didn't really have the corn growing here. We had to find people that we knew that was growing corn to go buy the corn. Then we learned how to hull the corn. We did interview some of our elders to get to know how to make the cornbread like Sarah Skenandore. They told us how to make the cornbread and the corn soup because we were still learning how to do it. That was the beginning of trying to get it from the elders.[7]

Jamie Betters explained how they had to hand shell all their corn before they purchased a machine to help with the shelling. "My hands have shelled thousands of pounds of white corn," she told me. "Yes, these hands have harvested and braided many, but we would all come together, the Tsyunhéhkwʌ and cannery staff and shell for two hours every Friday for at least ten years until they got a fancy smancy machine."[8]

Along similar lines, Randy Cornelius explained how a well-known cornbread maker back in the day washed her corn using a washing machine.

Later, the cannery decided to give that bit of technology a try. It now uses a washing machine to help process thousands of pounds of corn each year. "Sarah Skenandore was a renowned cornbread maker back in the day," Randy recalled. "After she passed, one of her relatives was going through the house and cleaning and he opened up the washing machine and there is corn in there. That's how she washed her corn! Instead of the old-time way with the basket, she threw it in the washing machine. So, they're doing that at the cannery and it's not as much work. Modern convenience, I guess."[9]

In 1982, the cannery began canning the white corn and selling that to the community.[10] The following year, they began selling canned pork corn soup. In 1985, they expanded even further by offering cornbread made with traditional, heirloom white corn to the community for Thanksgiving, Christmas, and Easter. From 1986 to 1988, the cannery produced canned corn soup for sale at the Oneida One Stop gas station and at Schroeder's, a small local grocery store. Vickie Cornelius, a former longtime cannery employee, described some of her work there beginning in the early 1990s.

> We grew up on a farm. We had a large garden. We had a large raspberry, strawberry pastures. We all had rows that we had to weed all the time. My mother canned and I had to help can. My dad also had chickens and pigs. It was a lifestyle. Having a garden is natural to me. When the position for the cannery became available in 1990 or 1991, I was encouraged by some of the community members to apply for it. I applied and I took that position. When I went to start to work there, I was the only employee, and the cannery was closed in 1990 because of a budget deficit. Carol Elm was working there before for many years, and she went to go work at Ortech and decided not to come back. When we opened, it opened under Art Skenandore at the elementary school because I didn't have the certain certification to run the equipment and they did. In the spring, I took all the training for the boiler and all the equipment there. Then I came back and started canning. I was there until 1998. I was the cannery supervisor until 1994, and then we got a grant and hired some agriculture workers. Then in 1994, we added the retail store and

> added on a small garden . . . I became the manager in 1994 until 1998. The programs changed a lot over the years. The products have changed over the years. I went back to the cannery in 2008, and I was there ten years and just left recently. I loved working there. I loved working with the people. I love doing the canning the workshops. It was very fulfilling for me.[11]

In 1994, a grant helped fund travel to attend a husking bee in New York State and to acquire Indigenous seeds. The following year, the cannery hosted its first husking bee. This event has since become annual with people from the greater community coming to help husk corn and learn and celebrate with the Oneida community. The husking bee has expanded to other workshops such as cornhusk doll making, composting, gardening methods, and talks by invited speakers about a wide array of topics, including health and wellness.

The primary goal of the cannery has always been to help Oneida families to become food self-reliant by helping them learn how to grow, prepare, and process their foods. Their focus is on self-sustainability and food security. The cannery staff process white corn for soup, cornbread, jams/jellies, salsa, pickles, and other fresh fruits and vegetables when in season. Over the years, with the help of staff in the Oneida Nation Grants Department, the cannery has secured a number of grants to help them carry out their goals. Some of the grants were for seed distribution, bedding plant vouchers and garden preparation, raised-bed gardens, video projects, and state-of-the-art commercial equipment such as food dehydrators, pressure cookers, and boiler-heated vats.

The first agricultural worker was hired through one of these grants. The cannery helped with gardens at several tribal government locations, at the homes of community members, and at community garden sites for those community members who did not have garden spaces at their homes. Jill Ninham, former outreach worker, described how she interacted with the community.

> When I first started growing the white corn, I was working for Tsyunhéhkwʌ. The most powerful thing about my work with Oneida Nation and Tsyunhéhkwʌ

> was that I was paid a living wage to learn about the most valuable parts of Haudenosaunee culture, specifically about the corn. I was an outreach worker at that time. My job was to help develop community garden sites, offer workshops, and encourage people to participate in providing sustenance for their families. As a program, our responsibilities were to encourage and provide any resources that we could for people. At that time, we were trying to establish who was growing and who wanted to grow. It was a lot about reaching out to people and reminding them about the white corn and how it is a living part of history. Whether it would be them, their families, their extended families, or their clans, we would find somebody in that family that would have those stories. It was an awakening in a sense for a lot of families and it reconnected families. It was about all the benefits that come with growing the corn and nurturing it and reflecting it out to those families and those relationships. That really strengthened this family bond. We had nests or pockets within the community where people were reawakening and continuing on those responsibilities with the corn.[12]

Similarly, Laura Cornelius, semi-retired culture teacher, explained how she was able to grow a garden with the help of Tsyunhéhkwʌ outreach efforts.

> When I moved to this neighborhood, I didn't have anywhere to plant. That was really hard because I always had a garden. Sugar Bear and I were raising heck with the Environmental people saying if they were going to build housing, they need to give us enough land to plant. It's nice that we have a home, but we don't need to be put on top of each other. For the sanity of the people in the community, we need our space. So that was a foreign concept to some of them over there because they didn't understand we were farmers. One thing to bring us back to the earth is to plant and get back in touch with the earth, our mother. We hollered around a lot with them. Well, that piece of land that's over there, I reclaimed it about five years ago when they decided that they were going to put a duplex there. I did a bunch of research, started a petition, and had everyone sign it in our neighborhood. That spring, I asked

> Tsyunhéhkwʌ to plow it up and I told them I was planting white corn there. Who was going to say something about an old lady planting white corn? Are they going to take that land away from me? They knew I would really raise heck. So, that's how I got my garden started the first year.[13]

The cannery and Tsyunhéhkwʌ started off as a single department within the Oneida Nation government. In 1995, the cannery staff conducted a visioning session and came up with a new name for their operations: Tsyunhéhkwʌ.

> Tsyunhéhkwʌ is the Oneida word that describes all that sustains our lives. These are gifts from Creation, the free and cultivated foods; the medicines; the soil; and the waters that sustain us. Together, they form our complete diet/ nutritional heritage and the sources of our well-being. In adopting this new name we are conveying the holistic nature of our work. We grow and harvest foods produce food products provide education, counseling and training in traditional diet and nutrition we conduct research and development into new forms for traditional foods.[14]

The following year, the cannery staff introduced a new name: tsiʔkutekhwayʌhe (place where they put the food away).[15] They continue to use this name today.

In 2015, the late Jeff Metoxen, former director of Tsyunhéhkwʌ, discussed community support in an interview with Wisconsin Public Radio. "Our program is so fortunate for all that we are able to provide here, and not just the white corn. We wouldn't be able to exist and continue to grow in any way or challenge ourselves if we didn't have the support of our community members . . . When people come on site, we work really hard to give them a hands-on demonstration."[16]

Tsyunhéhkwʌ grows foods such as beans, squash, and strawberries, along with tobacco. Its focus is on traditional, heirloom white corn. The staff also grow hay and have pastureland for their herd of grass-fed cattle. The farm is located on an 83-acre parcel of land near central Oneida. This location is where they host their annual husking bee and hold various workshops on gardening, fruit tree pruning, and medicinal herb walks throughout the year. They are open to the public and offer personal and educational tours. Kyle Wisneski, farm supervisor, explained how he and his wife, Jamie Betters, food-processor educator, host workshops and run community gardens. "Jamie and I started a community garden group that seventy-two community members joined," Kyle told me.

> We grew about an acre and a half. That's a new group new this year. I have four workshops that I run yearly including offering up white corn seed. White corn seed can be very hard to come by, so Jamie and I have been offering white corn seed for many, many years to families who want to try to start to grow it. We think it's important to have good seed because our corn is open pollinating corn. You want your neighbor to have just as good as seed as you . . . Jamie is a rockstar at producing food out of the white corn. She runs workshop after workshop throughout the year to try to encourage families to come in and eat the food. Maybe they don't want to grow it, but they can eat it.[17]

Today, the cannery and Tsyunhéhkwʌ work very closely together. With respect to corn, Tsyunhéhkwʌ grows the corn and the cannery processes it. Kyle and Jamie's young son, Braxton, loves to help out any chance he can get. Braxton described the work his parents do.

> My mom is called Jamie Betters, last name Betters. Nice worker. She works at the cannery, and she does have a lot of cool stuff making corn mush, corn soup, cornbread, and a lot of yummy stuff. Some of that stuff is from my dad right here and so a lot of stuff that my mom cooks is yummy. We love our beans, and our mom picks the beans at Tsyunhéhkwʌ where my dad works and I helped my dad at Tsyunhéhkwʌ for a lot of days and my mom visits there . . . The corn means a lot to me. I help my dad build a lot of corn this year and last year. Today, we need to start all over building the corn. We need to start all over. My dad's going to work really hard to build this corn, and a

> lot of people will be here to help because there's a lot of corn and my dad can't do it alone. My dad does a lot of stuff, and he does need helpers. And I'm proud of that.[18]

As Braxton pointed out, his parents, along with all the people who have worked at Tsyunhéhkwʌ and the cannery, dedicated so much time and effort to help our community have access to white corn and other traditional foods. Through their tireless endeavors, more people in our community have access to white corn than in recent memory. Through the cannery's educational outreach efforts, more people have the confidence to grow, harvest, cook, and preserve our traditional foods.

Oneida Market

Another essential Oneida Nation component to the efforts to make more corn available to community members is the Oneida Market. The Oneida Market began as the Tsyunhéhkwʌ Retail Store. It sells tea, herbs, spices, essential oils, vitamins and mineral supplements, healthy snacks, as well as regionally sourced food such as jams, honey, wild rice, eggs, and beef.[19] It is also the main outlet for the sale of a variety of white corn products including kanʌstóhale, dehydrated corn, mush flour, and kanʌstóhale flour. Vickie Cornelius explained the history of this store.

> The way I was raised, when we were sick, my grandmother would give us bergamot tea. I kind of forgot about those medicines as I grew and raised my family. Then one time I went to Albuquerque through the Indian Agricultural Council. Me and Sugar Bear went out there, and during the break we wanted to go to this grocery store to get stuff for our room and some snacks. I walked down the aisle and there were these jars of all these herbs and medicines. Just me walking down the aisle brought back that memory of how our grandparents used medicines to heal our sicknesses. I came back to our

> community and implemented our herbal medicine area within Tsyunhéhkwʌ department. I hired Cheryl Elm to create that department, and then I started doing more of the tinctures and aromatherapy and teaching those types of things. They are just as important. When you go through our Thanksgiving Address, it's just the most powerful thing that I ever experienced when I was learning my culture is that being grateful for everything.
>
> Everything has a place. Everything has a purpose. It's feeling that relationship. Let's say you need a blood cleanser. Burdock is going to show up at your house or a lot of dandelions because those are blood medicines. If you need a female medicine, well, the raspberry is going to show up at your house. I've had that happen at my house where those particular plants show up. I'm like, "Okay. That's the medicine I need to take and use at this time." It's like they know that this is what you need. It's so amazing to me that medicine would know that. One time I got poison ivy and I heard of jewelweed being the cure for that. I thought I should go look for some jewelweed. There was some right at my back door. It's also us being aware of that too and taking that time to learn those medicines and building that relationship.[20]

In addition to the traditional medicines, the Oneida Market is also the major distributor for corn grown at Tsyunhéhkwʌ and processed at the cannery. The market offers dehydrated white corn, fresh hull corn, cornbread large/small loaves, corn mush flour, and cornbread flour. In recent years, Tsyunhéhkwʌ and the cannery have done such a phenomenal job getting the Oneida community interested in eating more white corn, the demand often outpaces the supply. Paul "Sugar Bear" Smith, Oneida elder, and Vickie Cornelius talked to me about figuring out how much corn the community needs. "The corn became more popular, and it clearly seemed we were going to have to now organize to raise more corn because they were always buying out the community, all those that raised it," Sugar Bear told me. "Mr. Skenandore, Mr. Cornelius, or Mr. Danforth, those people were running out of what they could supply to the community because we were doing it in a new modern way with the cannery. The spurt of needing white corn became more and more and more eminent."[21] Similarly, Vickie recalled that they could keep up with demand early on.

> As long as the corn is growing and the weeds weren't as much at the time, we were able to keep up. As we started putting it out there more in our community and making it more available, and then working to get it into the school where they have corn soup in the school, and then eventually put the corn soup in the elderly services and the Headstart, everybody wants it now and now we can't keep up, which is a good thing. Now we want to know how much corn do you need to feed your community. That's the big question.[22]

Deborah Heckel, longtime corn grower and supplier to the cannery, mentioned to me in 2019, "I know that the cannery runs out of corn, and this past year I have been able to help them out with corn and I sold a number of quarts to them."[23] Kyle Wisneski recognized the need for more corn as well. He told me:

> I know the cannery is hoping to get anywhere between ten thousand to fifteen thousand pounds from us. We've never been able to grow over fifteen thousand pounds. The one year that we did produce ten thousand pounds was in 2007, it was the only year that we ever came close. There is still a huge void in the community for white corn and its products. Right now there is only dehydrated corn and kanʌstóhale. Those are the two products that the community has access to. On top of that, they got to pay top dollar. We talked about getting some corn into our emergency food pantry, and we have to do that very soon. That will be one more way to get access out there. I still think that the Oneida Nation as a whole has some work to do to get the white corn crop out to the community members. I think Tsyunhéhkwʌ can do a better job at getting some of the white corn out there, and I finally have the opportunity to try to work towards that. That's something that I can make happen now.

> I never had the opportunity to do that. I've worked there for so many years, but I haven't had that opportunity, and now I do. I think that's imperative that more and more products get put out to the community.[24]

While Tsyunhéhkwʌ staff are doing their best to try to produce more corn for the cannery to process and for the Oneida Market to sell, more community members are realizing that it may not be the role of tribal government to be the main supplier of white corn for the community at large. Together, Tsyunhéhkwʌ and the cannery offer assistance and educational services that will help community members have access to seeds, have their gardens tilled up, as well as learn how to care for, harvest, cook, and preserve their corn. Finding white corn products for sale at the Oneida Market is a convenience our community is fortunate to have.

Oneida Nation Farm

In addition to Tsyunhéhkwʌ, the Oneida Nation Farm is also responsible for agriculture. While its focus is more on conventional cash crops, it also raises beef and buffalo and operates an apple orchard. The Oneida government established the Oneida Nation Farm in 1989. It initially operated on three hundred fifty acres of land and had thirty-five head of cattle.[25] As the Nation prioritized reservation land reacquisition as a top goal, the Oneida Land Commission (previously the Oneida Land Committee) acquired a significant amount of land, the majority of which was agricultural land. The Oneida Nation Farm rapidly grew because most of the new acquisitions were handed over to the Farms for the staff to manage. Currently, the Oneida Farm has over six thousand acres under its care, primarily growing cash crops with grass-fed beef and a herd of buffalo. In addition to the cropped agricultural land, the Farms also manage a 3,100-tree apple orchard on forty acres of land the Nation acquired in 1994. In the early 2000s for a few years, the Oneida Farm, under the direction of the former Farms manager, Patricia Cornelius, grew between three and four acres of our traditional, heirloom white corn for the community to come and harvest for their families. In 2005, the Oneida Farm presented at the Harvard Project on American Indian Economic Development as part of their Honoring Nations project. When asked what the keys to success were for the Farms, Pat answered, "You need the backing of your [elected officials]. We need all the players to be involved, to support the project and to say that health is important, food is important, food security is important. It has to come from the top down."[26]

The Oneida Community Integrated Food System (OCIFS)

The Oneida Nation created the Oneida Community Integrated Food System (OCIFS) in 1994 to bring all food-related programs together and integrate all tribally produced foods back into the community.[27] The goals included maximizing tribal agricultural productivity with environmental sensitivity, maximizing self-sufficiency, and converting tribal food production to natural and organic operations. OCIFS was instrumental in establishing the Oneida Farmers Market as well as the Oneida Falling Leaves 4-H Club to teach the youth about agriculture, small-business entrepreneurship, health, and diet. The Oneida Emergency Food Pantry is also part of OCIFS. Marlon Skenandore, manager of the pantry, described the food pantry's recent efforts to plant a garden near the pantry.

> We planted like a 25-foot-by-25-foot plot, and we tried to do about thirteen different three sisters mounds. I wanted to highlight it because this is where we are from. This is our community connection. I didn't have enough time to get people in, so we were just tried to figure it out ourselves and it didn't work out well. We brought in some youth workers, and we were sending them out there weeding. One day I was wondering where all the beans went. A youth worker said, "Oh, I thought they were weeds." That's a learning curve, especially when you're working with youth that don't know nothing about

> it. So, making sure taking the time to go out there with them and showing them exactly what they are picking and how to care for them and take more time with that process is important.[28]

Conclusion

The Oneida tribal government has a long history of promoting traditional Indigenous foods with an emphasis on our white corn. So many tribal employees have been involved in this effort to celebrate and promote our foods. They worked tirelessly to deliver foods and programming to the Oneida community. The stories here told us how these people helped the community learn. It is one thing to provide corn for our community, but these programs and the people behind them have remained focused on educating our community. This goes back to our philosophy of one mind, when we put our minds together as one and we are stronger.

Through the efforts of our tribal government staff, people in our community have more access to white corn products and other traditional foods. People also have the support and encouragement to try to grow, harvest, and preserve their own foods, advancing the goals of these tribal programs. All these efforts support national development and community building. These programs have ensured that our people have access to our Indigenous foods; however, they have gone beyond access by empowering the community to work toward Indigenous food sovereignty. We cannot call ourselves a nation if we cannot help feed our people. Our ancestors knew this. George Washington and John Sullivan knew this.

Ohe·láku

(Among the Cornstalks)

NE· YAKʌ LATUHÁKWE THAT IN 2016, SEVERAL ONEIDA FAMILIES GOT TOGETHER to form a co-operative called Ohe·láku to grow white corn together. We saw a need to help meet the growing demands for corn in our community. We also recognized the need to step up and take responsibility for growing this corn instead of solely relying on the Oneida tribal government to grow and process corn for the community. Even though most of us were inexperienced with large-scale farming, our love for the corn helped us successfully grow more than we thought possible. This chapter describes the formation and organization of this grassroots community organization, including the voices of several group members.

CORN SHORTAGES AMONG THE YUKWANUHSYU·NÍ

The corn shortage concern is not unique to Oneida, Wisconsin. Community members realized the concern also exists out east in other Yukwanuhsyu·ní communities. In 2019, Jasmine Jimerson, Ohe·láku member, commented on corn shortages in Seneca territory.

> It's crazy how much and how far we have to go in reclaiming our traditional foods. Being out in the confederacy and seeing the need for corn is alarming. I always relied on other communities if we didn't have our corn. We could always look to other communities for corn. I am learning that it's not as abundant as I thought it was. A lot of communities are losing their corn ways. For instance, people recently started to grow it in my husband's community [Seneca] which is really inspiring. They're doing a really good job with it. When I first went into their community, there was only a non-Native farmer that lived near the reserve that would grow the corn for them. There was even a point where somebody was upset because it was their midwinter ceremony time and he didn't have enough corn for them. They were frustrated with him. I thought that was crazy. Why would it be his responsibility to make sure that you have corn? Maybe that person didn't know how to find corn, or they could have had corn growers in their family, but maybe they just weren't aware of it. So, I'm not speaking for their entire community. I'm talking about how inspiring it is to see how far their community is coming with their corn.[1]

Lea Zeise, Ohe·láku founding member, had a similar experience out east that fueled her desire to take charge and begin organizing corn growers in Oneida. Lea and Laura Manthe both explained their recollections of that encounter. Lea recalled:

> On my first visit to the Haudenosaunee homelands in 2014, I asked a fellow Haudenosaunee where I could get some white corn. I was directed down to the road to this guy. When I arrived, I was surprised to find that this guy was not Haudenosaunee. He was not ukwehúhwe.[2] He was white! I bought the corn anyway, not knowing what else to do in the moment. When I returned home to Oneida, I relayed the story to my mom and she was just as shocked as I was. I remember her voice raising as she turned her head and said, "*What?!?*

That's *it*. We're growing corn." And sure enough, that spring we planted our first crop as a family.[3]

Lea's mom, Laura, shared her take on this story.

> My daughter Lea works for the Intertribal Agricultural Council. She and Bruce Savage drove the Mobil Farmers Market Van to New York to learn about the Haudenosaunee communities and white corn. They took some dehydrated corn from Oneida to sell along the way. While they were in Seneca territory, they ran out of corn and wanted to buy more. The Seneca people sent them down the road to buy the white corn from this guy. He turned out to be a white guy. Lea couldn't believe it. The Senecas didn't grow their own white corn! They bought it from a white guy! What kind of hell is this? She came home a few weeks later and told me that story. I said "*What?!* No way. We are going to grow white corn and sell it to the Senecas." I was so mad, I convinced my husband, my kids, my friends Don Charnon and Ted Skenandore to grow corn with me. That is how I started growing white corn.[4]

Trial and Error

Prompted by their experience out east, Laura and Lea recognized the need to grow more corn and decided to gather a few people together to try to grow two acres. Lea described their unsuccessful endeavor in 2015.

> So, it was Mom, Robin, my little brother Greg, Don, and Ted. We were all growing two acres together at Ted's house. That was a lot for us to manage with just a small group of people. None of our equipment was working. We planted rows a certain way and then our cultivator was set up at a different way so we couldn't use our cultivator. If we would've just plowed some of the corn, we would have ended up with more than we had because we didn't cultivate. Harvest was terrible. It was like a jungle. Some of the weeds were

> taller than the corn. We had to kick the weeds down with our legs to even get to the cobs and then the cobs were these little, tiny, skinny things. We felt so bad for the corn, like we had let it down. Robin's grandchildren came to help and were reminding us of what we were supposed to be doing out there, because every time they would find a corn, they would say, "Thank you! Thank you so much for growing!" They reminded us that we shouldn't put the corn down for just growing a little bit. We should be thankful for whatever comes out of it.[5]

After this unsuccessful attempt, Laura and Lea recognized that they needed to find a way to organize people who were already growing white corn and those who wanted to grow white corn in their backyard gardens. They also needed to learn more about growing corn to see where they went wrong. "A major lesson looking back on it was that we weren't supposed to be growing white corn by ourselves," Lea explained.

> Growing corn with just one family is a really intensive endeavor, and if you really don't know what you are doing, you are not going to be able to grow more than a small plot in your backyard. So, we interviewed twenty-five to thirty people about how they were growing their corn and we realized that everyone else was growing a little tiny bit in their yards. We realized that no matter how much we were growing, we were all facing the same issues of animals wiping out the corn as it reached maturity. And so, everybody was putting all of this effort in and nobody was really getting enough corn out of it.[6]

Armed with information from the community, Laura and Lea got to work writing grants that would help fund the efforts to grow corn together. They obtained grants and financial support from Sustainable Agriculture Research and Education, the Great Lakes Commission, the Oneida Nation in Wisconsin, the Manzanita Fund, Cultural Conservancy, South Central Farmers Health and Education Fund, Wise Women Gathering Place, Mifflin Street Co-op,

Global Greengrant Funds, and the Intertribal Agriculture Council. They both described some of their early grant writing efforts. "When my daughter wrote the first grant for our project, we knew that we had to include culture and language in the grant writing process," Laura explained. "The funders needed to know why culture and language was so important because you couldn't have a traditional food like corn and not include all the ceremony that goes with it and all the responsibility that goes with it."[7] "We wrote a grant to do a research project with the corn to see what affect the fish emulsion had with the fertilizing," Lea recalled.

> Part of that grant was to do community outreach on soil health. We held a soil health and white corn workshop at Ridgeview Plaza, and forty people showed up to hear about soil health, how to improve the organic matter, and how to send the soil in for sampling. After that ended, we said if anyone was interested in growing as a group they should stay, and we could have our first meeting around that. About ten or twelve people stayed to have our first white corn growers' meeting. Mom pulled out the board [with a map] and said, "This is the land that the tribe identified that we could use for free for five years, and these are the seeds that we have." We asked if anyone else had seeds, and we pooled our seeds together. The first year was awesome and we were still learning a lot of lessons and we were still making huge mistakes, but we ended up with a ton of corn, and I think everybody was really excited about that. Then the following year we made a name for ourselves, Ohe·láku, and I think that really solidified things. Bev Scow facilitated our meetings to make sure that everybody's voice got heard and that everybody was included in the decision-making. We solved one problem at a time.[8]

Commitments and Responsibilities

Each year, we reaffirm our commitments and responsibilities to each other and to the corn. Our shared values are: 1) reclaiming the past to prepare for the future; 2) making the time to build consensus; 3) teamwork makes the dream work; 4) patiently learning and growing together as family; 5) nation building through sharing; and 6) mindfulness and respect for each other and the corn. While it isn't always easy, we are a family, and we need to get along with each other. If anyone is unable or unwilling to fulfill these commitments to each other and the corn, it jeopardizes the strengths we rely on as a group to come together to care for our corn. As a group, we share responsibilities and help each other out with the understanding that no single person can do this alone. As Jasmine Jimerson explained it, the group brings a sense of community responsibility.

> I think that I had the mentality like I have to do everything. I had to participate in everything. If I was ukwehúhwe, then I had to be sewing, and I had to be at every ceremony, and I had to be cooking, and I had to be in the garden, and I had to do all of these things. What I didn't learn until I got older was that being ukwehúhwe is having that community, helping each other, and understanding when one isn't able to do something, then another is able.[9]

Similarly, Laura Manthe described how we have an obligation to grow our corn together as an extended family, as a village.

> When Lea and I hosted the first White Corn Community Meeting in March 2016, we had a general idea of how we would grow corn together on the same field similar to other community gardens, but most of the people who wanted to grow white corn didn't have any seed to plant. That is when Don Charnon said, "We are not going to grow in family plots. We are going to pool our seeds together, we are going to plant together, harvest together, and eat together." I had to decolonize my mind and change my beliefs about ownership and embrace our traditional way of growing white corn on the spot. We grow our corn as a village, not as individuals.[10]

Ohe·láku doesn't have a formal leadership structure. Rather, we all have responsibilities to each other and to the corn. We discuss these responsibilities each year and reaffirm our commitments. We build on the knowledge of community members as well as each other's strengths. We have four main work groups within Ohe·láku: Tsiʔ niyukwalihotʌ (Our Ways), Tech, Taking Care of Business, and Back Achers.

The Tsiʔ niyukwalihotʌ group is responsible for sharing cultural and language resources with the group. At the beginning of each meeting, we practice introducing ourselves in the Oneida language. We also learn seed songs to sing to the corn, help organize the tobacco burning, process corn to give to the community during funerals, and ensure our seed is accounted for and properly stored at the homes of various group members. The Tech group is responsible for tracking the hours we work with the corn, organizing T-shirt fundraisers, and preparing materials for orientation as well as helping other groups form their own co-ops. The Taking Care of Business group is responsible for securing use of land, writing the grants, identifying fundraising opportunities, and organizing community events. The Back Achers group is responsible for ensuring the tractors and equipment are operational and for plowing, tilling, fertilizing, planting, and cultivating the fields.

Among our collective responsibilities, each family is tasked with weeding a number of rows of corn during the summer. Not only is this an effective way to divide up the work, but it also makes the task much more manageable. Before we divided up the rows, it felt like an impossible task when you looked at the whole three-acre field. Tony Kuchma described the friendly competition that went along with weeding our assigned rows. "My family was tasked with taking care of a number of rows and so is everybody else," Tony told me. "There's a little bit of friendly competition because you go out there and you're like, 'Oh, I see so and so maybe didn't weed this week,' or 'Boy, I better step my game up because our rows are not looking very good.'"[11]

Ohe·láku is not set up like community gardens where each family has a designated plot. Instead, we care for and harvest the entire field as a group.

We all keep track of how many hours we worked and distribute the corn after harvest according to how many hours our families contributed. At the beginning of the planting season, we all make a commitment to spend time caring for the corn. We need to fulfill those commitments and carry out our responsibilities in a manner the group decides is appropriate. For example, two main ground rules are that we don't allow drugs or alcohol to be used around the corn, and we use good words around the corn. We believe the corn hears us and responds in kind to our actions. We also believe she loves to hear laughter and understands our sense of humor as we tease each other, all in good fun.

To me, one of the most remarkable aspects of Ohe·láku is that it brings together people from different backgrounds and varying levels of experience with growing corn. Our common thread is our love for the corn and our commitment to help her grow and thrive. Jen Falck described how growing corn with the group was much more beneficial than she anticipated. "I'm really happy that this opportunity to grow corn with other families has come our way," she told me. "At first, when we started, it was going to be this cool way for us to learn how to grow corn. It's become much, much more than that . . . I think as far as my family goes, this is the first time in maybe a hundred years we are growing corn in our family."[12]

Adrianna Pelky and Bev Scow, founding members of Ohe·láku, both explained how they feel fortunate to be a part of the group. "Growing white corn together tied us to the community more," Adrianna told me. "I've got to meet so many more people in Oneida because of it. I heard the names and I have seen them from a distance, and yet I am now talking to them and now I know their names and I feel like I get to be a part of the community."[13] "It's a fun group of people that are drawn to being with the corn," Bev said. "I'm thankful for my kids to have those opportunities to connect with other people who understand the value of our food and our connection with the soil in the earth. I raised them in the longhouse, and so having that connection with the food and the ceremonies and having it be an actual practice meant a lot to me."[14]

Our group has relied heavily on those community members who hold the knowledge to grow our traditional foods. We are fortunate that they have been generous with their knowledge and expertise. Kwnwahta Smith, Oneida youth and son of founding Ohe·láku member Bev Scow, envisions how our group can pay it forward and help the community.

> I can see this organization going a hundred years from now with our people. I can see us encouraging and helping people build their own gardens. I can see us collaborating with Tsyunhéhkwʌ to build upon each other because it is good to have multiple sources of corn. If they don't have enough seed, or a lot of their corn died off or something, or their beans or squash something like that didn't make it, we could be that support and make sure that all of our people are provided for.[15]

Planting Sites

We currently have two sites that we plant our corn on. Robin John, Ohe·láku founding member, explained how our group got the opportunity to grow on tribal land.

> One day as I was filling up my car at the 54 One Stop, Bill Vervoort [Oneida food systems coordinator] saw me and walked over to chat. He said he heard we were looking for land to grow white corn on. He offered the use of the 4H field as no one was growing anything on it. My wife and I drove to the field to take a look. My brother Porky John used to grow hay on that field for his horses. We agreed that it would be a good place to grow white corn. If Bill didn't make that generous offer, we wouldn't have land to grow corn on today.[16]

We secured the use of another site the following year. We plant about three acres of corn at each site on a rotating basis. We call the first site the Uskah (one) field. We call the second site the Teken (two) field. We rotate where we plant corn at each field. The Uskah field is where we use conventional tractors to till and prep the field, to plant, and to cultivate. After the corn grows a couple of feet tall, the remainder of the process is done by hand. We hand-weed the field, we hand-harvest, and we hand-braid the corn so we can hang it up in the barn to dry. We don't use any pesticides or herbicides, and our fertilizers consist of horse manure, fish emulsion, compost tea, chicken crumbles (manure), and an organic mix from a local co-op. The seeds we plant are heirloom, Indigenous seeds. While our focus is on white corn, we also planted Hegowa corn, Iroquois blue corn, and Mohawk red flint corn. We also experimented with bringing squash and beans into our planting practices. We have a traditional tobacco burning before planting, and the women and girls sing seed songs during planting. The main goal is to incorporate as much traditional knowledge as possible into our conventional farming practices.

In the Teken field, we also use tractors, but we are aiming for a no-till practice with cover crops. Cover crops control soil erosion and runoff, amend the soil, promote biodiversity, control diseases and pests, and increase soil organic matter. No-till operations reduce soil erosion and runoff, lower fuel and labor costs, increase water filtration and retention, promote biodiversity in and around the soil, and fosters a living, healthy soil. We plant different cover crops in this field in the fall and plant corn between the cover crops in the spring, using specialized equipment that either crimps down the cover crop or mows it, depending on our cover crop of choice for that year. Then, the tractor attachment separates the soil just enough to plant a single kernel of corn and immediately pushes the soil back together. The different cover crops we used include rye, hairy vetch, oats, crimson clover, and cowpea.

The formation and execution of the plans for the Teken field are done in cooperation with the Oneida Nation Environmental Health and Safety Division. The Oneida Nation has a vested interest in reducing phosphorus runoff from agricultural fields into the surrounding surface waters of the Oneida Reservation. Jon Habeck, Oneida Nation Nonpoint Program Technician-Project Manager, and Tony Kuchma, Ohe·láku founding member and Oneida Nation Wetland Project Manager, described some of the runoff reduction efforts and concerns at the more remote Teken field. "With most of the Oneida Reservation draining into the lower Green Bay, one of the most affected areas in the Great Lakes, a plan was devised to use traditional ecological knowledge and mix it with new techniques to grow the traditional white corn," Jon explained.

> The plan was to use various cover crops to minimize exposed soil, reducing phosphorus an estimated eighteen pounds of phosphorus out of surface waters annually. The group partnership was awarded a $30,000 grant to do the phosphorus reduction over three years. The grant had an incentive payment built in for the group for each estimated pound of phosphorus reduced. The money then could be used to purchase equipment and supplies to increase their capacity to grow corn. Over the three years, the group tried different techniques, learning something new each year on how to reduce labor and nutrient runoff. At the end of the grant, the group surpassed the original estimated amount of phosphorus reduction from fifty-four pounds to more than an estimated one hundred eighty pounds.[17]

Similarly, Tony explained more runoff reduction efforts.

> The Teken field is the experimental field. We've been doing cover cropping out there. The first year worked pretty well. We grew a cover crop of rye and hairy vetch with the idea that we would come in and roll that down with a crimper and crush it and kill it. That worked really good for the rye, but it didn't work on the hairy vetch. The vetch provides a lot of nitrogen, but it's also an aggressive viney legume. It competed quite a bit with the corn early on. Eventually, the corn did okay. We had decent yields. This past year, we did a similar test with planting winter wheat in the springtime. That went in between the rows to keep the soil covered. It worked pretty good, but we had significantly less yield out there. We think it's a combination of four-legged predation on the corn, raccoons and deer, and maybe some two-legged harvesting going on out there. It's new. We've only been doing it for two years, so I think as the project goes forward, we will be hopefully proving that technique worthy.[18]

Harvest

One responsibility all group members share is harvest. For many gardeners, harvest time is their favorite time of year. It's a time for families and the community to come together to celebrate and reap the rewards of all their hard work. Harvest itself is a lot of work, but it's a joyous time often filled with food, family, friends, stories, laughter, music, and more food. It's a time for community members of all ages to gather. Ernest Stevens IV (twelve years old at the time) also talked about his experience with harvesting. He is the son of Stephanie and Ernie Stevens III. "I stayed there one night," Ernest told me.

> I sat there until I think it was ten o'clock, and we just braided corn and put it in that one thing, and you shell it in. It looks so cool and that was my favorite thing to use just putting corn in and shelling it and putting another corn in. I also watched the kids while my parents worked with the corn, and me and my brother would just go outside with the kids and play football and then we would go back inside, and we would help with the corn.[19]

Tony Kuchma, Ohe·láku founding member, also described the work that comes with every harvest. He described the wet weather we often face in the fall, as well as the effort involved with hand-harvesting and hand-braiding all the corn.

> The first image that comes to my mind during harvest time is that it's cold and wet and muddy, because that's usually when we are harvesting. It is usually the end of September, October, or even later sometimes. It's fun. It might be cold and wet and muddy, but everyone is out there. You pick as much as you can handle for that day, because we hand-pick, hand-husk, hand-braid, and hand-hang the corn. You can't leave it just sitting there, so you have to take care of everything that day. It's a communal event and it's a lot of fun. It's also hard work.[20]

When I asked Jen Falck, another founding member, to describe what harvest was like, she replied with one word: exhaustion. "It's husking and cleaning and packing for days and days and days," she recalled. "I think it's phenomenal how everybody in the group does it the best they can with the time that they have. I show up after work and I might bring a meal because I can't be there during the weekdays, but other people can. It's always a coming or going of people, but takes us about a month to finish the harvest. When we're done, we're tired, but the barn is full of corn."[21] Bev Scow, Ohe·láku founding member, described feeling serene during harvest. "I'm just really grateful to be a part of the project with Ohe·láku and the new people I'm working with," Bev told me. "Sometimes I'm busy with work and family, but when I can get to the barn, it just creates a serenity. It's almost meditative when you're getting into the rhythm of just husking or the braiding, and it's just good medicine all around."[22]

Ecuador

Involvement with Ohe·láku has brought many of our group members to travel across the United States to share our experiences with our corn and with each other. We traveled to food sovereignty conferences, to universities, and to Indian reservations to share what we learned. The most memorable trip so far was when a group of twenty-two of us went to Ecuador in March 2018. Through her connections at work, Lea organized the trip for a cultural exchange with Indigenous corn growers there. "We had twenty-two people flying to Ecuador to go on this three-week crazy bus ride through the mountains to visit all of these really tiny communities," Lea recalled.

> They knew we were coming, and they started to prepare for us. They saved really important events for our arrival, and they totally caught us off guard. Nobody communicated with us that it was going to be this huge thing. When

FIGURE 8. White corn harvest hanging in the barn in 2018.

we got off the bus in our grungy travel clothes, they were showering us in rose petals and singing us songs. We had a lot of translating back and forth between Quechua and Spanish and English, telling our stories and sharing our knowledge and singing songs, and then they rolled out this thirty-person buffet. Every woman there had a different corn meal, drinks made with corn, different tamales, soups, breads, tortillas. We just went down the line trying dish after dish after dish. Everything tasted totally different, and everything was super healthy, traditional food. They also opened up their seed house, which was not just a seed bank but a healing center. They brought us through that, and it was just a beautiful event. And that was just the first stop. It carried on from there, visiting their gardens and visiting all of their different sacred spaces that they welcomed us to. It really made me think about what we would do if they came to visit Oneida. What would we shower them with?

What songs would we sing to them? What sacred places would we take them to? and what would we feed them?[23]

One of the most notable aspects of the trip was how the people used all the available space to grow corn. Our own family was so inspired by the corn in Ecuador, we planted corn in our front yard after we came home. We've been planting corn in front of our house ever since. Don Charnon, Ohe·láku founding member and retired Tsyunhéhkwʌ worker, fondly described his first impressions. "It was absolutely wonderful to go to Ecuador and to find the similarities between the cooking process and the ways that people grew," Don told me. "Right when we got there, I saw cornfields and the red bud of a bean growing on the corn plant. I just about lost it. I was tearful."[24] Jasmine Jimerson recalled. "One thing that stood out to me was even when we were in large cities, there would be very little places to grow corn, but they found places to grow it anyway. Corn was everywhere."[25] Lea Zeise similarly recalled, "They had corn everywhere that you can plant corn. There was corn down hillsides that were incredibly steep. There was corn right outside the front door at the gas station. It was everywhere. That showed me that we need to reimagine our space and completely redefine all of our spaces to be ours and to represent us."[26]

Under the Wing

One of the phenomenal aspects of our group is that we have this great chemistry among the members. We may not always agree on every issue, but we understand we are like an extended family and we need to continue to work together in harmony for the benefit of the corn and so we can share corn with the community. We needed to think of a way to continue this delicate balance while allowing more community members to join the group.

Ohe·láku now has a process to bring in new members called "under the wing." If you have been a full member for two years, you have the opportunity to bring in a new group member. After harvest is complete and before planting begins, the group meets to discuss the plans for the coming year, including bringing in new members. If a group member wants to bring in a new member, they let the group know their intent and tell the group about this person and their family. The group then discusses whether this person will be a good fit, including whether they would embrace our philosophy.

People who are brought into Ohe·láku in this way work with us for a year, from planting to harvest. After harvest, the full group members discuss whether to accept the under the wing member as a full member. After being a full member for two years, that individual then has the opportunity to bring in an under the Wing member of their own.

Adrianna Pelky, Ohe·láku founding member, compares this process to braiding the corn. "When you make a braid of corn, you grab the husk of a cob and then you add another cob and weave it together, and then you add another one and you weave it together, and sometimes you have to grab an extra one to keep it stronger and you just keep building it up until you have a braid to hang and display to the world," she said. "I think of that braid as the group because we have this under the wing, and we're slowly bringing in people at a time and we're slowly putting things up."[27]

Toni House watched our group from the outside for the first couple of years. When we developed the under the wing process to take in new members, I took Toni under my wing. That was kind of ironic because in so many ways, she has been my mentor. I still go to her for my questions about longhouse protocols, about language, about our stories, about our foods, and about our medicines. "When I was watching Ohe·láku, I was so mad that I didn't jump in," Toni shared with me.

> I joined various groups over the years, and they always started and fell off. I remember being at TsyunhéhkwΛ and I would just be braiding all of their corn and harvesting and seed selecting. For years we did that. I would have fifty million ideas while I braided that corn. I tried to have plots with various families in different places and it just never went anywhere. Watching your group was really exciting to see because I remember being that excited. I haven't had that excitement in almost twenty years. The first time we grew our corn, I brought this one cob to longhouse because she was so big and long. I didn't want to take her out of the husk because she was so beautiful. I got to show Carol Elm. I probably consulted with her about corn. . . . Nobody had that same excitement that you had about this corn from when it grew every day. To see somebody else like I was, it was refreshing. You guys just had this niche. You had a nice chemistry, and I was just like, "Oh I want to be a part of that." And so now I am.[28]

Conclusion

Ohe·láku started out of a need for the community but grew into so much more. Not just for the members of their group but also for the entire community as well. Ohe·láku came together to help fulfill the community's need for corn. Most of us are new to growing our traditional foods and we are constantly learning with each new season. We are always taking advantage of opportunities to incorporate our language and culture into everything we do with the corn. We hope to be a part of our community's transition to more healthy, Indigenous diets. Together, we are reclaiming our past, claiming our future, and ensuring that people of all ages in our group and our community have more opportunities to learn about our corn.

Our group honors the gifts of each member. Just like our corn, Shukwayaʔtísu gave each of us a gift to contribute to our community and to Mother Earth. By splitting up the group into four main areas, we honor our member's gifts by allowing ourselves to exercise our true strengths. As our history has taught us, the colonizers have consistently put pressure on us to either not exist, or to exist in their image. Assimilate into the social norm, become laborers or slaves, kill the Indian, save the man. They attempted to take our foods, language, stories, ceremonies, and our very identity. They stole our power over and over again. Ohe·láku gives that power back both to our co-op members and to the community as a whole.

Yukwaliwisaʔáhtu

(How We Tie Our Matters Together)

NE· YAKʌ LATUHÁKWE MUCH LIKE THE CHIEFS WHO MAKE UP THE YUKwanuhsyu·ní Confederacy, everyone has a different perspective. When I talked to the people in our community about what the corn meant to them, they shared different viewpoints. One common theme I noticed was how people universally referenced the corn as being precious. Within that overarching theme, several other themes began to emerge. First, people talked about how corn is helping them reestablish historical trade routes. Second, people talked about how corn is helping our community work toward becoming more food sovereign. Third, people explained how growing and cooking our corn is helping them eat healthier. Fourth, in addition to healthy food healing our bodies, they talked about how corn is helping them heal our spirits.

Our Corn, She Is Precious

Stephanie Stevens, Ohe·láku member, explained how four generations of her family helped grow the corn and what that meant for her to watch the different generations sharing memories with the corn.

> I'd have my children in baby carriers while we were in the field. Sometimes they'd be nursing and I'd be working at the same time. They would be crawling in the muddy fields before they could walk, and as soon as they were walking, they were helping plant the seeds. I remember Orion using the corn stalks in the field to help himself stand up and maintain his balance My daughter and her great-grandmother were in the field together, as well as in the barn together, which means that work with the white corn spanned four generations. I remember sitting in the barn, watching them interact. Every time we work with the corn, something magical happens. It seems to lift our spirits, and it seems to connect us to something greater. My daughter was right next to her great-grandmother, and they were husking the corn. They were smiling, laughing, and telling stories. In the background, ceremonial songs were playing, and as they worked, they were also humming and singing along to those songs. That is ceremony. That is medicine. That is healing. That is tradition. That is food sovereignty. That is sacred.[1]

Stephanie's story demonstrates the power that corn has in bringing together the different generations to share in work, laughter, and stories. Corn has different meanings to different people, and we have a different relationship with corn depending on what we need in the moment. She can help us become more independent and interdependent as a people. She can help us learn new ways of growing and cooking. She heals our bodies and our minds. Corn helps connect us to community members and faraway friends, new and old.

The third year we grew corn, I tried to grow a purple Peruvian corn I received from Angela Ferguson at Onondaga Nation Farm. The corn was originally part of the Carl Barnes collection that Onondaga Nation Farm was now responsible for taking care of. The corn was so purple—even the cob was purple. I instantly thought of how purple her husks would be and envisioned making beautiful cornhusk dolls. I planted the corn and checked on her every day. She wasn't coming up. When I was getting done with the weeding, but still worrying over the corn, I got to my knees. I was still inspecting the ground real close to check whether I could see any signs of corn sprouting up.

It was a beautiful day out. The birds were chirping, the wind was blowing just a little bit, and the sun was shining. Then, I heard people talking, but I knew they weren't people. I was in shock. My stomach dropped. It reminded me of a reaction you might have when you see a car accident. Your mind asks, "Is this really happening? Am I really seeing this right now?" On this day, I asked, "Are those words? Are they really talking?" I couldn't believe that this was actually happening. I looked down and listened for a few seconds, my stomach churning. I had no idea what they were saying. The words reminded me of how when I hear Mohawk words. I sort of can tell what they are saying, but not really. The words slipped through my mind as familiar, but not enough to understand. I remember thinking that if I knew the Oneida language better, I would have understood what they were saying. When I looked up and got to my feet, I saw it was a group of crows gathered in a tree about a hundred yards away from the garden. All of a sudden, the talking stopped, and I heard nothing except the sound of the crows flying away.

The purple Peruvian corn never did grow that year. The seeds were sterile. I was still inspired to have colorful husks and set out to dye my corn husks that year. I made a few dozen beautiful cornhusk dolls of all sorts of colors. Looking back, at the time, I wasn't sure what the crows were saying. Writing this book has given me a new perspective on so many things. I can say with confidence that the crows were not making fun of me for worrying about my precious, dead seeds. They were rejoicing that more people were beginning to grow and care for our Indigenous foods again. Everything in creation has a responsibility. The crows were happy that more of us were picking up those responsibilities and sharing them with our community.

Reestablishing Trade Routes

Our original instructions teach us about how we are connected with the world around us. We have reciprocal responsibilities for all of creation. We are connected like a giant web. Prior to European contact, our trade routes looked like a giant web. Throughout North and South America, the people were trading goods and exchanging ideas. Lea Zeise, Ohe·láku founding member, and Jill Ninham, former Tsyunhéhkwʌ employee, both explain how our corn is helping to reestablish those historical trade routes and reconnecting Indigenous people. "I often think about how our corn is related to all the other corn that Native people grew and how our corn is actually really closely related to the corn that grows in Peru genetically," Lea explained.

> How did those trade routes so efficiently move corn from here to there on a sustainable, carbon-free economy? Our teachings tell us health care is for all, food is for all, shelter is for all. We are not supposed to limit access to that within our communities and from without our communities. People came to our communities, and we fed them. Whether or not that was a good idea all the time remains to be seen. I think about how to apply those teachings in a modern context. How do we equal the playing field again and make sure that everybody has access to health care, everybody is living a strong healthy life, everybody has a good mind, and everybody has access to corn? That's not just within our community. We are trading our corn again across Turtle Island.[2]

Similarly, Jill shared a story about a trade she helped me complete.

> I think that those trade routes that we had for from the beginning of time are really valuable to reintroduce and to investigate. Recently, I brought ten pounds of white corn to Tucson, Arizona, to trade to support their economy. In Tucson, there is an underground market made up of Indigenous people and people of color that grow their own food. They also have their own art that they trade and barter with. We traded the white corn for some variety of beans, including beans from Tohono O'odham. They are actually a variety that has been brought back from many, many, many generations ago. They grew it out and brought it back so much that it is in the community just like the white corn is in the community here. We also traded for red tepary beans,

white tepary beans, garbanzo beans, cocoa beans, Hopi beans, and some bitter root. It was a really great beginning for a revitalization of trade routes.[3]

These stories show how colonialism impacted us by creating artificial borders that severed long-standing ties with our near and far relatives. We are trying to revive those trade routes to make our foods more accessible and to support each other in our pursuits to revive our food systems. This realization really struck me when Ohe·láku went down to Ecuador in 2018 for a cultural exchange with the Indigenous corn farmers. When we were visiting one of the farming villages, we got ready to help cook a meal. We brought some of our white corn to share with them. I was explaining (through a translator) how we traditionally cooked our corn in ashes. After my explanation, they brought out a clay pot, filled it with water, put the corn and ashes in it, and nestled it over a bed of coals to cook. As it was cooking, I was talking with an elder. She explained that is exactly how they cook their corn. I was speechless. Then I felt a bit stupid. Because, why in the world wouldn't we cook our corn the same? We have been in contact with each other long before any of us came into contact with Europeans.

Strengthening Food Sovereignty

"Food sovereignty" is a phrase that a lot of people use, but not everyone has the same idea of what it means. To me and the community members I interviewed, food sovereignty means that Indigenous people should have access to healthy and culturally appropriate food, be able to engage in sustainable food production, and be able to safeguard their agricultural practices including planting, harvesting, and preservation.[4] Our community, like so many others, is taking advantage of the national food sovereignty movement to gain momentum to encourage more people to embrace and celebrate our food relatives.[5] The following stories from our community members explain how our corn can help us achieve increased food sovereignty. “It’s not only having access to the healthy foods but finding creative ways to generate economy,” Ohe·láku member Bev Scow began.

> We can get the kids involved in learning what it takes to put a project together and go beyond just feeding ourselves. We can, for example, make cornhusk dolls. There’s a way to use the product and have a creative expression and also maybe generate a little income for the kids. They could even grow it into a mini business of some kind, or the bartering part of it is exciting. Like being able to barter for artwork or for other Indigenous foods like rice. That’s freeing us from being dependent on the dollar.[6]

“Sometimes when people in our community hear about food sovereignty, they think it’s something that they don’t actually need to participate in,” Jasmine Jimerson explained.

> They think it is something that’s going to be done for them, that it’s going to be provided to them, and that it’s their right to obtain it. What is hard for people to understand is that if we want to be sovereign, we all have to work towards it, and you can’t obtain the benefits of it unless you’re contributing to it. When I talk about that, I’m kind of careful because I very much believe in the sense of community, but I think that the community needs to realize that they are a part of it and each individual needs to contribute somehow. We can’t have food sovereignty unless we are all united in that sense.[7]

Jamie Betters, food-processor educator for the Oneida Cannery, described her early involvement in the food sovereignty movement.

> On a professional level, it was about the right to regulate our own. Food sovereignty makes every bit of sense to me. When I started at the cannery, I had the opportunity to go on a work trip to Colorado. I was twenty-two years old, sitting in a small meeting room at Taos County Economic Development

> Corporation in Taos having no idea who the rest of the folks were. There and then was when we put together food sovereignty. I don't think anyone has a right to argue about the term "food sovereignty" unless they have been on the forefront defending our seed, sharing their own knowledge instead of sharing their own opinion of the work others have done. Here we were defining and putting together two words, "food" and "sovereignty." It was all about protecting our seeds, especially from Monsanto. Creating resolutions to bring back to each community to give to elected officials. Food Sovereignty began a movement because of those who were so passionate. It was also about regulating, to process our corn so we can integrate it back into our communities where the Bureau of Indian Affairs and the United States Department of Agriculture regulated our food. It was about taking control and taking back our rights. I watched the movement explode, smiling knowing how hard we worked in that room taking out a word, adding a word. It literally evolved different for each community but then the intent remained the same.[8]

Strengthening our community's food sovereignty can be a very empowering and liberating venture. After all, if a nation cannot feed its people, are they really a nation? It is pretty clear that George Washington and General Sullivan understood this concept well. If destroying our ability to feed ourselves is what they did to break our community, then reclaiming it may be how we rebuild. It appears to be working; growing corn can build community and bring people together toward a common goal. By becoming self-reliant, we are less susceptible to what goes on outside our boundaries. We have a greater control over our own future. With that empowerment, we can provide greater support to those who are growing and cooking corn and other Indigenous foods.

Growing, Cooking, and Eating for Health

Corn can help us become healthier in a number of ways. Getting out in the gardens and fields to plant, weed, and harvest can be great exercise. Cooking our Indigenous foods can be a great way to learn and put more thought into what we eat. Eating more Indigenous foods instead of highly processed, high-fat, high-sugar store-bought food can help reverse many chronic health conditions such as obesity, diabetes, and heart disease.[9]

With respect to growing our own foods, a number of people emphasized the importance of having gardens and knowing where our foods come from. Jen Falck, Ohe·láku founding member, explained that having large gardens and raising their own food has been a long-standing dream she has shared with her husband. "My husband and I have been talking about this essentially since we've been together over twenty years," Jen recalled. "This is really a dream come true. We've been talking and planning, and we are very interested in having our own food sources and knowing where our food comes from. Being responsible eaters and getting into agriculture makes sense to us and it is good for the environment."[10] Similarly, Stephanie Stevens, Ohe·láku member, explained how her children were learning the importance of caring for corn.

> I remember my husband and the boys working in the cornfield at the community garden. I remember it being so hot for a week, in the high nineties. And they would be out in the fields working. The boys would be hauling water to give to the corn. Back and forth, they were dripping sweat. It was grueling work, especially in the heat, but there were so many valuable lessons learned. Not only did they get quality time with their dad, [but] the boys saw those seeds that they placed into the ground grow into plants, and they knew those plants needed water as much as they did. They really put the work in, weeding and watering. And in the fall time, they saw firsthand the benefits of it. That jar of seeds we soaked and put into the ground became corn that we harvested and husked, which became heavy braids we held up with pride. It was so rewarding to make mush from that first harvest of corn. My whole family truly appreciated the entire process. Every one of us participated from start to finish, and it gave us all a full appreciation of the corn.[11]

Growing your own food has more benefits, but it takes more work. This might deter a lot of people from giving gardening a try. As these storytellers explained, the rewards far exceed the effort, especially considering the long-term health impacts of eating healthy foods. Recognizing the many benefits of growing our foods, we must also be mindful of giving thanks to those who grow the food and those who prepare the food. Randy Cornelius and chef Arlie Doxtator emphasize these points. Randy told me:

> We honor those people that prepare that food because you want to have good intentions when you're preparing that food and making that meal. You don't want to go in there with anger because then that food is not going to taste good. When you cook with a good mind, it's going to be yaweku, it's going to be delicious. So, we say that to the cooks, but it's also going to the Creator because the Creator is the one that made that possible. We say "yawʌ" when we are done with our meal or even just drinking water and thanking that spirit of the water because it's sustaining us.[12]

Arlie talked about being able to help the corn fulfill her responsibilities.

> Years ago, I was out in New York or Canada, getting ready to leave the kitchen professionally because I was having a hard time having a good mind and working in these European-style kitchens. You can't have a good mind and be in a European-style kitchen where they don't mesh because they are almost on opposite sides of the spectrum, and I was having a hard time fitting in. I told this elder about it and asked him what I should do. He told me all the things I work with had meaning: the squash, the corn, all those fruits, all those vegetables, all those meats. He said those are our relatives and they are part of the natural world. They know their responsibilities and they always want to fulfill their responsibilities. Part of that responsibility is as food and as medicine. They fill our stomachs with those good feelings and bring us together as family. He said, "Say you have a relative that knew their time was

> close and had maybe two or three responsibilities or duties left and they asked you to help. Would you help?" Yes. Obviously. He said as a chef, I had to do the same thing and help our food relatives fulfill their responsibilities. So that's how I look at cooking and working with corn. It is helping that corn fulfill its responsibilities to us. It's very humbling when you start thinking of it that way.[13]

Being thankful to our corn and our other food relatives. Even though we may not prepare our foods exactly as our ancestors did, many of our practices carry over to the present, including the responsibility to give thanks to those foods. We may use metal pots, gas stoves, and dehydrators to cook and preserve our foods, but we know those foods recognize we are helping them fulfill their responsibilities to sustain our minds and bodies.

A few storytellers explained some of their adventures in cooking with corn and experimenting with different recipes. Randy Cornelius shared that he has been swapping out certain ingredients in recipes for Indigenous foods like hulled white corn and green corn.

> I like experimenting with recipes, adding this and that and the other thing and seeing how it turns out. I especially like experimenting with our green corn and our Indian corn. My sister has a recipe for chili, and she used Indian corn instead of noodles and she used our buffalo instead of beef. Then she added zucchini, summer squash, and beans. I've been experimenting as well with my chili. I don't use noodles anymore either. Now I use green corn in my chili. Even in stews, I use green corn and just plain hulled corn instead of potatoes or rice. I haven't really expanded my other recipes with heirloom beans, but it's on my bucket list.[14]

Young elder Brian Doxtator told a story about how the elders were not too impressed with an experimental corn dish he served them.

When I was in my younger years, Kirby Metoxen started this program where they had house parties where people would get together and cook food, do beadwork, or make cornhusk dolls. It became a community event where bands would play throughout the summer and then he would get nonprofit groups in the community to cook so they could sell the food. Kirby always asked the Toto Club to cook. They were an organized group of grandmas and grandpas. One year, I decided that I was going to make a baked dish with white corn, zucchini, stewed tomatoes, and marinated pork cuts. I topped it with cheese and took it there. I was really interested and excited to hear what people thought of because I only grew up on cornbread and corn soup. Most of the people who were attending it were grandma and grandpas. They were all between the ages of sixty and eighty. I'd say there were about two hundred people there. Most of the younger people weren't raised here on the reservation. After everybody went through, I walked around and visited with quite a few of grandmas and grandpas. I asked what they thought about my corn casserole. They said it was okay. I was so bummed. They must have wondered what I did to their corn. At least that's how I took it. They must have been offended how I changed it up. The younger generation said it was awesome and asked how I cooked it. That's been my favorite white corn dish for the last twenty years and everybody likes it now.[15]

Oneida-language teacher Curt Summers described different ways to dress up corn mush.

I first encountered corn mush with some of our medicine societies. I remember the first time eating it and I was like, "Oh man, what is this?" There was so many different ways that people cooked it. Some were sweet with maple syrup, a little butter, berries, and nuts. Some had bacon grease in it. There was some that was just the corn mush and nothing else in it. There's a lot of different ways to make it just depending on who you're making it for and what you're making it for.[16]

Jasmine Jimerson, Ohe·láku member, talked about her young daughters and their adventures in the kitchen.

> My oldest daughter, she is six. She helps with making the corn soup and cleaning the corn. She comments on the way people clean their corn in a very nice way, but she still has something to say. She also notices the difference when people use ashes and when they use lye or baking soda. She's very open about it, so that's really funny. My younger daughter is four and, in her classroom, she is taught by first-language speakers and her classmates are first-language speakers. She gets pretty good vocabulary at school. I noticed she was starting to just only speak the language when she cooks. I think that must be something that they do at school. It's really encouraging to see how she understands.[17]

These stories about cooking show the different ways we can prepare our corn to nourish our minds and bodies. She is such a versatile food, and we can prepare her in so many ways. We can also trade out less healthy options in recipes for corn to make our dishes healthier. On the opposite end of the spectrum, Ohe·láku members Don Charnon and Toni House talked about how eating unhealthy food can cause us to become even hungrier and eat even more unhealthy food. They both described this vicious cycle. Don explained:

> If I buy five dollars [worth of food] at a junk food place and I just slam some carbs in my body, about a half an hour later I can probably eat the same meal again. I'm still starving. My body didn't get any nutrition and my hunger button isn't shut off. So I'm going to go blow another ten bucks. Some people say it's more expensive to eat organic food. I don't agree with them at all because I can go broke trying to feed myself and still be hungry on junk food. If I really did eat raw, nutritious food, I wouldn't eat as much, I wouldn't need as much, and my signals will say, "Oh yeah, we got enough."[18]

Toni shared a similar perspective.

> My mom, she always goes into the prophecies of how there isn't going to be any food. She always asks, "What are we going to do when there's no food?" I tell her we are in that day. Everyone is talking about obesity. Why do we have obesity in the world today and in our community? If you walk around and look at the kids and how obese they are at such a young age, it's running rampant. It's an epidemic in our community. I tell her, "It's because they are starving, mom!" She says they are not starving. I said, "Yes, they are. Go to the grocery store and see how much pure food you can get." I think there's two rows of it. Two small rows. All the rest is food that is being created in the world that has no nutritional content. Our bodies are very, very intelligent. They know that you didn't get what you needed, so they tell you to eat more. but when you break that all down, your body says you need to eat because you need this to function. You're getting kind of moody, you're getting kind of sluggish, and you're still hungry, so you keep eating and nothing is filling you up with what you need. Then you keep getting fatter and fatter because your body keeps telling you to eat. You can't stop eating because you keep eating noodles and bread and you don't stop and drink water. You don't go out and get corn. You don't eat venison because that's a lot of work. You can't go to Walmart and buy it.[19]

If you look at the nutrition of corn mush compared to cereal, you will notice a huge difference. It would take a lot of cereal to get to the same amount of nutrition in one bowl of corn mush. Add in real maple syrup, berries, and nuts to your corn mush, and it contains even more nutrients for your body. Unlike highly processed, high-sugar foods with countless preservatives in them, our foods are highly nutritious. Our foods might not be as accessible right now, but we are on the way to making them more available for everyone in the community. Making those foods more accessible will also lead to a healthier community.

HEALING

As we have seen so far in these stories, corn has responsibilities that extend beyond simply providing us with food. She also helps heal us. Whether it be a bowl of corn soup at a family gathering, digging your hands in the dirt to plant corn seeds, feeling the light brushes of the cornstalks on your shoulder in the cornfield, peeling back her dried husks to reveal beautiful cobs, or simply being present around the corn, the corn helps us heal. Elders Julie Barton and Stan Webster commented on how corn soup itself can be a medicine. "If things were down and out in your family or people were sick with things like mumps and measles and chicken pox and adults would have heart problems or when somebody would die, corn soup was part of the healing process," Julie explained. "Somebody would make this huge pot of corn soup and take it to the house. Corn soup would make you feel better."[20] "My understanding is that corn soup is a medicine," Stan similarly shared. "Whenever you might feel really ill, if your mind is not right, or if your emotions are not in the right place, if you have that corn soup, that helps you settle down and helps you spiritually to resolve the things that are inside. It helps you get the right balance back."[21]

In a sense, corn soup is like our chicken soup for the soul. So many of our community members have childhood memories where corn soup was present—usually at family gatherings and celebrations, or at funerals. While the association might not seem to be positive, sharing corn soup with family helps us heal. Many storytellers described other ways the corn can heal us. Oneida elder Laura Cornelius talked about how gardening can be a way to help many of her students at tribal school cope.

> Look at the epidemics right now in our community. I see the kids, and some of them were my former students. They are in their twenties and thirties now and they seem so lost, and their kids are so lost. Yesterday, I subbed in a culture class, and I asked how many of them have ever planted. None of their hands went up. Ninety percent of the sixth graders are either living in single-parent homes or are living with their grandma or grandpa. Their parents are the ones

> stuck in the opiate epidemic. Somewhere along the line, I think we need to ask these people if they want to come plant with us.[22]

Lois Stevens, an Oneida community member, talked about incorporating gardens of corn into a future treatment center in Oneida.

> Corn and our traditional foods can be very healing. Recent opiate epidemics are causing our people to suffer. We need to think differently. The other treatment programs that people go through are not working. We have something that could be so healing, that ties us to the land and that ties us to who we are as a people. We need to harness the power. That would be really great, to see a treatment center back on our reservation with a garden plot where they get to grow the corn. Just feeling the dirt on your hands is so healing. I would like to see the tribe harness the power of white corn because it's not just the food, it's not just the ceremony. It's very healing.[23]

Kwnwahta Smith, Ohe·láku founding member, talked about his own struggles and how corn understood his pain and helped heal him.

> It's very therapeutic for the youth because we have a lot of youth struggling with not just historical trauma and generational trauma, but their own trauma in the home. They don't know where to express their pain and their frustration. They express it out to each other and to their peers. It's a real struggle. I think working with corn and building character at a young age working with our traditional foods and our traditional ways and getting into the dirt can be really meditative and healing. I remember when I was a kid, I was pretty angry. I was pretty mad. One time I got upset, so I went to go work in the corn. People tell me you shouldn't work in the corn unless you have a good mind, a healthy mind, but sometimes I think our food can have positive energy so they can grow good and be healing to you and to each other. Not every time you can have a positive mind. I think the corn can understand that it's not directed towards them, and I think they would acknowledge your pain

> and help heal you. When I worked in the corn, I got that meditative aspect. I got a little healing out of it.[24]

These stories show how understanding and forgiving the corn can be. Throughout the interviews, many of the people were sharing similar experiences and stories. I tried my best to make sure that everyone's voice was heard and to not have any one voice be louder than the others. When I came across themes about our corn that I wanted to share, it was relatively easy to find places to trim out segments of an interview because someone else likely said something remarkably similar. The next set of stories discuss the grieving process and the comfort that the corn helped them find during such a challenging time in life. Linn Cornelius shared how her late mother is still making sure they take care of the corn.

> We had great corn stalks for my mom's last crop before she passed away. They were way over our heads. My mom waited until the first frost to go pick, but a bear was so smart, and he ate it. You actually could see where the bear would stay. He didn't sit on the edge of the cornfield. He sat in the middle and you could see how he brought the corn to him. Then he would move and sit. All we had was corn on the outside. When mom had passed, we had the corn hanging in her garage. My sister Kim and my brother Karrie decided to finish it. The first thing they said was that they wished they had the gloves that Mom would have when she used to take the kernels off the corn. When they were talking about it, they were in the garage by the house and one of the doors came open. That's where the gloves were. So, Mom is still alive, making sure that the corn is being taken care of.[25]

Toni House shared a story about her late friend and the wind.

> When Joy Ninham died, there was a storm. The corn blew over the night she died. I always equate it to her because I live in their house. I always thought she must have come here and visited one last time and she took my corn. It

FIGURE 9. Webster family with their white corn harvest. L-R Rebecca, Grace, Amelia, and Steve. Photo credit Stephanie Stevens.

> was right at green corn, so I picked it all. I was all sad because my corn blew over. I made a kettle of corn soup, and I took it over to Paul and Jill's, and so it ended up being for their family, for Joy Ninham.[26]

My husband, Steve Webster, talked about how the corn brought him to our ceremonies after his dad passed away.

> We harvested our first garden of white corn at home in 2015, which was months before my dad passed away. When he passed, it was the first time in my life that I couldn't just plow through a problem with just logistics. I was genuinely hurt and exposed where I was the weakest. I can honestly say that my temptation to drift toward drugs or drinking would have been so easy. I could have responded by overcompensating with anger or overconfidence, but for whatever reason, I was working with and learning about white corn for the first time in my life. The logistics or individual tasks that needed to

be done was a great diversion and allowed me to think through my hurt. I was surrounded by folks that had a totally different perspective than me and helped me heal spiritually in a good way. I attended my first ever ceremonies simply by chasing down knowledge of how to logistically plant better and more efficiently. Once I started going to ceremonies, I just ran into and connected with people who brought me even more peace. I'm still hardwired to figure out game plans with timetables and measurements, but I have learned to respect and take care of my spirit as well, and I am much happier because of it. All of this is thanks to the path the corn has taken me on.[27]

Jasmine shared how corn helped her heal after the passing of her uncle.

Last year was a year after we had been grieving the loss of my uncle. A long time ago, they said that you put off your work for a year while you're grieving. Last year after that time, it was still hard. I kept thinking it was going to be easier after the year, but it was still hard. Being out during harvest, harvesting among so many community members and among so much of our corn was healing for me. I was really appreciative of it, but I was even more appreciative of it this fall when I wasn't able to be in the garden and I wasn't able to harvest. I experienced depression because it was harvest time and I was inside all day long, and it was really hard for me, and even knowing that my community of corn growers were working really hard. That was uplifting for me, but at the same time, not being a part of it, I really felt the difference. Even my girls noticed the difference. They were able to come home for a short time and participate. They were just super happy about it. When they came back, they were just talking about it. Where we are living, there's not much corn growing. It's really interesting to see how my daughters value the corn. They value the corn because they told their friends that we had to go home because it's harvest time and we had to do so much work. They wanted to know how we were going to have our ceremony if we're not getting our work done, and yada yada yada.... It's really cool that they see that our food comes first, even if it's for a short while.[28]

Kyle Wisneski told a story about how one of his employees took comfort by sitting with the corn.

> Our community was going through some hard times. We had a young man that was taken away by a local police department. He was shot and killed, and his uncle was having a hard time, a really hard time. We were able to reach out to a couple of our spiritual advisers to see what we could do that would make [his uncle] happy. The thing that really came back to him that helped him was the corn and going into the field and just sitting out in the field. For three months, that was his outlet, the connection to the corn. He never had that either. He was a chef, so he was always cooking with corn. He always thanks me for that opportunity because I got to show him the seeds, the shelling, the planting, the cultivating. He had a unique opportunity to hang around with me for a year to get that from start to finish. I've never gotten the opportunity to teach anyone that, so that was kind of something new for me as well. He shared his story with me and told me that he would bring his whole family out there on weekends just to help the family get through that grief. It really put it into perspective for me the way corn is so much more than food. It is her responsibility to take care of us, and it's reciprocal for us to take care of her.[29]

These stories resonate with one of my own personal experiences with death, mourning, and corn. In the fall of 2019, I lost my uncle Jim. He was one of the few people in my immediate family who attended longhouse with us. The longhouse community, especially Bear Clan Chief Bob Brown, helped us with the arrangements, protocols, and in the overall mourning process. Before my uncle's final feast, I felt the need to offer something to Bob for being so kind and patient with our family, as many of my family members were only familiar with Christian funerals. Before the final feast started, I brought him our best cob of grandfather corn that we grew that year. A couple of months later, as I was conducting research for this book, I came across this passage in Arthur Parker's 1910 book *Iroquois Uses of Maize and Other Food Plants*: "in notifying people of the death feast, an ear or kernel of corn is given as a token. The person receiving it is bound to attend the ceremony."[30] I immediately began to think about recent research that revealed that historical trauma is in our DNA.[31] Many people throughout Indian Country soon responded that if historical trauma is in our DNA, our ancestral wisdom must be in there as well. With my heart pounding, I snapped a picture of the book passage and sent it to Bob Brown. He responded that until then, he had forgotten about that practice. He then relayed a story from when he was six or seven years old. He explained that he found a kernel of corn that his grandfather had dropped. He brought it to his grandmother and asked about it. She told him to give it to his grandfather. When he did, his grandfather said he was looking for it and told him that it meant he had to help with a condolence feast. His grandfather said it was like an invitation. Bob then told me how we don't do that here in Oneida anymore, but that he was curious to see whether the other communities out east still did that.

Corn fulfills so many roles for us. She is there to feed us. She is there to teach us. She is there to help us grieve and heal. These stories from our community illustrate how corn is so generous and giving. When we rely on her, we are helping her fulfill her responsibilities to feed our body and our minds. She helps sustain us. Louis Williams Jr., a former Tsyunhéhkwʌ employee, shared a story about how corn helped heal him. He was talking about how a coworker was teaching him about medicines, something that Louis was unfamiliar with at the time. "He told me about how our medicines work and what they are for," Louis explained.

> At the time, I was really struggling with drinking when I was working at the farm. There was a lot of times where I would come in hungover, and it would be a hazard for me doing the things I was doing while I was hungover. I was probably still drunk. When I was struggling with that drinking, I was also learning about Kaliwihyo. I started researching a little bit more and asking questions about Handsome Lake and the Kaliwihyo. The most important part

to me was realizing that these three sisters, especially the older ones, are a direct lineage to our ancestors since the beginning, in essence, since creation. They are our healing agents for our people. When I was there working is when I got sober. I was out there amongst the corn and doing those little braids and learning about the different medicines and societies and learning about different ceremonies and learning about different stories of Handsome Lake. It was at a time when I was really curious about the longhouse ceremonies, and I knew myself that I had to shape up a little bit.

I would encourage people if they are struggling with those kinds of things to contact somebody who does go to longhouse and have them bring them along with them. The relationships that we have with these things like the three sisters, it's all related into our ceremonies, in our culture, in our ways, in our medicines, and there's so many different things to learn from them. I can't even put a value on the things that I learned from the corn, especially when I was just getting clean and sober. It gave me that encouragement. It felt like the corn was communicating to me just as the corn communicated with Handsome Lake when he had his vision. I can totally identify with him when it comes to that. Shortly thereafter, I stopped cold turkey. It's been ten and a half years now. Every April is my sobriety anniversary. It seems like much longer. It seems like a lifetime ago. I've learned so much since then. I'm super thankful for our corn and experience that I had at Tsyunhéhkwʌ, just being around it and being able to absorb the energy and feel that love that it has for human beings and how it wants to be taken care of, and also how as human beings want to be taken care of by them. It's reciprocal. I don't know if I'd still be here now if I didn't stop drinking. I don't know if I wasn't working around the corn if I would have ever stopped drinking.[32]

Corn is a truly powerful sister with so many responsibilities. She has been with us during great prosperity as well as great tragedy. Through each phase of history and each phase of our lives, she helps us out in different ways. She helps heal our wounded bodies and our wounded minds.

Conclusion

Corn is embedded in every facet of our lives. She holds memory and partnership by reestablishing those trade routes and creating trust with members of all communities. She is providing purpose by looking past food security and sovereignty and reminding us that without community, we are not a people. She provides the nutritional means for every generation to be full and complete. She is giving us her hand, letting us know they we are not alone; we have her, we have our longhouse, we have our stories, we have our community. Through years of oppression, she has always been there, standing tall.

Corn is also helping us learn how to cook healthy meals by growing more of our three sisters and by cooking more meals with our Indigenous foods. She is healing our minds and our bodies by guiding us through the grieving process and helping us recover from destructive lifestyles. She is and has been our big sister, guiding us and picking us up when we have fallen.

Tsiʔ Nahte Olihwaka·yú· Okhale Oli·wásé

(Of What Old Matters and New Matters)

NE· YAKΛ LATUHÁKWE THAT IN SO MANY WAYS, THE STRUGGLE FOR BALANCE between traditional farming practices and contemporary farming practices mirrors the current situation many Indigenous people find themselves in when walking in two worlds. We want to hold on to and honor our history, but we also need to find ways to adapt to the changing world around us. This chapter features the voices of Oneida community members as they try to hash out how to find that balance. They talk about the point where the past meets the present and considers the future.

SEEDS

The process of planting and harvesting is a cycle, and it can be difficult to find an adequate place to start talking about farming practices. Since seeds hold future generations, they are a good place to start. Jamie Betters shared her passionate plea about protecting our seeds from predatory seed companies as well as from ourselves. She explained:

> The connection to who I am as an Oneida woman was the most important aspect of taking care of our white corn. Growing corn and saving seeds gave me a sense of purpose different than of a mother. Our corn at one time needed protection from our own people who had no connection and looked at it as a golden ticket out of gaming. We had no regulations on how we took care of her. We had no support on how to protect the seeds . . . Sometimes I was the only one fighting next with Kyle. Sometimes I didn't think we would ever get to where we are today. Sometimes, I didn't think I had enough fight in me. The people who I thought would be fighting with us and aside of us stayed behind, which left me resentful. I often thought, are we the only two people that care this much about protecting our white corn? I was discouraged, ready to give up the fight, until a woman who I respect immensely pulled me aside to talk with me and asked me why I was so passionate. She then reminded me that it was important to share my knowledge so I can get people connected. She told me to continue to teach and bring awareness to not only our white corn but all three sisters. She then helped me with a communication campaign, and all we did for a few weeks and months was just communicate to our community through social media the importance of our corn and how to care for her, with pictures, stories, and recipes. Food brings people together. While doing that I realized my attitude needed to change. Being resentful and bitter at so many who didn't get it was not the right path to take, but spending that time teaching and working with community brought us all closer together.[1]

Paul "Sugar Bear" Smith, Oneida elder and longtime corn grower, explained how we need to protect our corn from cross-pollination and be careful when we select cobs for seed.

> I went to elders, various older people that I knew. Anderson Cornelius, Hank Skenandore, Norbert Skenandore, and then also a gentleman with the last

name of Danforth. I looked for seed from some of the oldest people, including even Sarah Skenandore. Having those different seeds, I tried to generate a stronger, more sturdy corn. I was looking for traits that are necessary for corn. I did go to the University of Wisconsin–Madison and was trained there, and I certainly took agronomy. I was interested in our white flint corn and watching out for how you can avoid cross-breeding and inbreeding, and how you can also avoid ear placement where it is too low, and it is susceptible to mold and also looking for the husks to be very strong and sturdy. There is a mixture of several things that we have to watch out for even today in our seed selection especially with our corn seed. We got numerous types of corn seed. It's not just the white flint; there is yellow flint, blue flint, there is this snubbed-nose white corn, there is the Tuscarora white corn, and then you have the Oneida that's kind of in the middle of those particular two. There's a lot of different types of what we call white flint corn, and we have to be aware of that and we have to be aware of what we are planting it near. You got to watch for that dent corn because that dent corn is normally an animal corn, but it can also be a sweet corn. Things that are open pollinated are susceptible to the other flying pollen that will land on the hair of the corn. With the corn, you have to keep in mind it is also two in one. It is male and female. The female part is actually the hair that is coming out, so that starts first and then the pollen from the tassel. One pollen granule has to land on one hair on one ear in order to create one seed. That's how intricate this whole process is. It always has amazed me how that works.[2]

Lexi Levinson, a young Oneida woman, explained the relationship between a cob of seed corn and the female body. "The corn belongs to the woman," she explained. "She's real tall. Seed cobs have great big, uniform kernels. Certain parts of her are intended for seed. It's the same part on a woman as it is on the corn. There's a band in the middle where her belly or her uterus would be, and that is the part that you keep for seed."[3]

Our seeds hold future generations of corn. We need to keep our seeds safe to ensure we can continue growing and incorporating corn into our daily diets. This is becoming more difficult in recent times because of GMO seeds and different companies trying to place patents on our heirloom Indigenous seeds. Those threats make seed saving and seed keeping even more important practices. If we can keep those seeds safe, we can continue to grow them year after year.

Three Sisters Planting

Planting corn, beans, and squash together in mounds is part of our original instructions. The corn, the eldest sister, grows tall and strong and provides the main staple for Yukwanuhsyu·ní diets. The corn serves as a support system for the beans to climb up. The beans provide nitrogen to the soil. The squash spread out low, keeping moisture in the ground and suppressing weeds. Animals also don't like to cross through squash because of her prickly leaves and vines, protecting the corn and beans from animals. This method of planting contains ancestral knowledge that has been passed down since creation. Oneida people have had to occasionally lay down that practice for their survival, but we are once again able to pick it up and appreciate it for what it is, a scientifically sound and ingenious way to form the foundation for a healthy diet.

Carol Cornelius is an Oneida elder and author of *Iroquois Corn in a Culture-Based Curriculum*.[4] She acknowledges that "when we plant in mounds, we are saying 'This is the way our ancestors did this.' It's like when we are at the longhouse and doing ceremonies. I'm transporting back thousands of years. Our ancestors have always done this and here we are doing it again."[5] Likewise, Toni House recognized the ancient knowledge held in planting our three sisters together.

> My husband, Doug, and I have always bantered back and forth about planting a three sisters garden. Why would you question the three sisters? It's our ancient tradition. We were agriculturalists. We knew what we were doing.

> The way that we are raised in this community, we don't know. There's so many of us that don't have that connection to the corn, that don't have that connection to agriculture, that don't have connection to that knowledge. We are not connected up yet. I've been trying and trying to grow the three sisters and Doug laughs at me. There's got to be more to this. They're not called the three sisters for nothing. They are the three sisters for a reason. There is ancient knowledge there that I don't understand yet. I think as we grow the corn, we start to see how smart our people are.[6]

Some of the storytellers shared their techniques for making mounds. Sugar Bear talked about working with the directions and the sun when planting.

> When you talk about planting your three sisters, corn, beans, and squash together, squash do not like moist soil. So, when you go and you plant squash, they like being in well-drained soil, so we make a mound. When you plant squash, certainly you can't just plant them in the ground. They are going to hold that moisture too long and rot as a seed. That's why we make that mound and then plant your seeds at the top of that mound. The corn roots get another burst of energy and nutrition from that biodegraded fish. It's necessary to plant on the south side of the hill. You don't want to plant on the north side of a hill. There's no sun there until midsummer time. You got to work with the sun and the plants and all the other things with nature in order for all of it to work precisely the way it should. You got rows going horizontal and vertical and you also got rows going diagonally to the right and diagonally to the left.[7]

Eliza Skenandore, Ohe·láku founding member, explained how she carefully timed the planting of the corn and beans so they would support each other. "I just love the mounds we did at the Oneida museum," she shared. "The plants got more energy. We'd plant the white corn and then when the corn got about a foot tall, then we planted the beans around it and then the squash grew around the white corn. It helped with weed control. That was really powerful. It was the dream garden right there."[8]

In addition to the science of mounding up the dirt and planting the three sisters together, Sugar Bear mentioned placing fish in the mounds. Some people placed whole fish in the mounds and others placed the scraps after removing the meat. In either case, the fish provides nutrients to the soil to support the growing corn, beans, and squash. Along with Randy Cornelius and Louis Williams Jr., Sugar Bear elaborated on this practice, asking, "What does a plant need to eat in order to thrive enough for a start?" He was quick to answer:

> Our corn has always been around nitrogen, nitrogen, nitrogen, nitrogen. That's why fish are so important in our culture. Those fish were just as critical not only for our nutrition for our winter food but also for fertilizing our gardens. When you did that three sisters garden, the base of that was always a really good soil. What we would do is throw fish in that hole and then cover it up and then make a pile on top. Now that fish is rotting, and everything is in there. You got the calcium, you got the protein, you got the blood meal. It's a full set of nutritional pieces that things need to grow or to need to reproduce. They call that the NPK, your nitrogen and phosphorus and your potassium, and the fish has that.[9]

Randy described his experience growing a three sisters garden.

> They say you use fish to grow corn, so I went down to the quarry and I got a bucket full of fish. They were mostly Marblehead. I went home and dug a hole and put some fish in there. I put dirt on it. Then I put my seeds on it, usually two or three seeds in each hole. On the outside of the garden, that's where I put my squash. Down each row in between the corn, I put my beans so I would have all the different kinds of beans in each row like that. Most of them are climbers, so they would climb up the stalks.[10]

Louis shared how he used walleye in mounds.

> I helped with a garden back in Ontario. They would go walleye fishing in the spring. I think we got close to a hundred fish out of three different trips we took down to the river. They kept all those the fish guts and bones and stuff. We just put them in plastic containers, and I hauled it down to our garden. I dug holes. I was reading about it, and it said in order for the rodents and stuff to not be able to smell it and get it, you have to bury it between a foot and a half to two feet underneath the ground. I was digging out there by hand I didn't have no auger or nothing. I dug nine pits and put approximately a dozen fish in each one of those pits. Only one of them got dug up, then we had to try to fix it and fill up the holes and pack my dirt on it. If the raccoons smell it and know where it's at, it doesn't matter if you put another two feet of dirt on it. They know exactly where the thing is, and they will go right at it and take it back out again. For the next probably five to ten years, that garden is probably going to produce really, really good. I'm hoping that they are taking advantage of that back there.[11]

Young elders Vickie Cornelius and her brother Randy Cornelius switch back and forth between planting in three sisters mounds and planting in conventional rows. Vickie told a story about how she helped with a three sisters garden at the high school.

> I was going to plant a three sisters garden, but I think I'm so trained in the rows and how to do that that I end up just automatically doing that. Whenever we planted a three sisters garden with the high school, they had a beautiful garden. They planted the bear bean in there, too, so it was really beautiful because that beautiful red flower stood out against the green. Everyone in the building was so happy with the garden and always checking it out. When the wind came through and blew it down, the corn came back up by itself. It's unfortunate, though, that they didn't continue the gardens because I really feel like our high school and elementary school should be able to grow some of their own foods for them to eat. It's really important that they know

> where their food comes from and how to grow it. It's teaching them how to be self-sustainable.[12]

Randy shared a story about how he planted in conventional rows and, when the wind blew the corn down, it didn't stand up again because it didn't have the support it would normally have in the mound system.

> I got lazy this year and I tried to be conventional. I got the worst end of the deal there. Maybe the last ten years or so, I used that fish emulsion. When the plant sprouts out of the ground, that's when I put the first on, and then every two or three weeks after that. I put it on until it's up to my chest. This year I had a small garden plot and wanted to plant more corn in the same area. I just planted them every six inches apart in a row. My grandson helped me with that. He helped with the whole garden. He took one break about three or four rows in and then he came back and finished the rest of the garden. I swear every seed came up. I said, "You got a green thumb, my boy!" Every two or three weeks, I would fertilize it and I would weed it. I would mound it up and put that dirt around it to give it more stability. Being separated like that, when the wind came, it knocked everything flat. I didn't think anything of it because it happened before. It all came back up. But this time it wasn't coming back up. I went through it and I was trying to stand up the stalks and it was all mangled and I was breaking stalks. The stuff all on the outside came up but the stuff in the middle stayed down. This was when it was pollinating so the cobs were half full or half empty. I didn't get too many full cobs this year. When it was green, I went through and picked just about everything, and I ended up with six quarts of green corn this year. I just let everything else go. I probably got a quarter of what I got last year of Indian corn. It's still a good chunk. And it's a lesson to be learned. I never wanna do that again.[13]

Vickie's and Randy's stories demonstrate some of the reasons why more people are giving the three sisters planting methods a try. A handful of other storytellers explained how they thought that should be the goal. Lois Stevens and Ohe·láku members Lea Zeise and Jasmine Jimerson recognized the difficulties and impracticalities of growing using exclusively three sisters methods at the moment, but they all recognized that it would be a goal to work toward. "Planting the three sisters together makes more sense in my mind, not just only for our connection to the whole process but for the impact on the earth," Lois told me. "The more I study about our food system today, it's frustrating why everybody thinks that what we are all doing is sustainable. Why do we keep doing things this way? There's already plenty of literature on traditional growing methods and how it limits the impact on the earth. It drives me crazy that it's not more acceptable in mainstream society."[14]

Lea chimed in and emphasized community efforts.

> I think the traditional farming methods were really successful because everyone was involved in them. You didn't have to worry about getting out there to do it alone. Everybody knew that it was a part of their responsibilities. You didn't have to put flyers up around the longhouse to let them know that we were going to plant corn. Everybody was sleeping in the same place, and everybody was working in the same place. Now that we are in nuclear families, spread out, and we go to work to pay the mortgage on a nuclear family home. In our group, we are using the tractors now to meet our needs until we become more familiar with our responsibilities. It would be an awesome and fun day if we just had a hundred people out there planting fields and acres. It would take us the same amount of time that it takes us for the tractor to do the work.[15]

Jasmine also wanted to give the large community three sisters gardening a try. She said:

> It would be nice if we could go back to planting the traditional three sisters gardens with the mounds. I understand that times are changing, and we all have different responsibilities that we didn't have in the past. We don't have time for things that we once did. That's not [to] say that we couldn't make time. It would be a good goal to work up to. I understand if we need to use

> tractors, but it would be nice to eventually go back to planting our traditional three sisters garden. There is so much more of a connection with it because we spend that much time doing it and learning from it. We learn the importance of community. We learn the importance of the connections with the things around us. We learn how everything is interrelated. When we use a tractor to plant, we are missing out on that. Even though it still works, it gets the job done, it saves time, and it still teaches us, it doesn't teach us as much as when we plant the three sisters together. It's an experience that we should all have just so that we understand.[16]

They aren't alone in the desire to move toward more traditional planting methods, or in recognizing the need to have a balance in our lives between feeding more people and having less time to dedicate to agriculture than our ancestors had. The balance also came with our traditional methods and how we can use modern technology and equipment to help grow our foods.

Balance

When comparing traditional three sisters planting to more conventional methods, many of the storytellers talked about needing to find an appropriate balance. While three sisters planting is definitely the preferred option, sometimes we need to make compromises in order to fulfill our responsibilities to grow our foods. Chef Arlie Doxtator and my husband, Steve Webster, Ohe·láku founding member, both explained the occasional need for compromise. Arlie began,

> For me, everything is about balance. We have a large amount of people to feed, and nowadays people don't spend the time in the gardens like they used to. Growing up, it wasn't just the kids doing the garden work. The parents would also step out there. That was the time of visiting and for getting over with the neighbors. Once everybody would be done picking for that day, somebody

> always had the barbecue going. There was this family-oriented neighborhood event that would happen. It does happen today, but not like it used to. So, it is okay to use a machine if you're feeding a large amount people. Even some of the elders I've talked to said to go ahead and use machines, but always have that component of what you're teaching and you're remembering and you're not letting those responsibilities go by the wayside anymore. Those responsibilities that we have in the garden have a purpose. They are there for teaching us things. They teach us patience. They teach us that we have a relationship with the natural world starting with those little seeds all the way up to and beyond harvest.[17]

Steve Webster explained his thoughts on using machines for unconventional farming.

> I have found many very amazing teachers when it comes to growing our traditional foods. Things such as social media and texting allows us to be in contact with these folks, but in our Oneida community there are only a few growers. My personal observation is that the folks that are growing, harvesting, and consuming our foods are vastly outnumbered by the folks that don't know how to or are in situations where they cannot logistically do that. I am having this calling to change or at least influence that scenario. I believe the only way for a few to feed many is going to be using technology where it benefits the idea of getting more white corn and knowledge of white corn into our community. This can be a challenge due to the fact that many of the folks who are rich in knowledge of conventional farming methods and have the tools seem to struggle with the idea that we are not cash cropping. Their methods can actually hurt the very principles of why many are drawn to the corn, such as healthier/cleaner eating, spiritual/emotional connection with the corn, and the idea of doing something that connects you with your ancestors.
>
> I also feel that there is a challenge of traditional growing methods flourishing with things such as new invasive species, climate change, and previous farming practices that have stripped the soil of its ability to grow

> in. Going forward I see planting our gardens and working in the co-ops in mounds, burying fish, using planting sticks and shoulder blade hoes, using compost, while having the women sing seed songs. However, I will also be using tractors, tillers, trailers, UTVs, horse manure, fish emulsion, organic fertilizer, fancy tools to help with hand weeding to get people comfortable working with and growing our foods. I will not be using pesticides, herbicides, or farming for the purpose of selling our foods for cash. I will be forever open to any traditional practices that come up that could help address those new challenges and not be scared to give them a try.[18]

Regardless of the methods we use to care for our corn, we are fulfilling our responsibilities to grow our foods and helping those seeds fulfill their responsibilities to grow and provide us with sustenance. Kyle Wisneski, the Tsyunhéhkwʌ farms supervisor in Oneida, is responsible for ensuring that he delivers thousands of pounds of white corn to the Oneida Cannery each year. At this point in time, he cannot fulfill that responsibility without the assistance of modern technology. Tsyunhéhkwʌ also serves as a place for learning about our foods, so Kyle ensures that he cares for our foods in three sisters gardens each year. He is in a unique position to care for corn that he plants both with conventional tractors on a large scale and in three sisters gardens on a smaller scale. He explained that his relationship with the corn is the same, regardless of how he plants her. He told me:

> The cool thing at Tsyunhéhkwʌ is that every year, we grow both a small 25-foot-by-25-foot three sisters garden and then anywhere from six to ten acres of white corn grown conventionally. Conventional growing dominates at Tsyunhéhkwʌ, and we feel the effects of that like fertilizer runoff. As soon as you start row cropping, they start to support buying fertilizer from big companies instead of using manure from the cattle. In my case, the yield is much higher in the three sisters garden. We never have to move our garden when we are in three sisters. We are on a three-year rotation when we row crop. The three sisters garden is said to be able to plant twenty plus years in

> the same spot because of the symbiotic relationship that they share with helping each other out. I don't see any difference. I feel the same thing when I am in the three sisters garden versus when I'm in the row garden. I feel that connection to the corn. I can hear her talking a lot. I don't know if it was just this year why it was so loud, but everybody that went out to the field said that she was loud. She was really, really talking this year. I don't feel any difference with the special connection with row cropping or three sisters garden.[19]

Even though the Oneida community regularly pressures Tsyunhéhkwʌ to grow more and more corn each year, the staff members do their best to grow the corn in a way that maximizes use of their space while also caring for the long-term health of the soil and the seed stock. The community also sometimes compares the yields at Tsyunhéhkwʌ with local farmers growing GMO corn for animal feed or sweet corn. Louis Williams Jr. explained why such a comparison isn't realistic. Yield is not our top priority. Corn is our sister. Tsyunhéhkwʌ grows her to help meet the community's need for corn, not to exploit her to maximize profits. Louis said:

> Those corporate farms with their GMO corn like to plant them inches apart and get as many ears on each stalk that they can. That's what they're going for is the yield. with ours, we're not. We're trying to make it so that the corn is a healthy being, just as we would be treating another human being. We make sure it has its nourishment so that it has plenty of room and it has good soil and all those things. That's going to make it productive. It's like a relationship between us and the food. It's the corn that we had to think about. I know that it's been a topic of discussion for years and years in this community about why we aren't trying to get a better yield out of our white corn or why aren't we trying to get more corn out of the acreage.[20]

In addition to recognizing the importance of keeping our plants and soil healthy, we can also find ways to incorporate traditional practices into conventional methods. Kyle Wisneski and Tony Kuchma, Ohe·láku founding member, talked about some of those traditional practices and how community members are using modern technology to retain the benefits of those traditional practices. Traditionally, our ancestors soaked seeds in a medicinal tea, such as one made from mayapple leaves, to help protect the seeds against being eaten by other creatures. "We soaked the seeds in 2003, but what happened was they stuck together, and they were having a hard time coming through the planter," Kyle explained. "Now what we do is we mist them. Somebody will be pouring it in and somebody will have a mister and just spray it on so they're not soaking for hours, they are just kind of getting that coating on there. I feel like it's really helpful for any other insect or animal protection prior to germination. We use bitter root, white pine, and mayapple."[21] Tony Kuchma shared his experience with large acreage and soil health.

> It's hard to ignore the modern realities of the efficiencies that big equipment does bring. I think when your scale is over a couple of acres, it really is tempting to go that route. I think the traditional methods were right on soil health and soil fertility. I think we are heading back in that direction where we are not relying on fertilizers to supply everything that the corn needs. We are trying to make this soil healthy and have everything within it that the corn needs without having to rely solely on the fertilizer. I see it as a blend. Maybe it's applying traditional ecological knowledge, TEK, to it, and I see it working. We are adapting techniques with varying degrees of success, but it does seem to be working, so I'm excited about that.[22]

While we may be able to use conventional equipment like tractors to help us grow our corn today, that may not be an option for the future. To be prepared for that day, we need to understand how our ancestors grew our food. They did not have tractors, yet they were able to feed entire communities and have years' worth of food in storage. We need to keep those practices alive to honor that ancestral knowledge they passed down through the generations. There may come a day when their methods are the only viable options to feed ourselves. Laura Manthe and Bev Scow, Ohe·láku founding members, talked about these issues. "I think that we could explore more traditional growing methods," Laura said. "Our friends out east teach us that we can grow without implements. Who knows what the future holds. We may not have fuel to run our tractor, or if our tractor breaks down and we don't have another way to fix it, we might need to go back to those old ways."[23]

Bev expressed concern over how we are treating our fragile topsoil.

> Science is supporting the knowledge that our ancestors had with the interaction of the nutrients and how they support each. They were brilliant. The machines can help us right now with that, but going to those gatherings where we planted the field out in New York as a group was just really eye opening. In one morning, we had a big group of people plant the whole field. We might come to a point where we don't have gas for our tractors. We need to know how to grow the volumes of food in our own ways, so I'm also excited about experimenting with the no-till planting because we are dependent on those six inches of topsoil. If it's gone, we don't have any other options. We need to be very proactive in finding out how to keep that topsoil there.[24]

Our earth is strong and has survived for so many generations. It is scary when we think about how much damage people have caused to her in recent times. The earth can certainly survive without us, but we cannot survive without a healthy earth.

Conclusion

Our busy lives make it difficult for us to prioritize all our competing interests. We no longer have the lifestyles our ancestors had, and it would be quite difficult to completely revert back to that lifestyle. In picking up those practices our ancestors had to lay down, we often need to make compromises and strike a balance between preserving and practicing our ancient knowledge and traditions and working at a day job to pay our mortgage and keep the lights on. As we work toward learning more about our foods, it will become more natural, and we will be better equipped to balance those competing interests. Overall, it has become evident that we need lots of help from people with diverse skills who are ready to work hard.

Our ability to adapt is embedded in the corn. We have always been scientists or engaged in a scientific process when we grew our corn. Historically, our people were agriculturalists. Our knowledge wasn't stored in a textbook or in a library. Our knowledge was passed along by the community, and we learned how to communicate with nature and interact with nature in a reciprocal and respectful manner. This ability allowed us to continually adapt as we moved to different landscapes and continued to grow our corn.

While thinking about our past, present, and future, I created a cornhusk doll that embodied this span of time. This doll represents both our past and our future. She wears a traditional calico overdress, beaded wool skirt and leggings, and leather center-seam moccasins. Under one arm, she carries a braid of white corn. In addition to these traditional components, she carries a backpack and a math and science textbook in her other arm. On top of her head rests a pair of sunglasses. She represents our community today by showing how we can value knowledge from the past and present. But she also celebrates that we are finally being valued as doctors, scientists, and researchers, when these characteristics have always been traits of our ancestors. She represents our community today. Our culture was never meant to be preserved in a drop of sap and hardened into amber. We are an adaptive people, making use of available technology, all while doing our very best to celebrate our culture. In the cornhusk doll, we see our ability to adapt.

CHAPTER 15

Ohutu Yukwatkattuhati

(We All Are Looking to Our Future)

NE· YAKʌ LATUHÁKWE THAT OUR ANCESTORS WERE FORCED TO LAY DOWN SO much including our language, culture, agricultural practices, and cooking methods. Ne· yakʌ latuhákwe that we are the product of federal assimilation policies and repeated attempts to erase us. In spite of that history, we see a future where our community is at the helm. We are continuing to pick up those practices our ancestors had to lay down. When I interviewed Oneida community members for this book, one of the questions was, "What do you see for the future of white corn in our community?" This was an opportunity for our community to share our visions for what we wanted to see in our collective future. Our answers are realistic and hopeful at the same time. This chapter contains a chorus of our voices to paint a vivid picture for what we all anticipate our future to look like.

DOUBT FOR THE FUTURE

Despite the efforts I've described here and the numerous previous efforts that different departments within the Oneida organization have engaged in, some people have an understandably pessimistic view of the future of corn in our community. Kyle Wisneski dedicates his career to working with the white corn and has undertaken numerous initiatives to support and encourage families to garden more. He explains his rationale for not having an optimistic view of the future.

> Unfortunately, I don't see white corn in our community growing anytime soon. And by growing, I mean expanding. There is an opportunity that kind of slipped through the community's hands just recently. A family had an opportunity to kind of take over a farmstead and start their own little farm, but there's just no interest in the community for that farmstead. I think it's concerning. The knowledge of our white corn is at its highest peak. Even though more and more people know about it, I don't see anyone really jumping up, wanting to grow the white corn. I see the people wanting to eat it and be around it, which is great. I don't see people growing a whole lot in the future. I've had over thirty-five youth come through the farm over the last ten years, and I haven't been able to retain one. That's concerning for me. Our farm is not a conventional farm. You're not shoveling manure every day or working with cattle every day. It's a fun farm. I just have a hard time understanding why we can't retain farmers in our community. I don't see any family besides my son here who has really been interested in seed saving or farming or organic farming or food in general.[1]

Along similar lines, young elder Brian Doxtator noticed the current resurgence of growing corn in our community but expressed a concern that it may be a fad.

> People started to move back, and they wanted to get into gardening because they thought it was cool. It was another fad. Then Tsyunhéhkwʌ started taking off, which is kind of a remnant of the Iroquois Farms concept. They started and they got real big, and then all of a sudden they started to drop off. Pat Cornelius used to plant a field of white corn and never tell anybody where it was. When it was time to harvest, she put out the word, and if you

> wanted some, you could come harvest what you needed. My grandmother would always send me over to go get as much as we could for our own selves. When Pat retired, that ended too. I see the whole gardening, farming, and agriculture thing taking off again. I just hope this time it isn't a fad. I hope it actually continues. I don't care how many studies are done in the world, everybody points back to the fact that the food that you were genetically able to process and digest is the best food for you. It's also good for your mindset and spirituality. That's really where we need to go back to.[2]

Our community has a huge responsibility to make sure we continue on the path of growing more corn. It will not always be easy. It will not always be glorious. It will certainly not always be fun. To ensure this resurgence is not a fad, we must make commitments to our children, to ourselves, and to our community. We need to continue to grow and plant more corn until it truly becomes part of our daily lives. We also need to find ways to include corn in the food we make to ensure she fulfills her responsibility as our sister.

Listening to the Grandparents

Many of the people described the way that they feel connected to our corn sister. She is our relative. Our past, present, and future are intertwined. Just as we are finding ways to pick up what our ancestors had to lay down, our corn is also being picked up. More people of us are growing her and consuming her to heal our bodies and minds. As Deacon Deborah Heckel pointed out, we are dormant seeds. "I think things that have come down the generations are somehow instilled in us," she said. "As the generations go, even if they have only seen it and didn't participate in it, they knew that grandma used to do that. I think that it's another seed that is there. I believe that seed will begin to start to sprout within family members that have been a part of past generations. That's how it came to me later in life. Things don't come to us until we are ready for them."[3]

Chaz Wheelock talked about how we need to understand how our future is tied to that of the corn.

> The white corn speaks to us in a lot of ways. It's a metaphor for a lot of things about our growth and of our relationships with each other. It doesn't exist just by itself. The future of white corn is a reflection of the future of ourselves. It's about who we are and where we fit as Indigenous people among our alliances and networks with other efforts of a similar nature. It's beyond the Indigenous world, because we are realizing more and more the world is rather finite. What we do to it has impacts beyond just our immediate generations.[4]

Artley Skenandore, Oneida Nation High School principal, described how he helped make sure the kids were able to eat more corn and local foods.

> Here at the high school, we are looking at how to get more agriculturally engaged at the school. We got a group of students that are doing aquaponics right now. We have a goal of getting more of our food in a partnership with Tsyunhéhkwʌ and with the Farms for the number of buffalo and grass-fed beef we consume as a part of our daily diet in the school system. When I first came to the high school, we were under, I would say about 3 percent of food we were getting from local growers and from the stuff we grew ourselves. Now we are right around 30 percent, and we just keep moving and expanding.[5]

Even though schools in Oneida are making more efforts to make traditional foods available to students, this was not always the case. Carol Cornelius talked about how there was a time when seemingly no one valued that type of knowledge or education. Now, students are talking about how they remembered their grandmothers planting gardens. In turn, the adults have a responsibility to take our children into the gardens and teach them. Carol said:

> I just see our future with growing our food getting stronger and stronger. I see people expecting it to happen more and wanting to learn. Sometimes I

> run into people and think, "Well, they're going to put this down," or "they're not gonna want to learn more about our culture." Instead, they tell me how they remember grandma said something once and they start that reconnecting. Our ancestors kept all of that, and even though it was not valued by the church, by the U.S. government, or by the schools, they still kept that knowledge. We need to just keep working with our kids because there's so much that pulls them away from our culture. The big part is just doing it by example. "Get out there and plant corn with me." Tell them you don't care if they want to do something else, they're going to plant corn today.[6]

It has become increasingly important to hear the messages our corn brings to us. We have a long history with corn, and she stood by our side even when we were not able to or failed to appreciate her gifts. We have again learned the lesson of being thankful for her presence and helping her fulfill her responsibilities. When we look to the future, we also look to our future generations and hope to instill in them a respect and appreciation for our sister the corn.

Many of the people who talked about the future looked to the youth in our community. The youth are going to be the ones to inherit the fruits of our continued efforts to again celebrate our sister the corn and make her part of our daily lives again. Oneida elder Carol Cornelius described how she recently went to the longhouse and saw four generations sitting together. This was especially meaningful to Carol because she remembered being a part of the revival of our language and culture in the 1970s. "I'm seventy now and I can look back over generations and see what it takes to revive all of this," she said. "When we were in our twenties, we started to learn all of our ways and our language. Marj Stevens and I were in that original group that went to Canada to learn the original ceremonies. Marj's daughter Toni was raised this way. Toni's daughter, Jasmine, and Jasmine's daughter, Sakyrii, both stood up in the longhouse and spoke in the Oneida language. There it is! The perfect example of learning over the generations."[7] One of the people Carol spoke about, Toni House, Ohe·láku member, shared her story about how her children and grandchildren will go to the cornfield someday to be close with her. She said:

> It's really interesting to be with my second generation because I took my kids out to the cornfields. Jessica just wanted to be with me, but Jasmine always made it a great experience. She was on the news and being interviewed. Cole always asked why we had to do it. I said, "Someday, Cole, you're going to come out to this field and it's going to be the only place that you can find your mother. We are creating memories and bonding. You're going to remember those times when you were in the field." Now my daughter has her daughters and I bring them out there. It's really exciting to see them. Bringing my grandbabies out now, they're going to go out to that field someday and remember being out there with their grandma. Those will be fond memories.[8]

Similarly, young elder Chaz Wheelock described the joy in seeing generations of people in the cornfield working and socializing together. "Indigenous people have been saying since before contact that corn is a part of our way," he said. "It's a part of our ideology, religion, and lifestyle. White corn is a pretty interesting crop. When you see people in a field of white corn, there's a joy to see them, particularly the children out there, playing and helping when they can. There's a multigenerational experiential education that's going on."[9]

Laura Manthe, Ohe·láku founding member, talked about the importance of teaching the younger generations about growing our foods because there will come a day when their parents and grandparents can no longer grow foods for themselves. Ohe·láku members humorously remind one another that when we have our young children help in the fields or in the barn, it is not "child labor." Rather, it is "passing on traditions." "Right now, we have all these little people in our group, and we want them to be corn self-sufficient," Laura told me. "We didn't have that as children, so we bring them to these conferences and we teach them hands-on—this is how you plant it, this is how you pick the weeds, this is how you take the husks off, this is how you cook it. Hopefully there will be a day when we can just sit back and watch them do that, because we will be their elders and we won't be able to go out and do everything because of our age."[10]

Most of the people who talked about growing corn expressed an optimistic view of what our future would look like. In addition to more individual families growing in their backyard gardens, more families have been banding together to grow our foods. Randy Cornelius, Bear Clan Faithkeeper, described how growing corn together can help rebuild community connections.

> Corn growing used to be a communal thing. The clans worked together, harvested together, and then distributed all that corn through all the families. It's that group cohesiveness that's coming back together. We have stories from the WPA collection back in '39, and it talks about working bees. Back then, we would just have little farm homesteads. They would go from farm to farm to farm. They would help with the harvesting of the corn or whatever they got. It was community building. That's what I see what the corn growers are doing. It's more family oriented than a business. This is something that your children will grow up with and has been a big part of their life. I think that is just going to fan out more into the community and then come back to individual families doing that on their own as a family.[11]

Similarly, Vickie Cornelius runs the Indigenous Diet and Healing program at Oneida. She teaches community members how to plant and cook our Indigenous foods. Vickie talked about wanting to see more groups get together to help each other grow and harvest our foods.

> I would love to see more people growing white corn and taking a little more personal responsibility. We have to make sure that we have land to be able to do that, whether it's joining a co-op group to do it or growing in a community garden at Tsyunhéhkwʌ. I would love to see more community gardens throughout our reservation where people on the southside have a garden, the northside, the west, the east, they all have their gardens for their

> areas. It's a family thing with an opportunity for social time too. There's just so much relationship building that goes on in a garden.[12]

Other storytellers explained how everyone has a role to play in growing our foods. Jill Ninham, former Tsyunhéhkwʌ employee, talked about how we all have different ways in which we can contribute to the effort of growing corn.

> In the future, I hope to see that the corn is continuing to grow. It will be continuing by communities, families, and even programs in the Oneida Nation. There's no way you can grow it without respecting it, so it's a big teacher. Households will have room for it. There is so much space to grow the corn and to continue the corn. Everybody would benefit, whether they are growing corn or whether somebody next to them is growing corn. It connects people and it strengthens community. Everybody may not be able to grow the corn, but they might be able to cook it, they might be able to seed select, or they may be able to shell it. If they can participate in a part of the corn community, then that will help our community to heal and continue to find balance and wellness.[13]

Parents of Young Children

When talking about corn and the future generations, parents expressed that they are glad that their children are growing up with corn being part of their everyday lives. Jen Falck, Ohe·láku founding member, shared that for the first time in a hundred years, her family was now growing white corn again. All her efforts to relearn are directly benefiting her daughter, who now has the opportunity to grow up with corn as part of her life. "No one in my family has grown corn in probably over a hundred years," Jen shared. "We are raising corn now. We come here and now have a community, own land, have a house, and have a daughter where corn is just part of her life. Corn is not a mystery and it's not something strange that she wished she knew about, like I grew

FIGURE 10. Ohe·láku members Jen Falck, Toni House, and Rebecca Webster with their white corn harvest. Photo credit Tony Kuchma.

up thinking. I did all this muscling to pass this on to a new generation in my family of people who are now familiar with their culture."[14]

Similarly, Jasmine Jimerson, Ohe·láku member, described how her young daughters are developing a deep connection with corn at a young age.

> I feel like I was really rich growing up because I learned a lot about my culture. My girls are way beyond what I have experienced, especially from such a young age. Various people all throughout the confederacy teach them different things and we travel a lot. I didn't know how to sing seed songs and my girls can sing seed songs better than I can. They know a lot more songs than I do. So, we sing these at our traditional ceremonies. When my mother takes them out to the garden to help, they will sing the seed songs while they

> are working or while they are playing. They are pretty good about it. They know that when they are in the garden, that's the time to sing. It's actually really funny because when they are in the garden, they scold each other. If they are being a certain way, they are like, "Shh! They can hear you." I'm pretty proud of them because they really show how much our generations are learning. Even though it seems as though we are learning a lot of things, these younger generations are doing a lot of things that I didn't do, and that my mother didn't do. These things are coming back, and it's slower than we would like, but it's really good that we are starting to have those things in our community again.[15]

I can relate to these experiences because I have two teenage daughters. They have been involved in language and culture classes their whole lives. They have been helping us grow and cook corn and other Indigenous foods for over half their lives. The knowledge they have at their fingertips is knowledge that my husband and I did not have ready access to, even though we both grew up on the Oneida Reservation.

Adapting to Climate Change

Many of the people sharing their stories talked about needing to be prepared for whatever uncertainties the future would bring. They mentioned how returning to our traditional practices would help us survive into the future. In particular, a number of people mentioned climate change. Lois Stevens said she wanted to be a part of helping people adapt to our changing climate.

> For my PhD program, I am studying the impacts that the climate is having on our white corn. Just reading a little bit about it and seeing it for the last few years, it's not only happening now, but it is projected to get a lot warmer and a lot wetter in the future. I really want to understand how we can get ahead of the curve, because we are already behind. Some people are already doing

amazing things to alleviate the stress of the planet, and I think one of my goals is to get that information out there. We are not the only tribe suffering from climate impact, and I want to be another person that tells our story because we have a really unique story to tell.[16]

Steve Webster, Ohe·láku founding member, talked about how climate change or other disasters could impact the price of foods and drive more people to grow their own foods.

In my lifetime, I have watched giants of retail . . . shut down due to a change in how people shop online. These less glitzy/glamorous options often resulted in much cheaper prices, and once folks became comfortable buying online and the tools around them supported them buying online, it was game over for [the retail giants]. I'd like to think that as climate change continues to cause chaos and cash-cropping farming practices reach their unsustainable limit, food prices will increase. I believe food prices in the future will reach a point where the idea of growing/producing your own food will actually make economic sense. That a generation, sick of running the rat race at the cost of their health and time with loved ones just to afford to eat, will look for other solutions. The infrastructure changes for them are being created now with the cost of childcare and elderly who can no longer afford to retire will act as a method to really challenge this way of life. I feel that us preserving that knowledge, spreading that knowledge, keeping those seeds, selecting the ones that do the best as the climate changes, will once again be the foundation that the future generation will need in order to transition back to our corn. The same way those retailers lost their control due to e-commerce, I think growing our own will do that to the grocery stores.[17]

I conducted these interviews in 2018 and 2019, a year before the onset of the COVID-19 pandemic. It would be interesting to see how their answers would have changed or not changed had I asked these questions a year or two later. At our home, my husband and I shared Yukwanuhsyu·ní corn, bean, squash, and sunflower seeds with several dozen Oneida community members in the spring of 2020 and again in the spring of 2021 and 2022. We arranged porch trades with community members to ensure we followed proper social distancing protocols. The *New York Times* even covered a bit of those efforts in a piece titled "How Native Americans Are Fighting a Food Crisis."[18] Most of the people who came to get seeds from us never grew our traditional foods before. In that regard, many of the predictions of our community members that more people would grow our corn in the future came true sooner than they likely expected.

Inspiring and Helping Future Generations

Most of the people in our community are familiar with growing and harvesting white corn because of the annual husking bee held at Tsyunhéhkwʌ. Iris Hill, daughter of the late Jeff Metoxen, Tsyunhéhkwʌ director, and Jasmine Jimerson, Ohe·láku member, talked about wanting to inspire others to grow gardens. "Families coming together and working as a small community to continue what is always meant to be done is so cool and really inspiring," Iris said. "That is what my dad always talked about is his goal working at Tsyunhéhkwʌ. It was our goal to continue the traditional practices so we could teach other people and work together so that they could start doing it for themselves."[19] Similarly, Jasmine talked about our co-op.

> I hope people will be inspired by even our small group of corn growers. I hope we inspire groups of corn growers who are able to work together. I would like to see it branch off and have more community gardens and individual gardens. I think that our community is rich because we have different sources for our corn. More people have access to our corn. Also, if something bad happens, we have sources to find it. I want us to have seed banks so it's as spread out as possible. That's what I hope for.[20]

Marlon Skenandore, Oneida Food Pantry manager, recently started a garden at the pantry and talked about wanting to be a part of the corn movement in our community.

> I feel like it's going to grow. I feel like we're right on the cusp and there's a lot of people talking about it. A lot of different groups are trying to do it. I see a lot of different small plots in the community all over the place. I think it'll grow, and I'm hoping it does. We shouldn't have to go buy our corn from the Senecas or anybody else. We should just grow our own. I would say it's nice to see the resurgence of it all. You see so many different community members out there starting to grow it. I feel like I just want to be a part of that wave too. I'm just here to learn, and it's fairly early for me too. I went to school here and learned about that connection. When you're younger, it doesn't resonate with you. Then you get older one day and you're like, "Wow, this stuff they were teaching us, it does make a lot of sense." I was glad to have gone to school here and have all that knowledge before I actually got into [working with our foods]. Then, it really connected. I just want to try to learn as much as I can and go from there and see what the future holds.[21]

In addition to inspiring others to either grow their own food or form groups to help each other, the hands-on experience with corn can also bring new perspectives when we eat dishes that include corn. Lea Zeise, Ohe·láku founding member, talked about making better connections among our existing corn growers and consumers to gain an understanding of what it takes to grow corn.

> There is a lot of opportunity there to get people to start growing their own corn or supporting others who are growing corn to gain access to it. There is just a lack of connection that is happening. There is a lot of corn in the community that is available, but the vast majority of it is at Tsyunhéhkwʌ. People are constantly looking to fill those shelves and make sure that people

> have access to it. There's also a small stockpile in our group that could also be reaching people. There are members in our group that don't eat that much corn, and there could be connections there with more under the wingers that come into the group. If you don't know how much work it is to grow and harvest corn, you could think it could have come here from anywhere. We know it takes three hours just to pick and husk and braid one braid of corn. It's a pretty intensive process. I think we are really attached to it for that reason. If other people had that same attachment, they would treat the corn differently. They would probably fill up their bowls of soup differently.[22]

While most people spoke about community responsibility and the work that goes into growing our corn, a couple people mentioned how the Oneida government could do more to encourage community members to grow more corn and other Indigenous foods. Ernie Stevens III, Ohe·láku member and elected Business Committee member, proposed how different areas in the tribe could work together.

> In the future, I see at least a few dozen more families who got at least some kind of a garden. I see they will be learning how to expand. They will be starting to realize they can do more. People will say we don't have enough land, so we can only grow so much corn. I see that being potentially a good problem for the Nation, Land Commission, and Tsyunhéhkwʌ. People will come to them and tell them they want to do this. They will ask how they can do this. We will communicate and collaborate in this effort. That's the way I see it happening. We will have a sustainable system where people know what they can handle. They will know what's available for land. They will know what can be done so they can plan.[23]

Similarly, Lois Stevens explained how she would like to see more land used to grow corn. "I would like to see a certain percentage of tribal land dedicated to growing white corn instead of leasing out our land to other farmers," she said. "The tribe has invested in white corn significantly, I just don't feel like we should be leasing our land to others, especially non-Native farmers. We should be investing in that land."[24]

These sentiments are in line with current efforts to encourage more community members to lease tribal land to grow food. I serve on the Oneida Land Commission, an elected body responsible for making land acquisition and land use decisions on behalf of the Nation. We are continuing to work on ways to make smaller parcels of land available to individuals and co-ops at reduced or no cost. We are also working on ways to remove barriers to leasing smaller parcels of land, such as credit checks and lengthy agricultural plans that might not be relevant on a small-scale operation.

Young Adults Share Their Hopes

Corn has been with us since creation. She served as a staple for our people since the beginning. When talking about the future in our community, many people talked about how they hoped to see a revival of foods made with our Indigenous foods. Young adults all shared their hopes of bringing back more corn in our diets in the future. Lexi Levinson, Oneida Community member, emphasized how we need to continue to be mindful. "The more I learn about gardening, the more I learn about people who garden throughout the confederacy," she said. "It's like every year they are getting bigger. So, we are doing something right. I think that as long as we keep making an effort to do it and we keep being mindful of what we are doing, it could be really amazing. We need to make sure that we continue showing so much love and respect for the corn, and it will turn out really awesome."[25] Ruby Kuchma, daughter of Jen Falck and Tony Kuchma, predicted corn would become more important. "Growing the corn is good because you get to see how it's made and it's fun and it's not just one part of it, you get to do all of it," Ruby explained. "At harvest time, everyone just comes out and picks corn. At home now we have a bigger garden. I think growing corn will become more important as we keep doing it."[26] Similarly, one of my daughters, Grace Webster, looks forward to following more corn recipes.

> I see more people having their little gardens at their homes. I hope more people will join corn groups and even form their own groups to help each other out. People will be making more corn dishes at family and community events. I hope people start to share more recipes on how to cook corn so that we can try different ways to eat it. I hope those people that are new to growing our foods will start off with growing corn will then participate in more cultural events.[27]

My other daughter, Amelia Webster, spoke about bringing the community together. "I noticed that people are starting to understand the benefits of growing our traditional foods," she said. "Growing corn can connect you with your family and your ancestors. Gardening can put your mind at ease. More people are going to try growing it and it will bring the community together. We will trade more with each other and help each other out. I think we will be healthier because of it. Gardening is more work than going to the store and buying your food."[28] Ernest Stevens IV also looks forward to more community gatherings and sharing meals. "In the future, I see lots of people eating healthier because there's probably going to be more people growing corn in the future and over the years," he said. "I see us being more healthy, natural foods that was brought from way back, generations ago. That food helped bring us here today."[29]

In response to some of these young people's interest in having more ways to cook our foods, and in recognition of all the ways the past and present people in our community cook our corn, I included an appendix to this book. It contains a wide array of recipes to help in meeting the goal of incorporating more corn into our daily diets. The recipes span from those found in the accounts of the early European explorers to modern recipes from the community. There are even a number of recipes from the early 1900s that come from the Works Progress Administration (WPA) stories.

Perhaps one of the most powerful statements about bringing back traditions of growing corn came from a young Oneida man, Kwnwahta Smith. He succinctly described our history and talked about how we are going to move peacefully into the future, prepared to grow our food and celebrate our language.

> They tried to erase our culture. They tried to erase our history. They tried to erase us in general. We are still standing, and we are struggling because of their attempts to erase us. We are making progress because we are warriors bringing back our food, bringing back our culture, bringing back our ways. We are up against oppression, colonialism, imperialism. This is a fight for our ancestors and for our next seven generations. We are warriors, not with guns or war clubs, but with farming tools and our language.[30]

Our young people are going to be the corn growers and chefs of tomorrow. If the words of these storytellers is anything to go by, it seems our future is in good hands. We need to continue to protect and nurture our corn just as we do our children. We also need to continue to plan for the future to make sure it is secure for our children and the corn.

Ukwakhwa: Tsinu Niyukwayayʌthoslu (Our Foods: Where We Plant Things)

In 2017, our family purchased ten acres of vacant agricultural land. One portion of the land had been used as a recreational paintball field and was littered with dilapidated wooden structures, large plastic barrels, and over two thousand tires. We had the soil tested and found that previous conventional farmers had

FIGURE 11. Rebecca and Steve Webster by their farmstead sign, Ukwakhwa: Tsinu Niyukwayayʌthoslu (Our Foods: Where We Plant Things). Photo credit Stephanie Stevens.

not taken good care of the soil. We had a lot of work ahead of us and lots of ideas about how we could help celebrate our plant relatives.

With much help from family and friends, we built a farmstead. We also began to lay out our goals of serving as a place to host events where the community comes to learn about planting, growing, harvesting, seed keeping, food preparation, food storage, as well as making traditional tools and crafts. With these goals in mind, Oneida Faithkeeper Leander Danforth named our property Ukwakhwa: Tsinu Niyukwayayʌthoslu (Our Foods: Where We Plant Things). While our house was still under construction, we began to plant our expanded gardens. Our focus was on growing Yukwanuhsyu·ní varieties of corn, beans, squash, sunflowers, tobacco, and sunchokes. We also planted a number of different berries as well as fruit and nut trees. We recently built a kitchen to help the community have more access to Indigenous foods and to build their skills and confidence to process their own foods. To assist in our outreach and educational efforts, we started a YouTube channel, Ukwakhwa, and formed a 501(c)(3) nonprofit organization, Ukwakhwa Inc. We are just getting started on this new journey and are excited to see what the future will bring.

Conclusion

Our house is quite a busy place. People are always coming and going to see what we are up to. On one particularly busy day right before harvest was about to start up, we started the day by filming how we hull corn. My cousin and his wife were over to help. We had cameras set up and we were just having a great time cooking, hulling, and washing the corn. Then, another cousin and her husband stopped over for a while to visit to talk about our fall harvest. Then, my great-aunt brought her granddaughter and great-grandson over to our house to visit because they were in town from out east. It was a really great day and everyone was excited about what we were all doing with the corn.

After everyone left, the house was very quiet. My husband and I were talking about our future plans for our property and our foods. A little while later, I went outside into the garage to look for something. When I was out there, I looked up, and for a split second I saw a tall, thin man standing about fifteen feet in front of me. He was wearing a red, light jacket and dark pants. He had short dark hair. I didn't see him long enough to see his face, but I recognized him as Oneida. Anyone who has watched scary movies likely placed themselves in the movies and guessed at how they would react if something scary or supernatural happened to them. I always assumed I would either puke or scream if I saw something like that. I was surprised first at seeing this man, and second by my reaction to him. I wasn't at all frightened. I had the sense that he was just curious and wanted to see what was going on. We asked Bob Brown to come over and do a tobacco burning to explain what we were doing and to help anyone that might be hanging on so they can move along.

Looking back at this experience, I wonder if it was to show me why we do the work we do. I always have my vision set on the future and what this will mean to my daughter's generation and beyond. They will grow up with corn, culture, and language as part of their daily lives. They will not have to struggle to learn these things as adults. They will not have to be embarrassed because they don't know about our people or our ways. This experience taught me that maybe we do this work for those who have come before us who didn't have an opportunity to learn these things. They lived in a time when they were punished for speaking our language and practicing our ceremonies. They were deprived of our culture. I think they are taking notice of what our community is doing, and they are happy. They might be a little scared because of how they were brought up and the world they lived in, but I have to hope that a larger part of their thoughts is rejoicing that our people are free to be ourselves again. We can celebrate our corn, bean, and squash sisters again.

Our community painted a hopeful future that included more gardens and co-operative work while recognizing all the work that others had done to make that possible and that not all who came before us had the luxury to openly celebrate their culture. The future our community painted included more meals served with corn as a staple along with beans and squash. The people I interviewed expressed both hope and caution for what the unknown days ahead would bring. One thing is for certain: our corn is rejoicing in her return. We are relying on her now more than we have in recent times. She is resuming her place alongside us in our daily lives. She is continually demonstrating why we call her precious. We need to protect and care for her, and in turn she will care for and protect us. With that, I will end with a portion of the closing address as recited by Mohawk elder Tom Porter:

FIGURE 12. Harvest at the Ukwakhwa farmstead in 2021.

And then our Creator, when the world was new, planted for us the gardens and the vegetables that grow in the gardens. And the Creator chose the corn to be the leader of all the vegetables. He chose the beans to be number two. And then he chose the squashes and the pumpkin, the vines, to be a third leader of all the vegetables that grow in the gardens. And right now it is the middle of summer. And the gardens in my community are growing. They already are producing potatoes. They are already producing beans. They're already producing corn that we're eating. And so it is that the gardens grow that are the testimony, and we are the witnesses, of our Creator's wonderful world.

And so to the leaders, the Corn, the Beans, and the Squash, who represent all the vegetables that grow in all people's gardens, we the people today are of one mind. We send our greetings, our thankfulness and our love to the spirit of every Vegetable Plant that grows in our gardens, that brings nourishment to our bodies. We say thank you to them and to our Creator for that wonderful plan. And our mind is agreed.[31]

APPENDIX

Tsi Twakhunihe

(How We Cook Our Foods)

THIS APPENDIX CONTAINS RECIPES AND COOKING METHODS FROM A VARIETY of sources including notes from the early explorers, journals of Sullivan and his officers, WPA stories, as well as recipes from current Yukwanuhsyu·ní chefs. These recipes and cooking methods are organized into seven main categories: Green Corn, Green Cornbread, Hulled Cornbread, Soups and Stews with Hulled Corn, Casseroles, Mush, and Drinks. For each recipe and cooking method, this chapter cites the person providing the recipe or cooking source, the person's role, and the year of the recipe or cooking method. Since this book is not primarily a cookbook, most of these recipes haven't been professionally tested. If you decide to try them, be ready to adapt them to your preference.

GREEN CORN

There are basically two windows of time to pick corn: one is when the corn is still in its milky stage, and the other is when the sugars in the corn have turned to starch and there is no more milk in the kernels. The corn in its milky stage is called green corn. There are also a variety of corn types including sweet corn, dent corn, flint corn, flour corn, popcorn, and grandfather (pod) corn. There is also some debate over whether the most common type of corn in the Oneida community, Tuscarora white corn, is truly a flint corn or a flour corn. Debates aside, when Yukwanuhsyu·ní people cook their corn at the green corn stage, it is likely a sweet corn, a flint corn, or a flour corn. Even though the flint and flour corns turn starchy as they ripen and dry in the fields, when picked before they ripen, they have a sweet taste comparable to sweet corn. The cooking methods in this section describe basic cooking and preservation methods for green corn including green corn soup. There are several variations on green cornbread, so I included a separate section for that.

Roasted Corn, Arthur Parker, Seneca Anthropologist, 1910

This was the husked ear of green corn baked in hot embers. It is related that one of the old methods was to dig a long trench and place the ears across two slender green saplings and allow the heat of the hot coals to cook the corn. The ears could easily be turned over and the roasting made uniform.

Sometimes a husked ear of corn was encased in clay and baked. This was called Ogágoäḱwa or gago^{n}dūk. For roasting ears singly [one at a time] a sharpened stick was shoved into the stem and the ear held in the embers.

If kernels of the corn prepared in this way were sufficiently dried and parched, the entire ear or the shelled kernels were capable of long preservation. The writer [Parker] has found roasted corn on the cob, several centuries old, buried in pits that evidently once had been bark lined cellarettes. Parched shelled kernels are commonly found in caches in Indian village or lodge sites.[1]

Drying Sweet Corn, David Skenandore, WPA Collection, 1941–1942

Sweet corn is preserved by cooking green corn, and then you shell it and place the corn on the cloth, which makes it convenient to pick up if it is placed outside in sun. It can also be dried right in an oven, but it is more convenient outside if you have lots to dry. After it is thoroughly dry, you can put the corn in the paper bag or flour bag, which keeps it free from dust and flies, and it is put away for winter use; this makes a very wholesome food to eat during winter. This corn can be cooked with dried pumpkin, which makes a wonderful gruel. Small pieces of salt pork can be cut into it to add flavor, and it's incomparable to any other.[2]

Green Corn Soup, Guy Elm, WPA Collection, 1941–1942

This sweet corn, the Oneida women used to cook and dry it while the corn was still green and tender, then it's stored away to be used during the winter. This dried sweet corn makes a swell soup. When the women want to make a kettle of this kind of soup, they soak the corn in the water overnight, and in the morning it is ready to be put in the kettle. They let it boil for about thirty minutes, then they drain the water from it. The corn is washed with fresh clean water. The water is then put in the kettle with corn, and any kind of meat can be put in there to give the soup the right flavor. The soup is boiled again for about one hour. The soup is now ready to be eaten. And take it from me, it sure is good to eat. This used to be one of the favorite soups for the Oneidas at one time years ago, and the older Oneida people still dry the sweet corn for future use.[3]

Cracked Green Corn Soup, Nelson B. Cornelius's Wife, WPA Collection, 1938–1941

The different kinds of food, which the old-time people prepared for themselves is done away with. Take for instance cracked dried corn and pumpkins cooked together, which was made in soup form. It is sure a good meal to cook up. Fine one to eat. This cracked dried corn is cooked alone with meat, or if one desires to put milk with it, tastes good that way too. Cracked dried corn when cooked up changed its name. Onu·gáhle is a pumpkin. When the Indians used to hunt a lot of game, a hunter would often fill his pocket with cracked dried corn, and while hunting he would now and then eat a handful of the corn for his lunch; this would keep him from getting hungry while being out all day long in the woods.[4]

Green Cornbread

There are a number of ways to use green corn to make bread including boiling, frying, baking, using ashes or coals, and even drying the bread out for use later in the winter months.

Early Bread, Arthur Parker, Seneca Anthropologist, 1910

Before the corn was thoroughly dry in the autumn, it was plucked for making early bread. The unhulled corn was mixed with a little water in a mortar and beaten to a paste instead of a meal. Loaves were molded by the hands from the paste and boiled. This bread was considered a great delicacy and valued especially as a food for invalids.[5]

Leaf Bread Tamales, Arthur Parker, Seneca Anthropologist, 1910

This is prepared from green corn. The kernels are cut or scraped from the cob and beaten to a milky paste in a mortar. The corn used for leaf cake tamales should be too hard for green corn good for boiling and eating on the cob. The paste will then be of the proper consistency. The paste is patted into shape and laid in a strip on one end of a broad corn leaf, the free half being doubled over the paste. Other leaves are folded over the first, the ends all projecting uniformly from one end for tying. The oniắtcídắ was then tied three times laterally and once transversely and dropped into boiling water. When cooked (cooking requires about 45 minutes), the wrappings are removed and the cake is eaten with sunflower or bear oil, though in these modern days bacon grease or butter are more in vogue. Oftentimes, cooked beans are mixed with the mass before wrapping in the leaves. These impart their flavor and give variety.

Leaf cakes may be dried for winter's use if no beans have been used with the corn. In wrapping the leaf bread a bulbous shaped bundle is made resembling a large braid of hair doubled and tied, hence the name oniắtcídắ, derived from yēnyắtcídot, doubled braid of woman's hair.[6]

Fried Green Corn, Arthur Parker, Seneca Anthropologist, 1910

This dish was prepared by scraping the green corn, in the milk, from the cob, mashing it in a mortar and either patting it into cakes or tossing it in a basket to make a loose light mass. The corn was then ready for frying. The older Indians say that the frying could be done in a clay kettle and that corn so prepared was especially good if cooked in bear oil.[7]

Green Cornbread, Alma Thomas, WPA Collection, 1941–1942

Take green, white Indian corn and cut the kernels in half on the cob (this makes the corn finer), then you cut or scrape all the corn off the cob. Then butter a bread tin and put this corn mixed with salt, pepper, and red kidney beans, and bake for one (1) hour in a moderate oven.[8]

Green Cornbread, Mrs. Joshua Skenandore, WPA Collection, 1938–1941

(Skenandore described a very similar version using young beans. While she mentioned "frying" the bread, it seems she placed the cake pan of bread in the oven. It may be that the use of oil under the bread was the reason she described the method as "frying.")

Boil some young beans. Then scrape the green corn off some young Indian corn (white flint corn) and use a knife to scrape off the corn. Then mix the corn and beans. And you throw a little bit of salt. Then you stir it. Put some grease in a baking pan. Then you'll put it in and fry it for maybe one hour. Then you'll remove the bread and cool it. Then you will slice it and butter it for yourself. Boy, that's good tasting bread.[9]

Baked Scraped Green Corn Using Ashes, Arthur Parker, Seneca Anthropologist, 1910

The green corn is scraped from the cob with a deer's jaw or knife, pounded in a mortar or mashed in a wooden bowl with a stone, patted into cakes, sprinkled with dry meal and baked in small dishes. For baking in the ashes the cakes are wrapped in husk and covered with ashes. Embers are heaped over and a brisk fire built, this being kept going until the cakes were considered baked.[10]

Baked Green Corn Using Coals, Arthur Parker, Seneca Anthropologist, 1910

When the milk has set, Tuscarora and sweet corn is scraped from the cob and beaten to a paste in a mortar. This should be done just before the evening meal. After the housework is finished, the housewife lines a large kettle with basswood leaves three deep. The corn paste is then dumped in up to two-thirds the depth of the vessel. The top is smoothed down and covered by three layers of leaves. Cold ashes to a finger's depth are now thrown over the leaves and smoothed down. a small fire is built under the kettle which hangs suspended from a crane or tripod. Glowing charcoal is placed on the ashes at the top. The small fire is kept brisk and the coals at the top renewed three times. The cook may now retire for the night if her kettle hangs in a shielded place or in a fire pit. In the morning the ashes and top leaves are carefully removed and the baked corn dumped out. The odor of this steaming ogońsă [baked green corn] is most appetizing and it is eaten greedily with grease or butter. For winter's use the caked mass is sliced and dried in the sun all day, taken in at night to prevent dew from spoiling it and dogs or night prowlers from taking too much of it, and set out again in the morning to allow the sun to complete the drying. The ogońsă is then ready to be stored away for the winter. When ready for use, the winter's store of ogońsă was taken from storage and a sufficient quantity for a meal, thrown in cold water and immediately put on the stove. Boiling for a little more than a half hour produces a delicious dish. Ogońsă was one of the favorite foods of the Iroquois and remains so to this day. An Onondaga or Seneca can hardly mention the name without showing that it brings memories of the pleasant repasts that it has afforded.

In recent years the corn paste is prepared with a potato masher in a chopping bowl, or by running the corn as cut from the cob through a food chopper. Baking is done in shallow dripping pans in the oven. The food so prepared, however, lacks a deliciousness that makes the older method still popular.[11]

HULLED CORNBREAD

There are a number of recipes for bread made from hulled corn, especially in the WPA stories. There are three main ways to make this bread. The most common is to boil the formed cakes in water. Another way is to cook the formed cakes in ashes near a fire. The last way is to cook the formed cakes wrapped in corn husks. In all cases, the person preparing the bread first cooks the corn in ashes to remove the outer hull of the kernels. After cooking the corn in ashes, they wash and rinse the corn in clean water to remove the ashes and the hulls.

Cornbread, Elizabeth Doxtator, WPA Collection, 1938–1941

This is the way that I used to take care of myself a long time ago. Whenever I wanted cornbread for breakfast, then the day before I would cook my corn in ashes and wash it several times. Then I would keep my corn in the basket and hang it up to drain all the extra moisture out of the corn until the following morning. The following morning I would get up about 4 o'clock a.m. and I would pulverize the corn. Pulverizing the corn is hard work. You have to pound the corn and sift it. Then I put my loaves of bread into the boiling water for one hour. By that time maybe my husband is ready to haul pails and cans to the barn so we can milk the cows. By the time the milking is done, then my bread is also done too. We eat the hot cornbread and the broth of the cornbread.[12]

Cornbread, Alma Thomas, WPA Collection, 1941–1942

(Alma Thomas provided a recipe for cornbread that contained measurements. From personal experience, using boiling water to moisten the flour is essential.

If the water is not hot enough, your bread might break up when you cook it in the boiling water.)

Take six (6) quarts of white Indian corn and boil with three (3) cups of wood ashes and five (5) quarts of water for about twenty (20) minutes or until the corn starts to peel. Then you take a basket (a basket made especially for this corn) and pour the corn into it, then rinse it five or six times. This makes the corn real white. Then you take a meat grinder and grind the corn several times until you can put it through a fine sieve. This makes the corn about as fine as flour. Then you take about three quarters (3/4) of a quart of red kidney beans and mix with this corn flour, then pour enough boiling water into this to be able to shape it. Shape into round loaves. After the loaves are made, you put them into about ten quarts of boiling water, enough water to cover them, then let them boil steady for one (1) hour. This recipe makes five loaves of Indian cornbread.[13]

Dumplings, Arthur Parker, Seneca Anthropologist, 1910

Moisten a mass of cornmeal with boiling water and quickly mold it into cakes in the closed hand moistened in cold water. Drop the dumplings one by one into boiling water and boil for a half hour.

Dumplings were the favorite thing to cook with boiling meats, especially game birds. To fish the dumplings from the pot every one had a sharpened stick or bone. The dumplings were speared and held on the stick to cool and nibbled with the meat as it was eaten. The sticks after use were wiped off and stuck between the logs or bark of the wall for future use.

Many of the sharpened splinters of bone now excavated from village and camp sites are probably nothing more than these primitive forks, or more properly food holders. Oho^{ń}stă̄ was one of the foods of which children were very fond; nor did grown people despise it as a bread with their meat.[14]

Berry Kanʌstóhale, Rebecca M. Webster, 2018

I heard stories about people making cornbread with berries and maple syrup, but couldn't find any recipes, so I decided to experiment based on the typical cornbread recipes. To make this, you need to first get a kettle of water boiling. Here are the ingredients:

- 3 cups frozen berries (strawberries, blueberries, raspberries, etc.)
- 1 cup maple syrup
- 5 cups hulled white corn flour

Thaw out and heat up the berries and maple syrup before mixing each into the flour. Having hot ingredients helps make sure your cakes don't break apart in the water. Then add about 1 cup of boiling water. Mix it up. Shape the mixture into little cakes or little balls and boil them for 20 minutes. Serve hot with maple syrup or maple sugar. Save the water for drinking. We call the leftovers water samp.

Hulled Cornbread Cooked in Ashes, Elizabeth Huff, WPA Collection, 1938–1941

(Cooking the hulled cornbread in ashes begins similar to the process for boiling, except instead of placing the corn in the boiling water, the person cooking the bread places it in ashes. The heat from the ashes cooks the corn.) When you finish the dough, it will be about the size of a small saucer and then we put it under the ashes (dirt) for a short while; usually one mixes it with the ashes. Then you turn it over. When it is cooked, then you use a wet cloth and wipe off the ashes, and then you eat it.[15]

Hulled Cornbread Cooked in Coals, David Skenandore, WPA Collection, 1941–1942

Baking was done outside in open fire by placing dough under hot coals. The fire is being spread open in center of the fire bed and then dough is placed there, covered over with hot coals. This bread bakes just as good as in an oven. When this bread is done, then it is taken out of the fire and a knife is used to scrape the coals off until clean again.[16]

Wedding Bread, Arthur Parker, Seneca Anthropologist, 1910

Corn was prepared in the same manner as for bread but was wrapped in two balls with a short connecting neck like a handleless dumbbell wrapped in corn husk and tied in the middle. It was then ready for boiling. To complete the cooking required about one hour.

Twenty-four of these cakes were taken by the girl's maternal grandmother (by blood or by clan appointment, if the maternal grandmother was dead) to the door of the maternal grandmother of an eligible male. The recipient, who had previously conferred with the donor, if she favors the alliance suggested by the gift, tastes the bread and notifies her daughter that her (the daughter's) son is desired to unite with a certain young woman in marriage by the grandmother of that young woman. The mother of the boy must submit to her mother's wish if she can offer no substantial objection. The boy's grandmother then makes 24 wedding cakes and carries them to the girl's grandmother who then notifies her daughter that the girl must marry a certain man. If the suit is rejected at the first proposal, the wedding cakes are left untouched and the humiliated donor must creep back and reclaim the cakes. My informant says the rejected cakes were never eaten, but probably reserved as ammunition with which to pelt the offending old dowager, who had given reasons to believe that the suit was smiled upon. The bounds of a cake recipe forbid further discussion.[17]

Soups and Stews with Hulled Corn

Corn soup is one of the most common dishes using corn. As with all recipes, everyone makes their soup differently. People use a different amount of ashes to remove the hard outer hulls of the kernels of corn, and the amount you use often depends on the potency of the ashes. Once the corn is hulled, there are a wide variety of ways to use it in soups and stews. Ingredients can include different meats, vegetables, nuts, and even apples. People also use wildly different cooking times, with some cooking their corn for less than an hour while others cook their corn for four hours or more.

Corn Soup, Jonas Elm, WPA Collection, 1938–1941

We planted corn in the spring and then cut it in the fall. Then we husked it and dried the corn and made corn soup. When we made corn soup, we usually shelled about four quarts of corn. Then one'll put a kettle on the fire and the ashes are taken out and you put them in the kettle with the corn. Then it will boil for perhaps four hours. Next you remove the kettle and you rewash the corn and boil it again. It should boil until the ashes rinse off. Then you take out the soup and put in meat and salt and cook it until it is done. Then you put on the kettle with beans until it is quite done. Then you throw them in the soup and then you eat. Golly, it tastes so good.[18]

Corn Soup, Guy Elm, WPA Collection, 1941–1942

(Guy Elm described a similar process with special notations about using a special corn-washing basket. His description is also noteworthy because of the commentary that Oneida people kept white corn in storage throughout the year to be able to make this type of soup at any time.)

In making hull corn soup, the corn are shelled from the ears first. It takes about four quarts to make a nice big kettle of soup. Next procedure is to boil the corn with hard wood ashes, maple wood ashes if possible. They boil the corn until the hulls are loose, then they wash the corn several times. The corn is put back on the stove again to boil for about one hour. The corn is washed again with clean water. They used a basket made for that purpose.

The corn is put back in the kettle with fresh water, the beans are put in there, and salt pork. They let this cook together for an hour. The kettle is put aside ready for the hungry young braves, maidens, and the old buck. This kind of soup really comes handy at all times because it's so good and cheap to make it, you can't help but like it.

Most all the Oneidas still make this kind of soup, and they usually have this kind of corn in storage to be used whenever they run short of food.[19]

Corn Soup, Alma Thomas, WPA Collection, 1938–1941

(In describing how to make corn soup, Alma Thomas paid particular attention to the black bit coming off. This is the heart of the corn at the base of the kernel. The older generation says that if you don't get the black eyes off the kernels, that means you are a lazy cook.)

Take three (3) quarts of white Indian corn boil about three quarters (3/4) of an hour with three (3) quarts of water and one and one-half cups of ashes or until the peelings and the heart of the corn kernels which are black come off, then you pour this into a basket and rinse once or twice, then you boil it in water again for about an hour or until the corn looks clean, then rinse four or five times. Then boil the corn with pork ribs or shanks and red kidney beans, for three or four hours until the corn and meat is tender.[20]

Corn Soup with Nut Meats or Sunflower Seeds, Frederick Waugh, Anthropologist, 1916

Nut meats of various kinds may be added to corn soup; beechnuts were given by a Tonawanda informant as a popular ingredient there, also dried apples. The kernels are pounded in the mortar, sifted, and added to the soup, which is stirred from time to time and seasoned with salt and pepper.[21]

Sunflower seeds are pounded and sifted to a fine meal. Soup of ripe corn and beans is prepared in the usual way. The sunflower meal is added, forming a very rich soup. This is also seasoned according to taste.[22]

Venison Stew, Randy Cornelius, Oneida Bear Clan Faithkeeper, 2020

Randy Cornelius's tip for preparing this stew: the longer and slower the boil, the better all the flavors will blend into one heap of big, tasty stew.

Ingredients:

- 2 pounds of venison (or elk, buffalo, beef)
- 4 large carrots
- 1 medium/large rutabaga
- 1 large onion
- 2 tablespoons tomato paste
- ⅔ cups wild rice
- 2 cups hulled Indian corn or green corn
- 1 pound of green beans
- 4 stalks of celery
- 2 large red potatoes (optional)
- 4 cups beef stock
- 1 tablespoon maple syrup

- Salt and pepper, for seasoning meat [spice it up with a couple of shakes of cayenne pepper]
- ½ pound of all-purpose Indian corn flour, for dredging meat in and making baby dumplings
- Sunflower seed oil; for browning meat

Cooking instructions:

- Coat meat with seasoning, then dredge in flour. [Make baby dumplings with leftover flour.]
- Brown meat and diced onion in batches in cast iron with hot oil. Once all meat is brown, add into a larger kettle.
- Wash and chop the veggies and add to meat. Put beef stock and enough water to fully submerge the stew.
- Use herbs for flavoring: 3 springs each of fresh thyme and rosemary chopped **or** 1 tsp. of each dry.
- Add a couple of dashes of Worcestershire sauce, meat spice, and maple syrup. Add 2 more cups of water and bring to a rolling boil.
- Add wild rice and baby dumplings then cook over medium heat for 45 minutes (slow boil).
- Add diced green onions when stew is done.

Venison White Corn Stew, Rebecca M. Webster, 2018

This recipe is based on my mom's famous beef and barley soup. I mostly swapped out beef for venison and barley for white corn, with a few more modifications. We laughed about what to call it because the name "beef and barley soup with no beef and no barley" didn't seem to be a good fit. This is a two-day recipe, but you can start early in the morning if you want this for dinnertime.

Ingredients:

- Venison roast
- 1 packet of French onion soup mix
- 1 packet of ranch dressing mix
- 1 packet of brown gravy mix
- 1 pound of raw white corn
- 2 cups dried beans
- 1 onion
- 6 stalks celery
- 4 garlic cloves
- ¼ stick butter
- 1 bay leaf
- 1 small bag of frozen carrots
- 1 small bag of frozen green beans
- 2 cartons of beef stock
- ½ small can of tomato paste

The day before, prepare the stew according to the following cooking instructions:

- Cube up the venison and brown the cubes in butter in a saucepan.
- Place the venison and juices in a slow cooker. Add the three packets of mixes. Add 1 cup of the beef stock. Cook on low for 4 hours. Refrigerate overnight.
- Hull 1 pound of raw white corn in hardwood ashes. Refrigerate overnight.
- Wash beans. Cover beans by at least 3 inches of water and soak overnight.

The day of, finish the stew:

- Simmer the beans for about an hour until tender.
- Puree one onion, 6 stalks of celery, and 4 garlic cloves.
- Melt ¼ stick of butter in saucepan and add puree. Add bay leaf.

- Simmer on medium heat for about 10 minutes, stirring occasionally.
- Steam carrots and green beans in a separate pot.
- Add the beef stock to the slow cooker, adding more or less stock for desired thickness.
- Add all ingredients to the slow cooker. Set to low. The stew is ready once heated through. Remove the bay leaf.

Three Sisters Soup, Rebecca M. Webster, 2016

This recipe is great any time of year. It is a perfect addition to any event as a vegetarian/vegan option. This is a two-day recipe, but you can start early in the morning if you want this for dinnertime.

Ingredients:

- 1 pound of raw white corn
- 1 cup dry beans
- 1 winter squash
- 1 tomato
- 1 onion
- 2 celery stalks
- 2 garlic cloves
- 1 tsp. basil
- 1tsp. cumin
- 2 parsnips
- 4 carrots
- 2 cartons of vegetable stock

The day before, prepare the soup according to the following cooking instructions:

- Hull 1 pound of raw white corn in hardwood ashes. Refrigerate overnight.

- Wash beans. Cover beans by at least 3 inches of water and soak overnight.
- Cut the squash into cubes.
- Add to a slow cooker and cook overnight on low.

The day of, finish the soup:

- Simmer the beans for about an hour until tender.
- Puree tomato, onion, celery, and garlic.
- Transfer the puree to a cooking pot.
- Add the basil and cumin and simmer for 10 minutes.
- Add 1 carton of vegetable stock to the cooking pot.
- Chop up the parsnips and carrots and add them to the cooking pot. Simmer until tender. This can take an hour or more.
- Puree the squash. Add puree to cooking pot. Add white corn and beans to cooking pot. Add the rest of the vegetable stock, adding more or less for desired thickness.
- Simmer until heated through.

Nut and Corn Stews, John Gottlieb Ernestus Heckewelder, Missionary, 1876

Another very good dish is prepared by boiling with their corn or maize, the washed kernels of shell bark or hickory nut. They pound the nuts in a block or mortar, pouring a little warm water on them, and gradually a little more as they become dry until, at last, there is a sufficient quantity of water so that by stirring up the pounded nuts the broken shells separate from the liquor, which from the pounded kernels assumes the appearance of milk. This being put into the kettle and mixed with the pottage gives it a rich and agreeable flavor. If the broken shells do not all freely separate by swimming on the top or sinking to the bottom, the liquor is strained through a clean cloth before it is put into the kettle.[23]

Casseroles

Another way to prepare our corn is to bake it in a deep casserole dish with a variety of other ingredients.

White Corn Casserole, Brian Doxtator, Oneida Elder, 2020

(Brian Doxtator had been perfecting this recipe since the 1990s.)

Grill and cube a large turkey. Put it in a deep casserole dish. Add 12 cups of hulled corn, 6 sliced zucchini, 6 sliced yellow squash, 2 quarts stewed tomatoes, 2 quarts tomato juice. Stir to combine ingredients. Bake at 275 degrees for three hours.

Mush

Basic mush is typically prepared by parching or toasting mature, dried corn, grinding the corn into flour, and putting the flour in boiling water. A favorite in our house involves putting maple syrup in the water, bringing the water to a boil, and putting the mush flour in the water. I use a 3:1 ratio with 3 cups of water to 1 cup of mush flour. We cook it for about five minutes, then we put different combinations of chocolate chips, peanut butter chips, almonds, and fresh berries in it.

Mush for Babies, Ida Blackhawk, WPA Collection, 1941–1942

Many years ago the babies were never fed by a bottle. If a baby did not get enough from the breast of the mother or if the mother died, the baby was fed by a spoon such as gruel of the ground white corn, and later they used the liquid of the oatmeal, and then they used cow's milk too. After they had white doctors then they started to use bottles . . . the older people think that the prepared cereals are not very nourishing to a growing child. They would rather give them cornmeal mush.[24]

Meat and Mush, Pierre Espirit Radisson, Explorer, 1651–1654

(One explorer to Mohawk territory briefly described feasting on a dish with moose, beaver, and deer with corn mush and bear grease. It's not clear whether they were served together or as separate servings.)

They were waited on by a sort of young men, bringing downe dishes of meate . . . [beavers] and of red deer mingled with some flowers. The order of makeing was thus: the corne being dried between 2 stones into powder, being very thick, putt into a kettlefull of watter, then a quantity of Bear's grease.[25]

Haudenosaunee Fermented Corn Mush, David Smoke McCluskey, Akwesasne Mohawk Chef, 2020

Chef David Smoke McCluskey described his process of making fermented corn mush. He originally came across the idea to try to replicate a description in the journals of French explorer Samuel de Champlain. Chef David Smoke McCluskey explained:

> As a modern chef, my experiences with foods are widely varied, so when reading about Champlain's account of "putrid corn" being eaten, it piqued my

curiosity. Many years later, that curiosity especially because I know that our culture revered corn and would not "leave it festering in pools or puddles" as Champlain claimed . . . A lot of our foodways have been lost. What has been saved were the vehicles that we used to utilize our seasonally changing diets. I found that I like to ferment this corn whole after the lyeing with hardwood ash and pureeing or cracking as needed depending on my use. It's great whisked in as a secret ingredient as well as on its own. Fermentation can be stopped once you get it where you enjoy it by simply freezing it. If you don't have access to sassafras, you can substitute a cinnamon stick for a just as pleasant flavor.[26]

For the Ferment:

- 1 pound lyed Iroquois white corn (nixtamalized)
- 12 cups spring water

Simmer the corn in the water until tender and allow to cool overnight on the stove top. Pour into a glass jar, and allow to ferment for another day or two, or until you have a flavor that you like. I sometimes start this and allow it to ferment for weeks or months under refrigeration.

For the Mush:

- 8 ounces Iroquois white corn, fermented
- 4 cups spring water
- a few pieces of sassafras stick (or ground bark to taste)
- 2 ounces pecans, roasted and chopped
- 2 ounces fat (examples: butter, bacon fat, lard, bear)
- 2 tablespoons maple syrup, or more if desired
- Salt to taste

Method: With the back of a chef's knife or a rolling pin, or even a mortar and pestle, smash corn into a coarse texture. Meanwhile, add the water to a saucepot, add the salt, sassafras or cinnamon stick, and bring to a boil. Allow to simmer for a few minutes, then add the fat, corn, and half of the pecans.

Simmer gently until a soft mush or "grits" are formed. Add the maple syrup to taste and serve in bowls garnished with the remaining pecans and more maple syrup if desired.

Corn and Pumpkin Pudding, Frederick Waugh, Anthropologist, 1916

The pumpkin is boiled, as before, to a thin mush. A quantity of ripe corn is parched, pounded in the mortar, and sifted to a fine meal. The latter is then stirred into the pumpkin with a paddle until it is of the proper thickness. Maple sugar is added to sweeten, also a little lard. The mass thickens up like a pudding, after which it is ready for eating.[27]

Corn and Pumpkin Pudding, Arthur Parker, Seneca Anthropologist, 1910

This favorite pudding was made from parched or yellow cornmeal mixed with sugar and boiled pumpkin or squash.[28]

Onyúsha otsiskwáʔ okhale wáhtaʔohses tekahsohkwayéstu, Arlie Doxtator, Oneida Chef, 2020

In English, Arlie calls this recipe "Squash and Corn Pudding and Maple Nut Glaze." Onyúsha talks about the long squash or butternut squash and otsiskwáʔ talks about corn mush (pudding) that is made from our corn that has been roasted (parched) and ground. Wáhtaʔohses tekahsohkwayéstu talks about maple syrup that has nuts mixed in it.

Ingredients:

- 1 cup roasted corn mush flour

- 2 cups water
- ¾ cup real maple syrup or sugar (¼ cup for the squash and ½ cup for the corn mush flour)
- 2 cups diced butternut squash
- ¼ cup roasted corn flour
- 4 tablespoons chopped walnuts

Instructions:

- In a pot, put enough water to cover the squash by 1 inch.
- Boil until squash is soft enough to mash.
- Add sweetener and flour and mix until smooth.
- Fill 8 ounce ramekins half full.
- Bring the water to a boil and add flour, stirring 3–5 minutes.
- Remove from heat and stir in sweetener.
- Top the squash with the mush and refrigerate for 4 hours or overnight until pudding is set. Top with nuts and drizzle with real maple syrup.

Drinks

There are two main types of drinks made from corn: samp and parched corn coffee. The Oneida word for samp is onʌstokli. The dried silks from the corn can also be used to make a tea.

Samp, David Skenandore and Jonas Elm, WPA Collection, 1941, 1938–1941

(After describing cornbread, David Skenandore describes how people use the water that is left over. He mentions soup, but then goes on to describe a cooking method that our community members follow today.)

And the gruel that's left in kettle from this bread is used for soup. And the coarse siftings is also been made to gruel, or it is ground over for more flour, which is very good, and in this gruel, buttermilk can be added to give a different taste to eat with sugar or without as you desire. This method is still carried on by most of the older Indians.[29]

(Jonas Elm describes how to make hulled cornbread in the typical fashion. At the end, he also explains how they save the water to drink.)

Then take out the bread and store it away for gruel soup. They usually take some along when they go hunting. One drink will last him all day so he won't get hungry.[30]

Parched Corn Coffee, Arthur Parker, Seneca Anthropologist, 1910

Corn was well burnt and parched on the coals, scraped from the cob and thrown in a dish. Upon this boiling water was thrown and the dish or kettle placed over the fire again. To produce the burnt corn drink, the boiling was continued for about five minutes.[31]

Glossary

Áhsʌ nyaʔtekutʌhnu·téleʔ—three sisters. This refers to corn, beans, and squash.

Deganawida—two river currents flowing together. He brought the message of Kayanláslaʔkowa to the Yukwanuhsyu·ní. Commonly referred to as the Peacemaker.

Hayé·wateʔ—he's always awake. He helped bring the message of Kayanláslaʔ-kowa to the Yukwanuhsyu·ní. Another common spelling is Hiawatha.

Hotahéy—(unknown translation). He was the guardian of the celestial tree/tree of life in the Sky World. He became the husband to Yotsiʔtsísaʔas (Sky Woman).

Kaliwihyo—good words. Also referred to as "The Code of Handsome Lake."

Kanʌstóhale—a type of boiled cornbread using ground corn flour.

Kayanláslaʔkowa̲—great matters. Also referred to as the Great Law of Peace.

Kanehelatúksla—to extend greetings and thankfulness. Also referred to as the Thanksgiving Address.

Iohsótha̲—his grandmother. Also lotihsótha̲, their grandmother. This is how we refer to Yotsiʔtsísaʔas when we are talking about the twins.

Ne· yakʌ latuhákwe—and so it is, they say. This is a tribute to all those who have said these things in the past. It is also a recognition that I am writing and interpreting other people's stories and sharing my own story based on my understanding at this particular moment in time.

Ohe·láku—among the cornstalks. A co-operative of Oneida families growing Indigenous corn together.

Ohero:kon—under the husk. This is an Akwesasne Mohawk rites of passage initiative lead by Louise Wakerakats:se Herne, Bear Clan Clanmother.

Okwiláse—sapling. Also referred to as the right-handed twin. When he and his brother are done creating, we refer to him as Shukwayaʔtísu (he made our bodies). The Four Messengers that appeared to Skanatalihyo referred to him as Shukwalihunte (he appointed us). In contemporary references, we sometimes call him Tehaluʔyawáku (he holds the sky).

O·nʌsteʔ—corn.

Shawíhskla—flint. Also referred to as the left-handed twin.

Skanatalihyo—Handsome Lake.

Tehototálho—he was the evil sorcerer in the Kayanláslaʔkowa̲ (Great Law). Other common spellings of his name include Tadadaho, Tadodaho, and Tadodahoh.

Tetwatunhatenyehse—we are changing our lives. A group dedicated to reestablishing traditional cultural teachings of rites of passage to help prepare our young ukwehúhwe (Indigenous) men and women for their transition into adulthood.

Tsikusaseh—she has a new face. She helped bring the message of Kayanláslaʔkowa to the Yukwanuhsyu·ní. Another common spelling of her name is Jigonhsasee.

Tsyunhéhkwʌ—life sustenance. The Oneida Nation department responsible for growing white corn for the Nation.

Ukwakhwa: Tsinu Niyukwayayʌthoslu—Our Foods: Where We Plant Things. This is the name of our ten-acre farmstead on the Oneida Reservation.

Ukwehúhwe—Indigenous.

Yenʌhliʔnése̲—she leads the groups. She was the daughter of Yotsiʔtsísaʔas.

Yotsiʔtsísaʔas—mature flower. In contemporary references, we often call her Sky Woman.

Yukwanʌ́ste—our corn and our precious.

Yukwanuhsyu·ní—we all build a house.[1] More commonly referred to as Haudenosaunee or Haudenosaunee Confederacy. Previously referred to as Iroquois, Iroquois Confederacy, League of the Iroquois, or Six Nations.

Notes

PREFACE

1. The spelling of the word "yukwanʌ́ste" in the book title borrows from the Mohawk language, a sister language to the Oneida language. Where there is a caret "ʌ" in the Oneida language, the Mohawk language uses "en" to represent the same sound. Using this replacement helps ensure special characters will not appear as a "?" when searching or viewing the book title online. As a compromise, the title includes the spelling as "yukwanénste."
2. Bob Brown, personal communication, December 5, 2018.

CHAPTER 1. TSIʔTSYOTÁSHAWAU (OF WHERE IT BEGAN)

1. More commonly known as Haudenosaunee. See the glossary for further explanation.
2. Demus Elm and Harvey Antone, *The Oneida Creation Story* (Lincoln: University of Nebraska Press, 2000).
3. Elm and Antone, *Oneida Creation Story*, 2.
4. Elm and Antone, *Oneida Creation Story*.
5. Elm and Antone, *Oneida Creation Story*.
6. John Mohawk, *Iroquois Creation Story: John Arthur Gibson and JNB Hewitt's Myth of the*

Earth Grasper (Buffalo, NY: Mohawk Publications, 2005).

7. While his story briefly mentions the Sky World, a large portion of the story occurs before Yotsiʔtsísaʔas (mature flower, also referred to as Sky Woman) had her pregnancy cravings and eventually fell through a hole to the earth below. A large portion of the story also takes place after the twins are done creating.
8. Amos Christjohn, "Creation Story," Oneida Nation, https://oneida-nsn.gov/our-ways/our-story/creation-story/.
9. Mohawk, *Iroquois Creation Story.*
10. Gibson's version explained that she made the mush from chestnuts.
11. Loretta Webster, personal communication, December 31, 2018.
12. For a discussion on artwork containing the celestial tree, see Arthur C. Parker, "Certain Iroquois Tree Myths and Symbols," *American Anthropologist* 14, no. 4 (1912): 608–620.
13. J. J. Cornplanter, *Legends of the Longhouse* (Ontario: Iroqrafts, 1986).
14. Jane Mt. Pleasant, "Traditional Iroquois Corn: Its History, Cultivation, and Use," Natural Resource, Agriculture, and Engineering Service, Cooperative Extension (2010).
15. Mohawk, *Iroquois Creation Story.*
16. Tom Porter, *And Grandma Said . . . Iroquois Teachings, as Passed Down through the Oral Tradition* (Bloomington, IN: Xlibris Corporation, 2008), 58.
17. Carol Cornelius, *Iroquois Corn in a Culture-Based Curriculum: A Framework for Respectfully Teaching about Cultures* (Albany: SUNY Press, 1999).
18. When Yotsiʔtsísaʔas was a young girl, she was protected as all young children were. We refer to this as being "under the husk." Much like a cob of corn is protected by the husks, so are our young children. Parents, aunts, uncles, and grandparents are responsible for slowly introducing children into adulthood, educating them about the transition, and ensuring that they support the young people's transition.
19. Mrs. Thomas Elm to Ida Blackhawk, Folder 6. This segment is part of the WPA collection more fully described in chapter 9.
20. The term "longhouse" refers to both the style of houses we lived in as well as our belief system and government. We practiced our ceremonies and gathered for meetings in a central longhouse in each village. Carol Elm, personal communication, January 8, 2019.
21. Vickie Cornelius, personal communication, November 21, 2018.
22. Stephanie Stevens, personal communication, April 7, 2018.

23. Mohawk, *Iroquois Creation Story*, 21–22.
24. Mohawk, *Iroquois Creation Story*, 22.
25. Mohawk, *Iroquois Creation Story*, 23.
26. Mohawk, *Iroquois Creation Story*, 40–41.

CHAPTER 2. KANEHELATÚKSLA (TO EXTEND GREETINGS AND THANKFULNESS)

1. Curt Summers, personal communication, November 13, 2018.
2. Lexi Levinson, personal communication, December 26, 2018.
3. Toni House, personal communication, November 21, 2018.
4. *Yawʌ* means "thanks."
5. Randy Cornelius, personal communication, November 15, 2018.
6. John Mohawk, *Iroquois Creation Story: John Arthur Gibson and JNB Hewitt's myth of the Earth Grasper* (Mohawk Publications, 2005), 90–91.
7. Mohawk, *Iroquois Creation Story*, 87–88.
8. *Iroquois Creation Story*, 90.
9. Oneida Indian Nation Language and Cultural Centre, "The Seven Dancers," https://oneidalanguage.ca/story/seven-dancers/.
10. Brian Doxtator, personal communication, December 23, 2018.
11. Ernest Stevens IV, personal communication, April 7, 2018.
12. *Tsyunhéhkwʌ* means "life sustenance." It is the name of the Oneida Nation's organic farm that grows traditional, heirloom white corn for the community. See chapter 11 for more discussion about Tsyunhéhkwʌ.
13. Kim Nishimoto, personal communication, January 29, 2019.
14. Randy Cornelius, personal communication, November 15, 2018.
15. See also J. Mt. Pleasant, "The Iroquois Sustainers: Practices of a Longterm Agriculture in the Northeast," in J. Barreiro, *Indian Corn of the Americas: Gift to the World*. Cultural Encounter II. *Northeast Indian Quarterly* (1989).
16. Curt Summers, personal communication, November 13, 2018.
17. Arthur Caswell Parker, *Iroquois Uses of Maize and Other Food Plants*, volume 144 (Albany: University of the State of New York, 1910), 31–32.

18. Laura Manthe, personal communication, October 17, 2018.
19. Don Charnon, personal communication, November 28, 2018.
20. Bev Scow, personal communication, December 4, 2018.
21. Kwnwahta Smith, personal communication, November 18, 2018.
22. Bev Scow, personal communication, December 4, 2018.
23. Braxton Wisneski, personal communication, January 15, 2019.
24. Eliza Skenandore, personal communication, April 9, 2018.
25. A Nesco is a brand name of an electric roaster oven, typically holding eighteen quarts of food or liquid. Schuyler Ryerse, personal communication, April 8, 2018.
26. Parker, *Iroquois Uses of Maize and Other Food Plants*, 80–88.

CHAPTER 3. KAYANLÁSLAʔKOWA̲ (GREAT MATTERS)

1. They say that the Peacemaker will come back someday if we need him to. To get him to come back, we need to yell his name into the woods. Some people choose to call him Peacemaker when talking about him to ensure that when we call out his name, he will know when we mean for him to come back. Others choose to use his name with the understanding that he is smart enough to know the difference. His name is Deganawida.
2. John Arthur Gibson, "Concerning the League: The Iroquois League Tradition as Dictated in Onondaga by John Arthur Gibson," newly elicited, edited, and translated by Hanni Woodbury in collaboration with Reg Henry and Harry Webster on the basis of AA Goldenweiser's Manuscript (Syracuse, NY: Syracuse University Press, 1992), 10.
3. Tom Porter, *And Grandma Said . . . Iroquois Teachings, as Passed Down through the Oral Tradition* (Bloomington, IN: Xlibris Corporation, 2008).
4. Gibson, "Concerning the League," 103–108.
5. Arthur Caswell Parker, *The Constitution of the Five Nations* (Albany: University of the State of New York, 1916), 61.
6. Porter, *And Grandma Said*, 279.
7. Jasmine Jimerson, personal communication, January 4, 2019.
8. Toni House, personal communication, April 10, 2020.

9. Porter, *And Grandma Said*, 287.
10. Gibson, "Concerning the League," 34–35.
11. Gibson, "Concerning the League," 41–42.
12. Oniagara is likely an early spelling of "Niagara" and describes the place where Lake Erie narrows into the strait of the Niagara River to Lake Ontario. John N. Jackson, *The Mighty Niagara: One River-Two Frontiers* (Buffalo, NY: Prometheus Books, 2003). Arthur C. Parker, *The Life of General Ely S. Parker: Last Grand Sachem of the Iroquois and General Grant's Military Secretary* (Buffalo, NY: Buffalo Historical Society, 1919).
13. Bob Brown, personal communication, March 6, 2020.
14. The Gibson text contains the written version of the Great Law in the Seneca language, followed by an English translation. The phrase "peace chief" is followed by a footnote in the Gibson text noting that modern speakers are unsure of the translation.
15. Gibson, "Concerning the League," 91–94.
16. Gibson, "Concerning the League," 191–192.
17. Gibson, "Concerning the League," 192.
18. Parker, *Constitution of the Five Nations*, 82.
19. Parker, *Constitution of the Five Nations*, 82.
20. Gibson, "Concerning the League," 194–195.
21. Parker, *Constitution of the Five Nations*, 82.
22. Gibson, "Concerning the League," 294–296.
23. Gibson, "Concerning the League," 458.
24. Susan M. Hill, *The Clay We Are Made Of: Haudenosaunee Land Tenure on the Grand River*, volume 20 (Winnipeg: University of Manitoba Press, 2017).
25. Arlie Doxtator, personal communication, November 8, 2018.

CHAPTER 4. WAHUTATYA·THEWÉWE (THEY ARRIVED)

1. William Stetson Merrill, "The Catholic Contribution to the History of the Norse Discovery of America," *Catholic Historical Review* 13, no. 4 (1928): 589–619, 594.
2. William Henry Babcock, "Recent History and Present Status of the Vinland Problem," *Geographical Review* 11, no. 2 (1921): 265–282. See also Merritt Lyndon Fernald, "Notes

on the Plants of Wineland the Good," *Rhodora* 12, no. 134 (1910): 17–38. Juul Dieserud, "Norse Discoveries in America," *Bulletin of the American Geographical Society* 33, no. 1 (1901): 1–18. See also Fridtjof Nansen, "The Norsemen in America," *Geographical Journal* 38, no. 6 (1911): 557–575.

3. Douglas R. McManis, "The Traditions of Vinland," *Annals of the Association of American Geographers* 59, no. 4 (1969): 797–814.
4. Merrill, "Catholic Contribution," 593.
5. Victoria Dickenson, "Cartier, Champlain, and the Fruits of the New World: Botanical Exchange in the 16th and 17th Centuries," *Scientia Canadensis: Canadian Journal of the History of Science, Technology and Medicine/Scientia Canadensis: Revue canadienne d'histoire des sciences, des techniques et de la médecine* 31, no. 1–2 (2008): 27–47.
6. Arthur Caswell Parker, *Iroquois Uses of Maize and Other Food Plants* (Albany: University of the State of New York, 1910), 15.
7. Dickenson, "Cartier, Champlain, and the Fruits of the New World," 27–47.
8. A signoc is a horseshoe crab. Parker, *Iroquois Uses of Maize and Other Food Plants*, 17.
9. Parker, *Iroquois Uses of Maize and Other Food Plants*, 16.
10. Parker, *Iroquois Uses of Maize and Other Food Plants*, 16. Citing Gabriel Sagard, *Le grand voyage du pays des Hurons situé en l'Amérique vers la mer douce, ès derniers confins de la Nouvelle France dite Canada* (Paris: Tross, 1865), 135.
11. C. T. Gehring and W. A. Starna, eds., *A Journey into Mohawk and Oneida Country, 1634–1635: The Journal of Harmen Meyndertsz van den Bogaert* (Syracuse, NY: Syracuse University Press, 2013).
12. Gehring and Starna, *Journey into Mohawk and Oneida Country*, 4.
13. Gehring and Starna, *Journey into Mohawk and Oneida Country*, 17. See also chapter 5 of this book for a discussion of the Kaliwihyo and the practice of feeding guests.
14. Adriaen Cornelissen Van der Donck, "Description of New Netherland 1653," in *In Mohawk Country: Early Narratives about a Native People* (Syracuse, NY: Syracuse University Press, 1996), 104–130, 121.
15. S. Lewandowski, "Three Sisters—A Iroquoian Cultural Complex," in J. Barreiro, *Indian Corn of the Americas: Gift to the World*, Cultural Encounter II, *Northeast Indian Quarterly* (1989).

16. Lewandowski, "Three Sisters," 42.
17. Paolo Andreani, "Travels of a Gentleman from Milan 1790," in *In Mohawk Country*, 318–333, 319.
18. Parker, *Iroquois Uses of Maize and Other Food Plants*, 17.
19. Parker, *Iroquois Uses of Maize and Other Food Plants*.
20. D. K. Richter, *The Ordeal of the Longhouse: The Peoples of the Iroquois League in the Era of European Colonization* (Chapel Hill: University of North Carolina Press, 2011), 104.
21. Laura Antoniou, *The Documentary History of the State of New York*, volume 1 (Albany, NY: Weed, Parsons and Company, 1849), 238–239.
22. Rachel B. Herrmann, "'No Useless Mouth': Iroquoian Food Diplomacy in the American Revolution," *Diplomatic History* 41, no. 1 (2017): 20–49.
23. Grace Webster, personal communication, March 31, 2020.

CHAPTER 5. WOHOTILIWAHOKÉNHA (THEY TANGLED OVER MATTERS)

1. Barbara Graymont, "The Oneidas and the American Revolution," in *Oneida Indian Experience: Two Perspectives*, ed. Jack Campisi and Laurence M. Hauptman (Syracuse, NY: Syracuse University Press, 1988).
2. This wouldn't be the last time the Yukwanuhsyu·ní fought against each other in battles. In the War of 1812, the Yukwanuhsyu·ní Confederacy did not take sides, but individual warriors were able to choose a side. With the confederacy being split between the United States and Canada, there were Yukwanuhsyu·ní on both sides of the war. See Reginald Horsman, "The Origins of Oneida Removal to Wisconsin, 1815–1822," in *The Oneida Indian Journey: From New York to Wisconsin, 1784–1860*, ed. Laurence M. Hauptman and L. Gordon McLester (Madison: University of Wisconsin Press, 1999), 53–69.
3. Karim M. Tiro, "A 'Civil' War? Rethinking Iroquois Participation in the American Revolution," *Explorations in Early American Culture* 4 (2000): 148–165.
4. Graymont, "Oneidas and the American Revolution."
5. Herrmann, "No Useless Mouth."

6. Joseph T. Glatthaar and James Kirby Martin, *Forgotten Allies: The Oneida Indians and the American Revolution* (New York: Macmillan, 2006).
7. Tiro, "A 'Civil' War?"
8. Glatthaar and Martin, *Forgotten Allies.*
9. Graymont, "Oneidas and the American Revolution."
10. Tiro, "A 'Civil' War?"
11. Bob Brown, personal communication, March 27, 2020. The framers of the U.S. Constitution modeled the Yukwanuhsyu·ní Confederacy when they set up the lawmaking process in the House and Senate, with the president making the final decision to sign the bill into law or veto it.
12. Glatthaar and Martin, *Forgotten Allies.*
13. *Forgotten Allies.*
14. Letter from Officer Louis de Tousard to Lieutenant Colonel Marinus Willett, April 7, 1778, Myers Coll., NYPL.
15. Glatthaar and Martin, *Forgotten Allies*, 199.
16. "Polly Cooper: Oneida Heroine," Oneida Indian Nation, http://www.oneidaindiannation.com/polly-cooper-oneida-heroine/.
17. Glatthaar and Martin, *Forgotten Allies.*
18. Glatthaar and Martin, *Forgotten Allies*, 208.
19. Glatthaar and Martin, *Forgotten Allies.*
20. "Polly Cooper: Oneida Heroine."
21. Glatthaar and Martin, *Forgotten Allies.*
22. Herrmann, "No Useless Mouth."
23. Tiro, "A 'Civil' War?," 157.
24. Frederick Cook, *Journals of the Military Expedition of Major General John Sullivan against the Six Nations of Indians in 1779: With Records of Centennial Celebrations; Prepared Pursuant to Chapter 361, Laws of the State of New York, of 1885* (Auburn, NY: Knapp, Peck and Thomson, Printers, 1887), 252. This entry by Reverend William Rogers explained that the twenty-five Oneidas would join Brigadier General James Clinton, who would later join up with Sullivan.
25. Cook, *Journals of the Military Expedition*, 264.

26. Cook, *Journals of the Military Expedition.*
27. Cook, *Journals of the Military Expedition*, 421.
28. Cook, *Journals of the Military Expedition*. The record notes 160,000 bushels of corn. Using sixty pounds of shelled corn per bushel, this totals 9.6 million pounds of corn.
29. Richter, *Ordeal of the Longhouse.*
30. Bob Brown, personal communication, March 27, 2020.
31. Cook, *Journals of the Military Expedition*, 112. Sergeant Major George Grant.
32. Cook, *Journals of the Military Expedition*, 99–100. Major Jeremiah Fogg.
33. Cook, *Journals of the Military Expedition*, 164. Lieutenant Colonel Adam Hubley.
34. Cook, *Journals of the Military Expedition*, 336.
35. Cook, *Journals of the Military Expedition*, 379.
36. Graymont, "Oneidas and the American Revolution."
37. Herrmann, "No Useless Mouth."
38. Jack Campisi and Laurence M. Hauptman, eds., *The Oneida Indian Experience: Two Perspectives* (Syracuse, NY: Syracuse University Press, 1988).
39. Graymont, "Oneidas and the American Revolution."
40. Graymont, "Oneidas and the American Revolution," 39.
41. Elijah Skenandoah was likely a relative of Chief Skenandoah. He was a pine tree chief, meaning he was an ambassador who could talk on behalf of other nations. J. L. Jourdan, "Wampum: Our Historical Record. Oneida Cultural Heritage, Oneida Nation," https://oneida-nsn.gov/dl-file.php?file=2016/04/WAMPUM-OUR-HISTORICAL-RECORD-9.13.pdf.
42. Tehanetorens, *Wampum Belts of the Iroquois* (Onchiota, NY: Six Nations Indian Museum, 1983).
43. Jourdan, "Wampum."
44. Native American Graves Protection and Repatriation Review Committee Meeting, November 1–3, 1996, Myrtle Beach, SC, volume 2, https://irma.nps.gov/DataStore/DownloadFile/630486.
45. Kwnwahta Smith, personal communication, November 18, 2018.
46. Arlie Doxtator, personal communication, November 8, 2018.

CHAPTER 6. KALIWIHYO (GOOD MESSAGE)

1. Different speakers refer to the lessons or prophesies within the Kaliwihyo with different terms, such as "sections," "articles," "verses," or "matters." For ease of consistency, this chapter uses the term "section."
2. Jacob E. Thomas and Terry Boyle, *Teachings from the Longhouse* (Toronto: Stoddart, 1994), 21.
3. Alex F. Ricciardelli, "The Adoption of White Agriculture by the Oneida Indians," *Ethnohistory* 10, no. 4 (1963): 309–328.
4. William Edmundson, *A Journal of the Life, Travels, Sufferings, and Labour of Love in the Work of the Ministry, of That Worthy Elder, and Faithful Servant of Jesus Christ, William Edmundson, Who Departed This Life, the Thirty First of the Sixth, Month, 1712. Eighteenth Century Collections Online*. London: Printed and sold by the assigns of J. Sowle, in White Hart-Court in Gracious Street, and at the Bible in George-Tard, Lombard-Street, 1715.
5. The Stockbridge and Brothertown are tribes that traveled to Wisconsin from the east around the same time the Oneidas were moved west. Jeremy Belknap and Jedidiah Morse, "Report on the Oneida, Stockbridge, and Brothertown Indians, 1796. No. 54" (Museum of the American Indian, Heye Foundation, 1955), 22–23.
6. Belknap and Morse, "Report," 30.
7. Karim M. Tiro, "'We Wish to Do You Good': The Quaker Mission to the Oneida Nation, 1790–1840," *Journal of the Early Republic* 26, no. 3 (2006): 353–376.
8. Louis Williams Jr., "Handsome Lake and Kaliwihyo," Oneida Nation, https://oneida-nsn.gov/our-ways/our-story/historic-timeline/handsome-lake-and-kaliwihyo/. Spelling of Oneida words has been revised with the inclusion of special Oneida characters for consistency.
9. *Niawe* means "thanks." Arthur C. Parker, "The Code of Handsome Lake," New York State Museum Bulletin 163 (1913), 36.
10. Thomas and Boyle, *Teachings from the Longhouse*, 56.
11. Nicholas Reynolds, personal communication, January 27, 2019.
12. North American Indian Travelling College, *Traditional Teachings* (Akwesasne, ON: North American Indian Travelling College, 1984), 78.
13. Parker, "Code of Handsome Lake," 39 fn 3.
14. Thomas and Boyle, *Teachings from the Longhouse*, 82.

15. Parker, "Code of Handsome Lake," 45.
16. Harriet S. Caswell, *Our Life among the Iroquois Indians* (Boston: Congregational Sunday School and Publishing Society, 1892), 211.
17. Parker, "Code of Handsome Lake," 53–54.
18. Randy Cornelius, personal communication, November 15, 2018.
19. Parker, "Code of Handsome Lake," 47.
20. Thomas and Boyle, *Teachings from the Longhouse*, 68–69.
21. Parker, "Code of Handsome Lake," 38.
22. North American Indian Travelling College, *Traditional Teachings*, 82.
23. Thomas and Boyle, *Teachings from the Longhouse*, 46.
24. See also Marilyn Holly, "Handsome Lake's Teachings: The Shift from Female to Male Agriculture in Iroquois Culture. An Essay in Ethnophilosophy," *Agriculture and Human Values* 7, no. 3–4 (1990): 80–94.
25. Caswell, *Our Life among the Iroquois Indians*, 212.
26. North American Indian Travelling College, *Traditional Teachings*, 85.
27. Parker, "Code of Handsome Lake," 54.
28. Parker, *Iroquois Uses of Maize and Other Food Plants*, 25.
29. Thomas and Boyle, *Teachings from the Longhouse*, 59–60.
30. Thomas and Boyle, *Teachings from the Longhouse*, 60–61.
31. Parker, "Code of Handsome Lake," 54 fn 1.
32. Thomas and Boyle, *Teachings from the Longhouse*, 60.
33. Parker, "Code of Handsome Lake," 54.
34. Parker, "Code of Handsome Lake," 54 fn 1.
35. Thomas and Boyle, *Teachings from the Longhouse*, 61.
36. North American Indian Travelling College, *Traditional Teachings*, 95.
37. Thomas and Boyle, *Teachings from the Longhouse*, 68–69.

CHAPTER 7. WAYUKHINUKULHAʔTE OKHALE WAYUKHINATÓ·LI· (THEY DISMISSED OUR THINKING AND THEY DISRUPTED OUR TOWNS)

1. Alex F. Ricciardelli, "The Adoption of White Agriculture by the Oneida Indians," *Ethnohistory* 10, no. 4 (1963): 309–328.
2. Doug Carroll, "Tribal Lands: In N.Y., 6 Million Acres Hang in the Balance . . . ," *Washington Post*, September 24, 1979, https://www.washingtonpost.com/archive/politics/1979/09/24/tribal-lands-in-ny-6-million-acres-hang-in-the-balance/a370e054-974f-43c2-ab8a-f239bbe92b2e/.
3. Laurence M. Hauptman and L. Gordon McLester, *Chief Daniel Bread and the Oneida Nation of Indians of Wisconsin*, volume 241 (Norman: University of Oklahoma Press, 2002).
4. Bloomfield lived in Oswego, New York. In writing her classic book *The Oneidas*, she relied heavily on the works of Ellen Goodnough, wife of a missionary to the Oneidas, and Susan Fenimore Cooper, an author from Cooperstown, New York. L. Gordon McLester III, Laurence M. Hauptman, Judy Cornelius-Hawk, and Kenneth Hoyan House, eds., *The Wisconsin Oneidas and the Episcopal Church: A Chain Linking Two Traditions* (Indiana University Press, 2019). Julia Keen Bloomfield, *The Oneidas* (New York: Alden Brothers, 1907), 149–150.
5. John C. Calhoun, *Papers of John C. Calhoun, 1818–1819*, volume 3 (Columbia: University of South Carolina Press, 1967), 95.
6. Ricciardelli, "Adoption of White Agriculture."
7. Oneida Castle was a major fortified Oneida village. Guy Elm, Folder 16. Works Progress Administration.
8. Hauptman and McLester, *Chief Daniel Bread.*
9. Charles C. Trowbridge, *Journal of C. C. Trowbridge's Trip to Green Bay in Company with the Oneida Indians of New York*, 1821, https://exploreoneida.com/wp-content/uploads/2018/09/11-Jan-1-Sept-1821Journal-of-CC-throwbridge-Trip-to-Green-Bay-.pdf.
10. Hauptman and McLester, *Chief Daniel Bread.*
11. Reginald Horsman, "The Origins of Oneida Removal to Wisconsin, 1815–1822," In *The Oneida Indian Journey: From New York to Wisconsin, 1784–1860*, ed. Laurence M. Hauptman and L. Gordon McLester (Madison: University of Wisconsin Press, 1999).

12. D. Shames, *Freedom with Reservation: The Menominee Struggle to Save Their Land and People* (Madison, WI: National Committee to Save the Menominee People and Forests/ Wisconsin Indian Legal Services, 1972), 7.
13. R. E. Bieder, *Native American Communities in Wisconsin, 1600–1960: A Study of Tradition and Change* (Madison: University of Wisconsin Press, 1995).
14. Guy Elm, Folder 16. Works Progress Administration. There does not currently exist a single, word-searchable, electronic version of the complete collection of Oneida WPA stories. I used several sources for the stories, including a collection from the late Oneida historian Sue Daniels (noted with reference to folders); a digital collection maintained by the University of Wisconsin Madison (noted with reference to a letter and number); and old unpublished Oneida Nation pamphlets and booklets (no additional references noted). Each citation includes the individual storyteller and the individual recording the story. Where there is only one individual listed, that individual recorded their own story.
15. Bloomfield, *Oneidas*, 176–177.
16. Laurence M. Hauptman and L. Gordon McLester, eds., *The Oneida Indian Journey: From New York to Wisconsin, 1784–1860* (Madison: University of Wisconsin Press, 1999).
17. Treaty with the Oneida, 1838. 7 Stat., 566.
18. Hauptman and McLester, *Oneida Indian Journey*.
19. Hauptman and McLester, *Chief Daniel Bread*.
20. Papers of John C. Calhoun, 564–565.
21. John C. Calhoun to chiefs and headmen of Onondagas, Senecas, Tuscaroras, Oneidas, and Stockbridge Indians about treaty at Green Bay, October 27, 1823. Ontario County Historical Society, Canandaigua, NY, Jasper Parrish Papers. https://exploreoneida.com/wp-content/uploads/2018/07/1823-Letter-to-Oneidas-and-other-tribes-about-treaty-in-Green-Bay.pdf.
22. Onudake, or Onudaga, was a county in New York. Mrs. Thomas Elm to Stadler King, S2. Works Progress Administration.
23. Tom Elm to Mr. Basehart and Stadler King, Folder 15.
24. Laura Manthe, personal communication, October 17, 2018.
25. Aaron House to Oscar H. Archiquette, Folder 17. Works Progress Administration. Archiquette collected this story in 1941 when Aaron was eighty-eight years old.

26. Rachel Swamp to Dennison Hill, D6.
27. Amelia Webster, personal communication, March 31, 2020.
28. Hauptman and McLester, *Oneida Indian Journey*, 15.
29. Karim M. Tiro, *The People of the Standing Stone: The Oneida Nation from the Revolution through the Era of Removal* (Amherst: University of Massachusetts Press, 2011).
30. Hauptman and McLester, *Oneida Indian Journey*, 16.
31. Bloomfield, *Oneidas*, 242–243.
32. Hobart Church is now known as the Church of the Holy Apostles or the Stone Church.
33. Bloomfield, *Oneidas*, 268.
34. J. Campisi, "The Wisconsin Oneidas between Disasters," in Hauptman and McLester, eds., *Oneida Indian Journey*, 70–84, 82.

CHAPTER 8. WAYUKWAHUTSYÁKWA OKHALE WAYUKHIWILÁHKWA (THEY HAVE TAKEN OUR LAND AWAY AND THEY HAVE TAKEN OUR CHILDREN AWAY)

1. It is difficult to pinpoint when the boarding school era began and ended. Oscar Archiquette noted that the first group of Oneida children were sent off to boarding school in 1884 and most of the government boarding schools were abolished in 1918. Oscar H. Archiquette, Folders 17, 15. In 1972, Congress passed the Indian Education Act in an attempt to give tribes greater control over the education of their people. While there are still boarding schools today, they are generally controlled by tribal governments and orient their curriculum toward Indigenous culture.
2. Day schools were schools located near children's homes. The children went there for the day and came home after school. Boarding schools were often located far away from children's homes. The children often lived at the school the entire school year, occasionally coming home for breaks.
3. Minutes of conference held by Inspector McLaughlin, Supervisor Brandon and Superintendent Hart with Indians of the Oneida Reservation at Oneida, Wisconsin, Tuesday, August 7, 1917, 55.
4. Herbert S. Lewis and L. Gordon McLester, eds., *Oneida Lives: Long-Lost Voices of the Wisconsin Oneidas* (Lincoln: University of Nebraska Press, 2005).

5. While the Dawes Allotment Act stated that allottees would become citizens after they received fee patents, it is important to note that the federal government didn't make all Native Americans eligible for citizenship until 1924. Indian Citizenship Act of 1924, 8 U.S.C. ch. 12, subch. III § 1401b. However, states maintained the right to determine who was eligible to vote. It wasn't until 1970 when Congress passed the Voting Rights Act that major restrictions to Native American voters were removed in every state. 84 Stat. 314. F. W. Merril, *The Church's Mission to the Oneidas*, 2nd ed. (Green Bay, WI: P. B. Haber Printing, 1902), 42.
6. Andrew Beechtree, Folder 4.
7. Merril, *Church's Mission to the Oneidas*.
8. Merril, *Church's Mission to the Oneidas*, 51–52.
9. Minutes of 2nd Conference with Oneida Indians, August 14, 1917, https://868b826de7.nxcli.net/wp-content/uploads/2022/02/1917-Letter-to-Inspecter-McLaughlin.pdf.
10. Merril, *Church's Mission to the Oneidas*.
11. Anderson Cornelius to Guy Elm, Folder 15.
12. Mr. Powless to Guy Elm, Folder 6.
13. Given Beechtree's animosity toward the boarding schools, by these "ideal" conditions I can only assume he meant that the children had food, shelter, and clothing. Andrew Beechtree, Folder 27.
14. Andrew Beechtree, Folder 23.
15. William Metoxen, Folder 1.
16. Anderson Cornelius to Guy Elm, Folder 15.
17. Porter, *And Grandma Said*.
18. Porter, *And Grandma Said*, 388.
19. Andrew Beechtree, Folder 27.
20. Andrew Beechtree, Folder 4.
21. Guy Elm, Folder 20.
22. Stadler King, Folder 11.
23. Porter, *And Grandma Said*, 387.
24. General Allotment Act, 25 U.S. Code ch. 9 (1887) §§ 331 et seq.
25. Arlinda Locklear, "The Allotment of the Oneida Reservation and Its Legal Ramifications," in *The Oneida Indian Experience: Two Perspectives*, ed. Jack Campisi and

Laurence M. Hauptman (Syracuse, NY: Syracuse University Press, 1988), 83–93.

26. Burke Act, 25 U.S. Code ch. 9 (1906) § 349.
27. Minutes, August 7, 1917, 14.
28. Minutes, August 7, 1917, 15.
29. Minutes, August 7, 1917, 33–34.
30. Minutes of 2nd Conference with Oneida Indians, August 14, 1917, 11. Interpreted by Mr. Webster.
31. Minutes, August 7, 1917, 46.
32. Minutes, August 7, 1917, 52.
33. Oscar Archiquette, Folder 17.
34. Oscar Archiquette, Folder 17.
35. I omitted the name of the individual in this quote. While these stories are not confidential, I did not feel it was appropriate to repeat an accusation made over eighty years ago. The individual's descendants could take issue with the accusation. I included the story because it helps us understand what was going on during this period of time, that there were factions, and that the allotment of the reservation hurt their families. Joel Reed to Oscar Archiquette, Folder 7.
36. 701 Comprehensive Planning Program, Oneida Indian Reservation. 1973.
37. Jones Hill to Oscar Archiquette, Folder 5.
38. Martin Hill to Tillie Baird, T45.
39. Frank Danforth to Guy Elm, Folder 3.
40. Ida Blackhawk, Folder 11.
41. Tom Elm to Mr. Basehart and Stadler King, Folder 15.
42. James McLaughlin to the secretary of the interior, August 31, 1917.
43. Locklear, "The Allotment of the Oneida Reservation."
44. Stadler King, Folder 15.
45. Merril, *Church's Mission to the Oneidas*, 54.
46. Merril, *Church's Mission to the Oneidas*, 54.
47. Andrew Beechtree, Folder 21.
48. Ida Blackhawk, Folder 1.
49. Wilson Cornelius to Stadler King, Folder 12.

CHAPTER 9. WAYUKHINIKUHLÁʔKHÁSHYI (THEY HAVE SEPARATED OUR MINDS)

1. Johnson O'Malley Act of 1934 25 U.S.C. §§ 452–456 et seq. Indian Reorganization Act of 1934 25 U.S. Code ch. 14, subch. V (1934) §§ 461 et seq.
2. Lewis Meriam and Hubert Work, *The Problem of Indian Administration: Report of a Survey Made at the Request of Honorable Hubert Work, Secretary of the Interior, and Submitted to Him, February 21, 1928*. No. 17 (Baltimore: Johns Hopkins Press, 1928).
3. Oscar Archiquette, Folder 15.
4. Oscar Archiquette, Folder 15.
5. Francis Skenandore, "William Skenandore," in *The Oneida Indian Experience: Two Perspectives*, ed. Jack Campisi and Laurence M. Hauptman (Syracuse, NY: Syracuse University Press, 1988), 126–130.
6. Skenandore, "William Skenandore," 127.
7. Andrew Beechtree, Folder 21.
8. Oscar Archiquette, "The Indian New Deal at Oneida," in *A Nation within a Nation: Voices of the Oneidas in Wisconsin*, ed. L. G. McLester III and L. M. Hauptman (Madison: Wisconsin Historical Society, 2014), 37. Interview with Oscar Archiquette in 1971.
9. Ida Blackhawk to Guy Elm, Folder 21.
10. Andrew Beechtree, Folder 21.
11. Guy Cornelius to Guy Elm, Folder 3. When I first read this story, I didn't see the humor. I asked around the community to see what I may have missed. A couple of people thought something must have gotten lost in translation, but this story was written directly in English. To the best of my understanding, the grandpa genuinely wanted to understand the IRA. His grandson didn't support it and was giving his grandpa a sarcastic response. The grandpa got mad, and they fought for a bit.
12. Guy Elm, Folder 11.
13. Andrew Beechtree, Folder 11.
14. Guy Cornelius to Guy Elm, Folder 3.
15. Nick Denny to Guy Elm, Folder 8.
16. Guy Elm, Folder 17.
17. Oscar Archiquette, Folder 17.

18. Laurence M. Hauptman, *The Iroquois and the New Deal* (Syracuse, NY: Syracuse University Press, 1988).
19. Jack Campisi and Laurence M. Hauptman, eds., *The Oneida Indian Experience: Two Perspectives* (Syracuse, NY: Syracuse University Press, 1988).
20. Hauptman, *Iroquois and the New Deal.*
21. Hauptman, *Iroquois and the New Deal.*
22. Floyd Lounsbury, "Recollections of the Works Progress Administration's Oneida Language and Folklore Project," in Campisi and Hauptman, eds., *Oneida Indian Experience*, 131–134.
23. Hauptman, *Iroquois and the New Deal.*
24. Hauptman, *Iroquois and the New Deal.*
25. Lounsbury, "Recollections."
26. Hauptman, *Iroquois and the New Deal.*
27. This is the equivalent of $9.63 per hour or $866.78 per month in 2021 dollars. See https://www.minneapolisfed.org/about-us/monetary-policy/inflation-calculator.
28. Lounsbury, "Recollections."
29. Hauptman, *Iroquois and the New Deal.*
30. Hauptman, *Iroquois and the New Deal.*
31. Lounsbury, "Recollections," 132–133.
32. Lewis and McLester, *Oneida Lives.*
33. Lewis and McLester, *Oneida Lives.*
34. Tom Elm to Mr. Basehart and Stadler King, Folder 15.
35. Oscar Archiquette, Folder 17.
36. R. M. Webster, "The Wisconsin Oneida and the WPA: Stories of Corn, Colonialism, and Revitalization," *Ethnohistory* 68, no. 3 (2021): 407–427.
37. Hyson Doxtator, Folder 1.
38. Andrew Beechtree, Folder 17.
39. Rachel Denny to David Skenandore.
40. Mrs. Nelson B. Cornelius to Dennison Hill, D-90.
41. Jessie Peters to Stadler King, S9.
42. Lucy Rose to Guy Elm, G18. Chapter 5 also contains two short stories about red ears of corn in relation to the Revolutionary War and the corn remembering her relatives.

43. Ida Blackhawk, Z34.
44. Celecia Hill to Ida Blackhawk, I-5.
45. Dennison Hill, D20.
46. Tom Elm to Guy Elm, G40.

CHAPTER 10. OHUTSYO·KÚ· WAHATIHA·WÍHTE (THEY TOOK IT TO UNDER THE EARTH)

1. Mike Hoeft, *The Bingo Queens of Oneida: How Two Moms Started Tribal Gaming in Wisconsin* (Madison: Wisconsin Historical Society, 2014).
2. Laurence M. Hauptman, *The Iroquois Struggle for Survival: World War II to Red Power* (Syracuse, NY: Syracuse University Press, 1986).
3. Nancy O. Lurie, "Recollections of an Urban Indian Community," in *The Oneida Indian Experience: Two Perspectives*, ed. Jack Campisi and Laurence M. Hauptman (Syracuse, NY: Syracuse University Press, 1988), 83–93.
4. Study Poverty of the Oneidas, *Milwaukee Journal*, January 26, 1953, 11.
5. Martin C. Carey and Beverly Paigen, "Epidemiology of the American Indians' Burden and Its Likely Genetic Origins," *Hepatology* 36, no. 4 (2002): 781–791.
6. Julie Barton, personal communication, January 6, 2019.
7. Stan Webster, personal communication, January 31, 2018.
8. Chicago Corners is a neighborhood on the reservation.
9. Gerald Danforth, personal communication, November 14, 2018.
10. Stan Webster, personal communication, December 31, 2018.
11. Loretta Webster, personal communication, December 31, 2018.
12. Julie Barton, personal communication, January 6, 2019.
13. Julie Barton, personal communication, January 6, 2019.
14. Carol Elm, personal communication, January 8, 2019.
15. Artley Skenandore, personal communication, December 5, 2018.
16. Chaz Wheelock, personal communication, November 29, 2018.
17. Linn Cornelius, personal communication, November 15, 2018.
18. Brian Doxtator, personal communication, December 23, 2018.
19. Gerald Danforth, personal communication, November 14, 2018.

20. Brian Doxtator, personal communication, December 23, 2018.
21. Linn Cornelius, personal communication, November 15, 2018.
22. Kim Nishimoto, personal communication, January 29, 2019.
23. Arlie Doxtator, personal communication, November 8, 2018.
24. Brian Doxtator, personal communication, December 23, 2018.
25. Deborah Heckel, personal communication, February 5, 2019.
26. Michele Doxtator, personal communication, April 12, 2020.
27. Nicholas C. Peroff, *Menominee Drums: Tribal Termination and Restoration, 1954–1974* (Norman: University of Oklahoma Press, 2006).
28. Julie Barton, personal communication, January 6, 2019.
29. Bob Brown, personal communication, December 5, 2018.
30. Randy Cornelius, personal communication, November 15, 2018.
31. Leander Danforth, personal communication, January 22, 2019.

CHAPTER 11. ONA WAEKWATAHTASKENHÁ (NOW WE HAVE THE MEANS TO HELP OURSELVES)

1. Oneida Reservation Comprehensive Plan, revised October 1, 2008, 4–114, https://oneida-nsn.gov/dl-file.php?file=2016/02/Comp-Plan-which-includes-Land-Policy-Framework.pdf.
2. Oneida Reservation Comprehensive Plan.
3. Chaz Wheelock, personal communication, November 29, 2018.
4. Artley Skenandore, personal communication, December 5, 2018.
5. Oneida Reservation Comprehensive Plan.
6. Jamie Betters, personal communication, April 14, 2020.
7. Carol Elm, personal communication, January 8, 2018.
8. Jamie Betters, personal communication, April 6, 2018.
9. Randy Cornelius, personal communication, November 15, 2018.
10. Oneida Reservation Comprehensive.
11. Vickie Cornelius, personal communication, November 21, 2018.
12. Jill Ninham, personal communication, January 9, 2019.
13. Laura Cornelius, personal communication, April 6, 2018.

14. Oneida Reservation Comprehensive Plan, 4–118. Citing a presentation titled "Tsyuhehkwa Center (All of the Things That Sustain Our Life)" by Vickie Cornelius, Manager; Carol Elm, Food Processing Supervisor; Paul Smith, Agric. Food Production Coordinator; Cherie Elm, Holistic Health Developer, March 12, 1996.
15. Jamie Betters, personal communication, April 14, 2020.
16. Jeff Metoxen, "Wisconsin Life: Oneida White Corn," Wisconsin Public Radio, 2015, https://www.wpr.org/listen/794816.
17. Kyle Wisneski, personal communication, January 15, 2019.
18. Braxton Wisneski, personal communication, January 15, 2019. Braxton was six years old at the time of this interview.
19. V. Cornelius and J. Betters, "Oneida Cannery Year in Review," Kalihwisaks, December 15, 2016, 20; J. Metoxen, Tsyunhéhkwʌ, "Updates," Kalihwisaks, June 2, 2016, 12.
20. Vickie Cornelius, personal communication, November 21, 2018.
21. Paul "Sugar Bear" Smith, personal communication, November 19, 2018.
22. Vickie Cornelius, personal communication, November 21, 2018.
23. Deborah Heckel, personal communication, February 5, 2019.
24. Kyle Wisneski, personal communication, January 15, 2019.
25. Oneida Reservation Comprehensive Plan.
26. Patricia Cornelius, Harvard Project on American Indian Development, https://nnigovernance.arizona.edu/honoring-nations-pat-cornelius-oneida-nation-farms.
27. Oneida Reservation Comprehensive Plan.
28. Marlon Skenandore, personal communication, December 28, 2018.

CHAPTER 12. OHE·LÁKU (AMONG THE CORNSTALKS)

1. Jasmine Jimerson, personal communication, January 4, 2019.
2. *Ukwehúhwe* means "Indigenous."
3. Lea Zeise, personal communication, November 24, 2018.
4. Laura Manthe, personal communication, October 17, 2018.
5. Lea Zeise, personal communication, November 24, 2018.
6. Lea Zeise, personal communication, November 24, 2018.
7. Laura Manthe, personal communication, October 17, 2018.

8. Ridgeview Plaza is an Oneida Nation government building with open meetings spaces on the Reservation. Lea Zeise, personal communication, November 24, 2018.
9. Jasmine Jimerson, personal communication, January 4, 2019.
10. Laura Manthe, personal communication, October 17, 2018.
11. Tony Kuchma, personal communication, March 9, 2019.
12. Jen Falck, personal communication, March 9, 2019.
13. Adrianna Pelky, personal communication, January 3, 2019.
14. Bev Scow, personal communication, December 4, 2018.
15. Kwnwahta Smith, personal communication, November 18, 2018.
16. Robin John, personal communication, October 17, 2018.
17. John Habeck, personal communication, April 16, 2020.
18. Tony Kuchma, personal communication, March 9, 2019.
19. Ernest Stevens IV, personal communication, April 7, 2018.
20. Tony Kuchma, personal communication, March 9, 2019.
21. Jen Falck, personal communication, March 9, 2019.
22. Bev Scow, personal communication, December 4, 2018.
23. Lea Zeise, personal communication, November 24, 2018.
24. Don Charnon, personal communication, November 28, 2018.
25. Jasmine Jimerson, personal communication, January 4, 2019.
26. Lea Zeise, personal communication, November 24, 2018.
27. Adrianna Pelky, personal communication, January 3, 2019.
28. Toni House, personal communication, November 21, 2018.

CHAPTER 13. YUKWALIWISAʔÁHTU (HOW WE TIE OUR MATTERS TOGETHER)

1. Stephanie Stevens, personal communication, April 7, 2018.
2. Lea Zeise, personal communication, November 28, 2018.
3. Jill Ninham, personal communication, January 9, 2019.
4. Rebecca Webster, "Food Reservations at the Reservation?," in *Translating National Policy to Improve Environmental Conditions Impacting Public Health through Community Planning*, 131–153 (Cham: Springer, 2018).

5. D. A. Mihesuah, E. Hoover, and W. LaDuke, *Indigenous Food Sovereignty in the United States: Restoring Cultural Knowledge, Protecting Environments, and Regaining Health* (Norman: University of Oklahoma Press, 2019).
6. Bev Scow, personal communication, December 4, 2018.
7. Jasmine Jimerson, personal communication, January 4, 2019.
8. Jamie Betters, personal communication, April 6, 2018.
9. Webster, "Food Reservations."
10. Jen Falck, personal communication, March 9, 2019.
11. Stephanie Stevens, personal communication, April 7, 2018.
12. Randy Cornelius, personal communication, November 15, 2018.
13. Arlie Doxtator, personal communication, November 8, 2018.
14. Randy Cornelius, personal communication, November 15, 2018.
15. Brian Doxtator, personal communication, December 23, 2018. A version of this recipe can be found in the appendix of this book.
16. Curt Summers, personal communication, November 13, 2018.
17. Jasmine Jimerson, personal communication, January 4, 2019.
18. Don Charnon, personal communication, November 28, 2018.
19. Toni House, personal communication, November 21, 2018.
20. Julie Barton, personal communication, January 6, 2019.
21. Stan Webster, personal communication, December 31, 2018.
22. Laura Cornelius, personal communication, April 6, 2018.
23. Lois Stevens, personal communication, December 28, 2018.
24. Kwnwahta Smith, personal communication, November 18, 2018.
25. Linn Cornelius, personal communication, November 15, 2018.
26. Toni House, personal communication, November 21, 2018.
27. Steve Webster, personal communication, April 7, 2018.
28. Jasmine Jimerson, personal communication, January 4, 2019.
29. Kyle Wisneski, personal communication, January 15, 2019.
30. Arthur Caswell Parker, *Iroquois Uses of Maize and Other Food Plants*, volume 144 (Albany: University of the State of New York, 1910), 88.
31. Mary Annette Pember, "Trauma May Be Woven into DNA of Native Americans," *Indian Country Today Media Network* 20 (2015).

32. Louis Williams Jr., personal communication, November 5, 2018.

CHAPTER 14. TSIʔ NAHTE OLIHWAKA·YÚ· OKHALE OLI·WÁSE̲ (OF WHAT OLD MATTERS AND NEW MATTERS)

1. Jamie Betters, personal communication, April 6, 2018.
2. Paul Smith, personal communication, November 19, 2018.
3. Lexi Levinson, personal communication, December 26, 2018.
4. Carol Cornelius, *Iroquois Corn in a Culture-Based Curriculum: A Framework for Respectfully Teaching about Cultures* (Albany: SUNY Press, 1999).
5. Carol Cornelius, personal communication, November 20, 2018.
6. Toni House, personal communication, November 21, 2018.
7. Paul Smith, personal communication, November 19, 2018.
8. Eliza Skenandore, personal communication, April 9, 2018.
9. Paul Smith, personal communication, November 19, 2018.
10. Randy Cornelius, personal communication, November 15, 2018.
11. Louis Williams Jr., personal communication, November 5, 2018.
12. Vickie Cornelius, personal communication, November 21, 2018.
13. Randy Cornelius, personal communication, November 15, 2018.
14. Lois Stevens, personal communication, December 28, 2018.
15. Lea Zeise, personal communication, November 24, 2018.
16. Jasmine Jimerson, personal communication, January 4, 2019.
17. Arlie Doxtator, personal communication, November 8, 2018.
18. Steve Webster, personal communication, April 7, 2018.
19. Kyle Wisneski, personal communication, January 15, 2019.
20. Louis Williams Jr., personal communication, November 5, 2018.
21. Kyle Wisneski, personal communication, January 15, 2019.
22. Tony Kuchma, personal communication, March 9, 2019.
23. Laura Manthe, personal communication, October 17, 2018.
24. Bev Scow, personal communication, December 4, 20198.

CHAPTER 15. OHUTU YUKWATKATTUHATI (WE ALL ARE LOOKING TO OUR FUTURE)

1. Kyle Wisneski, personal communication, January 15, 2019.
2. Brian Doxtator, personal communication, December 23, 2018.
3. Deborah Heckel, personal communication, February 5, 2019.
4. Chaz Wheelock, personal communication, November 29, 2018.
5. Artley Skenandore, personal communication, December 5, 2018.
6. Carol Cornelius, personal communication, November 20, 2018.
7. Carol Cornelius, personal communication, November 20, 2018.
8. Toni House, personal communication, November 21, 2018.
9. Chaz Wheelock, personal communication, November 29, 2018.
10. Laura Manthe, personal communication, October 17, 2018.
11. Randy Cornelius, personal communication, November 15, 2018.
12. Vickie Cornelius, personal communication, November 21, 2018.
13. Jill Ninham, personal communication, January 9, 2019.
14. Jen Falck, personal communication, March 9, 2019.
15. Jasmine Jimerson, personal communication, January 4, 2019.
16. Lois Stevens, personal communication, December 28, 2018.
17. Steve Webster, personal communication, April 7, 2018.
18. Priya Krishna, "How Native Americans Are Fighting a Food Crisis," *New York Times*, April 13, 2020, https://www.nytimes.com/2020/04/13/dining/Native-americans-coronavirus.html.
19. Iris Hill, personal communication, November 16, 2018.
20. Jasmine Jimerson, personal communication, January 4, 2019.
21. Marlon Skenandore, personal communication, December 28, 2018.
22. Lea Zeise, personal communication, November 24, 2018.
23. Ernie Stevens III, personal communication, April 7, 2018.
24. Lois Stevens, personal communication, December 28, 2018.
25. Lexi Levinson, personal communication, December 26, 2018.
26. Ruby Kuchma, personal communication, March 9, 2019.
27. Grace Webster, personal communication, April 7, 2018.

28. Amelia Webster, personal communication, November 8, 2018.
29. Ernest Stevens IV, personal communication, April 7, 2018.
30. Kwnwahta Smith, personal communication, November 18, 2018.
31. Tom Porter, *And Grandma Said . . . Iroquois Teachings, as Passed Down through the Oral Tradition* (Bloomington, IN: Xlibris Corporation, 2008), 396.

APPENDIX. TSI TWAKHUNIHE (HOW WE COOK OUR FOODS)

1. Arthur Caswell Parker, *Iroquois Uses of Maize and Other Food Plants*, volume 144 (Albany: University of the State of New York, 1910), 78.
2. David Skenandore, Folder 7.
3. Guy Elm, Folder 9.
4. Nelson B. Cornelius's Wife to Dennison Hill, D89.
5. Parker, *Iroquois Uses of Maize and Other Food Plants*, 72.
6. Parker, *Iroquois Uses of Maize and Other Food Plants*, 66.
7. Parker, *Iroquois Uses of Maize and Other Food Plants*, 68.
8. Alma Thomas, Folder 2.
9. Mrs. Joshua Skenandore to Walter L. Skenandore, W7.
10. Parker, *Iroquois Uses of Maize and Other Food Plants*, 68.
11. Parker, *Iroquois Uses of Maize and Other Food Plants*, 67.
12. Elizabeth Doxtator to David Skenandore, WPA Collection. Another version of this story is in the catalogue as V34.
13. Alma Thomas, Folder 2.
14. Parker, *Iroquois Uses of Maize and Other Food Plants*, 73.
15. Elizabeth Huff to Tillie Baird, T33.
16. David Skenandore, Folder 7.
17. Parker, *Iroquois Uses of Maize and Other Food Plants*, 71–72.
18. Jonas Elm to Morris Swadesh, Z7.
19. Guy Elm, Folder 9.
20. Alma Thomas, Folder 2.
21. Frederick Wilkerson Waugh, "Iroquois Foods and Food Preparation" (Ottawa: Government Printing Bureau, 1916), 90.

22. Waugh, "Iroquois Foods," 90.
23. John Gottlieb Ernestus Heckewelder, *History, Manners, and Customs of the Indian nations: Who Once Inhabited Pennsylvania and the Neighboring States*, volume 12 (Historical Society of Pennsylvania, 1876), 194.
24. Ida Blackhawk, Folder 6.
25. Pierre Espirit Radisson, "Voyages of Pierre Espirit Radisson 1651–1654," in *In Mohawk Country: Early Narratives about a Native People* (Syracuse, NY: Syracuse University Press, 1996), 62–92, 70.
26. David Smoke McCluskey, personal communication, April 13, 2020.
27. Waugh, "Iroquois Foods," 88.
28. Parker, *Iroquois Uses of Maize and Other Food Plants*, 75.
29. David Skenandore, Folder 7.
30. Jonas Elm to Morris Swadesh, Z2.
31. Parker, *Iroquois Uses of Maize and Other Food Plants*, 77.

GLOSSARY

1. I use this term to describe our people. Each nation has their own language and has different ways to describe themselves and the collective of the Six Nations. A few decades ago, when the people were getting ready to go to the Geneva Conference, the chiefs met to talk about how they were going to present themselves. Since the Onondaga are the central fire, they decided to use the Onondaga word *Haudenosaunee* (people who build the house). In this book, I wanted to find a term that was more inclusive, since the *Kayanlásla?kowa̲* (great matters, or Great Law of Peace) was meant to be inclusive. When I expressed concern about how people would receive this word, Toni House emphasized its inclusiveness. Bob Brown agreed and stated, "We gotta have resistance, otherwise nothing gets done." Bob Brown, personal communication, April 16, 2020.

Bibliography

Andreani, Paolo. *Travels of a Gentleman from Milan 1790, in Mohawk Country: Early Narratives about a Native People*. Syracuse, NY: Syracuse University Press, 1996.

Antoniou, Laura. *The Documentary History of the State of New York*. Vol. 1. Albany, NY: Weed, Parsons and Company, 1849.

Babcock, William Henry. "Recent History and Present Status of the Vinland Problem." *Geographical Review* 11, no. 2 (1921): 265–282.

Belknap, Jeremy, and Jedidiah Morse. *Report on the Oneida, Stockbridge, and Brotherton Indians, 1796. No. 54.* Museum of the American Indian, Heye Foundation, 1955.

Bieder, R. E. *Native American communities in Wisconsin, 1600–1960: A Study of Tradition and Change*. Madison: University of Wisconsin Press, 1995.

Burke Act, 25 U.S. Code ch. 9 (1906) § 349.

Calhoun, John C. *Papers of John C. Calhoun, 1818–1819*. Vol. 3. Columbia: University of South Carolina Press, 1967.

Campisi, Jack, and Laurence M. Hauptman, eds. *The Oneida Indian Experience: Two Perspectives*. Syracuse, NY: Syracuse University Press, 1988.

Carey, Martin C., and Beverly Paigen. "Epidemiology of the American Indians' Burden and Its Likely Genetic Origins." *Hepatology* 36, no. 4 (2002): 781–791.

Carroll, Doug. "Tribal Lands: In N.Y., 6 Million Acres Hang in the Balance . . ." *Washington Post.* September 24, 1979. https://www.washingtonpost.com/archive/politics/1979/09/24/tribal-lands-in-ny-6-million-acres-hang-in-the-balance/a370e054-974f-43c2-ab8a-f239bbe92b2e/.

Caswell, Harriet S. *Our Life among the Iroquois Indians.* Boston: Congregational Sunday School and Publishing Society, 1892.

Christjohn, Amos. "Creation Story." Oneida Nation. https://oneida-nsn.gov/our-ways/our-story/creation-story/.

Cook, Frederick. *Journals of the Military Expedition of Major General John Sullivan Against the Six Nations of Indians in 1779: With Records of Centennial Celebrations; Prepared Pursuant to Chapter 361, Laws of the State of New York, of 1885.* Auburn, NY: Knapp, Peck and Thomson, Printers, 1887.

Cornelius, Carol. *Iroquois Corn in a Culture-Based Curriculum: A Framework for Respectfully Teaching about Cultures.* Albany: SUNY Press, 1999.

Cornplanter, J. J. *Legends of the Longhouse.* Ontario: Iroqrafts, 1986.

Dickenson, Victoria. "Cartier, Champlain, and the Fruits of the New World: Botanical Exchange in the 16th and 17th Centuries." *Scientia Canadensis: Canadian Journal of the History of Science, Technology and Medicine / Scientia Canadensis: Revue canadienne d'histoire des sciences, des techniques et de la médecine* 31, no. 1–2 (2008): 27–47.

Dieserud, Juul. "Norse Discoveries in America." *Bulletin of the American Geographical Society* 33, no. 1 (1901): 1–18.

Elm, Demus, and Harvey Antone. *The Oneida Creation Story.* Lincoln: University of Nebraska Press, 2000.

Edmundson, William. *A Journal of the Life, Travels, Sufferings, and Labour of Love in the Work of the Ministry, of That Worthy Elder, and Faithful Servant of Jesus Christ, William Edmundson, Who Departed This Life, the Thirty First of the Sixth, Month, 1712. Eighteenth Century Collections Online.* London: Printed and sold by the assigns of J. Sowle, in White Hart-Court in Gracious Street, and at the Bible in George-Tard, Lombard-Street, 1715.

Fernald, Merritt Lyndon. "Notes on the Plants of Wineland the Good." *Rhodora* 12, no. 134 (1910): 17–38.

Gehring, C. T., and W. A. Starna, eds. *A Journey into Mohawk and Oneida Country, 1634–1635: The Journal of Harmen Meyndertsz van den Bogaert*. Syracuse, NY: Syracuse University Press, 2013.

General Allotment Act, 25 U.S. Code ch. 9 (1887) §§ 331 et seq.

Gibson, John Arthur. "Concerning the League: The Iroquois League Tradition as Dictated in Onondaga by John Arthur Gibson. Newly Elicited, Edited and Translated by Hanni Woodbury in Collaboration with Reg Henry and Harry Webster on the Basis of AA Goldenweiser's Manuscript." Syracuse, NY: Syracuse University Press, 1992.

Glatthaar, Joseph T., and James Kirby Martin. *Forgotten Allies: The Oneida Indians and the American Revolution*. New York: Macmillan, 2006.

Graymont, Barbara. "The Oneidas and the American Revolution." In *The Oneida Indian Experience: Two Perspectives*, ed. Jack Campisi and Laurence M. Hauptman, 31–44. Syracuse, NY: Syracuse University Press, 1988.

Hauptman, Laurence M. *The Iroquois and the New Deal*. Syracuse, NY: Syracuse University Press, 1988.

———. *The Iroquois Struggle for Survival: World War II to Red Power*. Syracuse, NY: Syracuse University Press, 1986.

Hauptman, Laurence M., and L. Gordon McLester. *Chief Daniel Bread and the Oneida Nation of Indians of Wisconsin*. Vol. 241. Norman: University of Oklahoma Press, 2002.

Heckewelder, John Gottlieb Ernestus. *History, Manners, and Customs of the Indian Nations: Who Once Inhabited Pennsylvania and the Neighboring States*. Vol. 12. Historical Society of Pennsylvania, 1876.

Herrmann, Rachel B. "'No Useless Mouth': Iroquoian Food Diplomacy in the American Revolution." *Diplomatic History* 41, no. 1 (2017): 20–49.

Hill, Susan M. *The Clay We Are Made Of: Haudenosaunee Land Tenure on the Grand River*. Vol. 20. University of Manitoba Press, 2017.

Holly, Marilyn. "Handsome Lake's Teachings: The Shift from Female to Male Agriculture in Iroquois Culture. An Essay in Ethnophilosophy." *Agriculture and Human Values* 7, no. 3–4 (1990): 80–94.

Horsman, Reginald. "The Origins of Oneida Removal to Wisconsin, 1815–1822." In *The Oneida Indian Journey: From New York to Wisconsin, 1784–1860*, ed. Laurence M. Hauptman and L. Gordon McLester, 53–69. Madison: University of Wisconsin Press, 1999.

Jackson, John N. *The Mighty Niagara: One River-Two Frontiers*. Buffalo, NY: Prometheus Books, 2003.

Jourdan, J. L. "Wampum: Our Historical Record. Oneida Cultural Heritage, Oneida Nation." Oneida Nation. https://oneida-nsn.gov/dl-file.php?file=2016/04/WAMPUM-OUR-HISTORICAL-RECORD-9.13.pdf.

Lewandowski, S. "Three Sisters: A Iroquoian Cultural Complex." In *Indian Corn of the Americas: Gift to the World*, ed. J. Barreiro. Special issue, *Northeast Indian Quarterly* (1989): 41–45.

Lewis, Herbert S., and L. Gordon McLester, eds. *Oneida Lives: Long-Lost Voices of the Wisconsin Oneidas*. Lincoln: University of Nebraska Press, 2005.

Locklear, Arlinda. "The Allotment of the Oneida Reservation and Its Legal Ramifications." In *The Oneida Indian Experience: Two Perspectives*, ed. Jack Campisi and Laurence M. Hauptman, 83–93. Syracuse, NY: Syracuse University Press, 1988.

Lounsbury, Floyd. "Recollections of the Works Progress Administration's Oneida Language and Folklore Project." In *The Oneida Indian Experience: Two Perspectives*, ed. Jack Campisi and Laurence M. Hauptman, 131–134. Syracuse, NY: Syracuse University Press, 1988.

"Kayanlaˀ Kówa—Great Law of Peace." Oneida Nation. https://oneida-nsn.gov/our-ways/our-story/great-law-of-peace/.

McLester, L. Gordon, III, Laurence M. Hauptman, Judy Cornelius-Hawk, and Kenneth Hoyan House, eds. *The Wisconsin Oneidas and the Episcopal Church: A Chain Linking Two Traditions*. Bloomington: Indiana University Press, 2019.

McManis, Douglas R. "The Traditions of Vinland." *Annals of the Association of American Geographers* 59, no. 4 (1969): 797–814.

Meriam, Lewis, and Hubert Work. *The Problem of Indian Administration: Report of a Survey Made at the Request of Honorable Hubert Work, Secretary of the Interior, and Submitted to Him, February 21, 1928*. No. 17. Baltimore: Johns Hopkins University Press.

Merril, F. W. *The Church's Mission to the Oneidas*. 2nd ed. Green Bay, WI: P. B. Haber Printing, 1902.

Merrill, William Stetson. "The Catholic Contribution to the History of the Norse Discovery of America." *Catholic Historical Review* 13, no. 4 (1928): 589–619.

Mihesuah, D. A., E. Hoover, and W. LaDuke. *Indigenous Food Sovereignty in the United States:*

Restoring Cultural Knowledge, Protecting Environments, and Regaining Health. Norman: University of Oklahoma Press, 2019.

Minutes of 2nd Conference with the Oneida Indians, August 14, 1917.

Minutes of Conference Held by Inspector McLaughlin, Supervisor Brandon and Superintendent Hart with Indians of the Oneida Reservation at Oneida, Wisconsin, Tuesday, August 7, 1917.

Archiquette, Oscar. "The Indian New Deal at Oneida." In *A Nation within a Nation: Voices of the Oneidas in Wisconsin*, ed. L. G. McLester III and L. M. Hauptman. Madison: Wisconsin Historical Society, 2014.

Mohawk, John. *Iroquois Creation Story: John Arthur Gibson and JNB Hewitt's Myth of the Earth Grasper*. Buffalo, NY: Mohawk Publications, 2005.

Mt. Pleasant, J. "The Iroquois Sustainers: Practices of a Long Term Agriculture in the Northeast." In *Indian Corn of the Americas: Gift to the World*, ed. J. Barreiro. Special issue, *Northeast Indian Quarterly* (1989): 33–39.

———. "Traditional Iroquois Corn: Its History, Cultivation, and Use." Natural Resource, Agriculture, and Engineering Service, Cooperative Extension, 2010.

Nansen, Fridtjof. "The Norsemen in America." *Geographical Journal* 38, no. 6 (1911): 557–575.

Native American Graves Protection and Repatriation Review Committee Meeting. November 1–3, 1996, Myrtle Beach, SC, vol. 2, https://irma.nps.gov/DataStore/DownloadFile/630486.

North American Indian Travelling College. *Traditional Teachings*. Akwesasne, ON: North American Indian Travelling College, 1984.

Parker, Arthur C. "Certain Iroquois Tree Myths and Symbols." *American Anthropologist* 14, no. 4 (1912): 608–620.

———. "The Code of Handsome Lake." *New York State Museum Bulletin* 163, 1913.

———. *The Life of General Ely S. Parker: Last Grand Sachem of the Iroquois and General Grant's Military Secretary*. Buffalo, NY: Buffalo Historical Society, 1919.

———. *Iroquois Uses of Maize and Other Food Plants*. Vol. 144. University of the State of New York, 1910.

Parker, Arthur Caswell, and Seth Newhouse. *The Constitution of the Five Nations*. No. 184. Albany: University of the State of New York, 1916.

Pember, Mary Annette. "Trauma May Be Woven into DNA of Native Americans." *Indian*

Country Today Media Network 20, 2015.

Peroff, Nicholas C. *Menominee Drums: Tribal Termination and Restoration, 1954–1974.* Norman: University of Oklahoma Press, 2006.

"Polly Cooper: Oneida Heroine." Oneida Indian Nation, March 2, 2017. http://www.oneidaindiannation.com/polly-cooper-oneida-heroine/.

Porter, Tom. *And Grandma Said . . . Iroquois Teachings, as Passed Down through the Oral Tradition.* Bloomington, IN: Xlibris Corporation, 2008.

Radisson, Pierre Espirit. "Voyages of Pierre Espirit Radisson 1651–1654." In *In Mohawk Country: Early Narratives about a Native People*, 62–92. Syracuse, NY: Syracuse University Press, 1996.

Ricciardelli, Alex F. "The Adoption of White Agriculture by the Oneida Indians." *Ethnohistory* 10, no. 4 (1963): 309–328.

Richter, D. K. *The Ordeal of the Longhouse: The Peoples of the Iroquois League in the Era of European Colonization.* Chapel Hill: University of North Carolina Press, 2011.

Sagard, Gabriel. *Le grand voyage du pays des Hurons situé en l'Amérique vers la mer douce, ès derniers confins de la Nouvelle France dite Canada.* Paris: Tross, 1865.

Shames, D. *Freedom with Reservation: The Menominee Struggle to Save Their Land and People.* Madison, WI: National Committee to Save the Menominee People and Forests/Wisconsin Indian Legal Services, 1972.

Skenandore, Francis. 1988. "William Skenandore." In *The Oneida Indian Experience: Two Perspectives*, ed. Jack Campisi and Laurence M. Hauptman, 126–130. Syracuse, NY: Syracuse University Press.

Stevens, Lois, and Joseph Brewer. "Ka?tshatstʌ́sla: 'Strength of Belief and Vision as a People'—Oneida Resilience and Corn." *Journal of Agriculture, Food Systems, and Community Development* 9, no. B (2019): 1–14.

Tehanetorens. *Wampum Belts of the Iroquois.* Onchiota, NY: Six Nations Indian Museum, 1983.

Thomas, Jacob E., and Terry Boyle. *Teachings from the Longhouse.* Toronto: Stoddart, 1994.

Tiro, Karim M. "A 'Civil' War? Rethinking Iroquois Participation in the American Revolution." *Explorations in Early American Culture* 4 (2000): 148–165.

———. "'We Wish to Do You Good': The Quaker Mission to the Oneida Nation, 1790–1840." *Journal of the Early Republic* 26, no. 3 (2006): 353–376.

———. *The People of the Standing Stone: The Oneida Nation from the Revolution through the Era of Removal.* Amherst: University of Massachusetts Press, 2011.

Treaty with the Oneida, 1838. 7 Stat., 566.

Trowbridge, Charles, C. *Journal of C. C. Trowbridge's Trip to Green Bay in Company with the Oneida Indians of New York*, 1821. https://exploreoneida.com/wp-content/uploads/2018/09/11-Jan-1-Sept-1821Journal-of-CC-throwbridge-Trip-to-Green-Bay-.pdf.

Van der Donck, Adriaen Cornelissen. "Description of New Netherland 1653." In *In Mohawk Country: Early Narratives about a Native People*, 104–130. Syracuse, NY: Syracuse University Press, 1996.

Waugh, Frederick Wilkerson. *Iroquois Foods and Food Preparation.* Ottawa: Government Printing Bureau, 1916.

Williams, Louis, Jr. "Handsome Lake and Kaliwihyo." Oneida Nation. https://oneida-nsn.gov/our-ways/our-story/historic-timeline/handsome-lake-and-kaliwihyo/.

Webster, Rebecca. "Food Reservations at the Reservation?" In *Translating National Policy to Improve Environmental Conditions Impacting Public Health through Community Planning*, 131–153. Cham: Springer, 2018.

———. "The Wisconsin Oneida and the WPA: Stories of Corn, Colonialism, and Revitalization." *Ethnohistory* 68, no. 3 (2021): 407–427.

Index

Page numbers in *italics* refer to figures.